W9-BXD-636

THE GENEALOGIST'S HANDBOOK

Modern Methods for Researching Family History

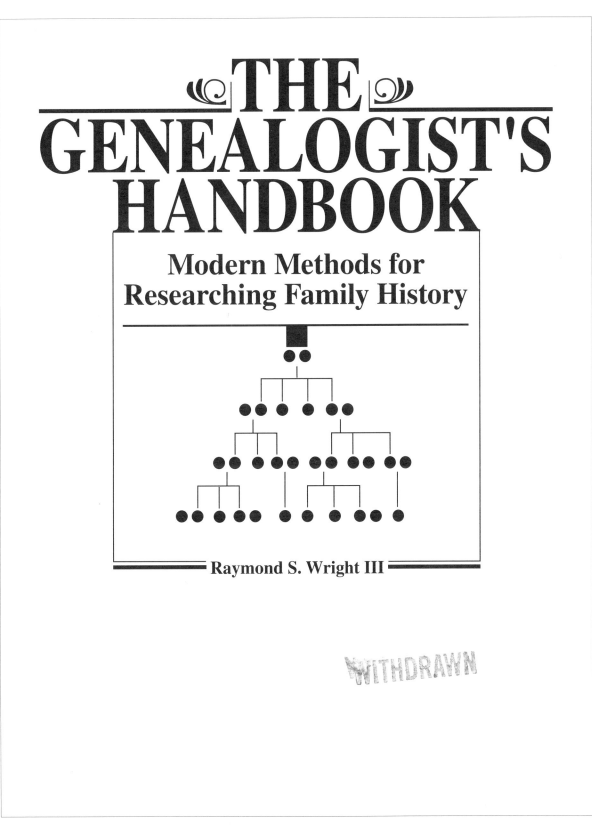

Raymond S. Wright III

AMERICAN LIBRARY ASSOCIATION
CHICAGO AND LONDON 1995

Managing Editor: Joan A. Grygel

Cover design: Richmond Jones

Text design: Publishing Services, Inc.

Composed by Publishing Services, Inc. in ITC Berkley
    on Xyvision/Linotype L330

Printed on 50-pound Glatfelter, a pH-neutral stock,
    and bound in Holliston Roxite cover stock
    by McNaughton-Gunn, Inc.

The paper used in this publication meets the minimum
requirements of the American National Standard for
Information Sciences—Permanence of Paper for Printed
Library Materials, ANSI Z39.48-1992. ∞

FamilySearch, Personal Ancestral File, International
Genealogical Index, Family History Library Catalog, and
Personal Ancestral File are trademarks of the Church of
Jesus Christ of Latter-day Saints.

Library of Congress Cataloging-in-Publication Data

Wright, Raymond S.
    The genealogist's handbook : modern methods for
    researching family history / Raymond S. Wright III.
        p.   cm.
    Includes bibliographical references and index.
    ISBN 0-8389-0625-7
    1. Genealogy.   I. Title.
CS9.W74   1995
929'.1—dc20   93-29750

ISBN 0-8389-0625-7

Printed in the United States of America.

99 98 97 96 95   5 4 3 2

To my mother

Contents

Figures

Acknowledgments

Authors, perhaps more than others, realize that their ideas are the product of their own thought processes and of associations with others. Much of the inspiration for this book has come from friends, colleagues, and teachers.

I am grateful to former coworkers at the Family History Library in Salt Lake City for all that I learned from them during nearly twenty years of association. Since 1979 I have also been able to learn from and exchange ideas with members and supporters of the American Library Association's Genealogy Committee. P. William Filby, Gunther Pohl, Ottilia Koel, and other early members established a tradition of inquiry and learning that still survives. These two circles of friends have played key roles in the genesis of this book.

Several persons shared valuable time with me by reading the manuscript and suggesting important changes and additions: Kip Sperry (Brigham Young University), David Heighton (Family History Library), Dr. Richard Anderson (Brigham Young University), Judith Reid (Library of Congress), J. Carlyle Parker (California State University, Stanislaus), Jayare Roberts (Family History Department—Church of Jesus Christ of Latter-day Saints), Kenneth Nelson (Family History Library), and Dr. V. Robert Westover (Brigham Young University). I thank them for essential contributions to this work and for their friendship. My thanks also to Dr. Denise M. Glover (Court Education Division, Federal Judicial Center) for reviewing the sections dealing with African-American family history and for sharing valuable suggestions with me.

Several persons helped provide copies of important documents used as figures in the book. Herbert White and Diana Briggs and their coworkers at the Granite Mountain Record Vault of the Church of Jesus Christ of Latter-day Saints provided photographs of several documents shown in chapter 6. Additional documents for chapters 6 and 7 were produced with the aid of Brigham Young University's instructional graphics and micrographics departments. The map of principal meridians and baselines (figure 18) was furnished by the United States Department of the Interior, Bureau of Land Management. My thanks to Donald A. Buhler, Chief of Cadastral Surveys at the Utah State Office of the Bureau of Land Management for help in obtaining the map and answering questions about federal land records.

My wife, Jo Ellen, read the manuscript many times and served as my personal editor and critic long before other eyes viewed these pages. When we met as students more than thirty years ago, she gave new meaning to the word "homework." She is still the reason I prefer to work at home.

Student assistants seldom receive the credit they deserve for the hours of research, typing, and proofreading they do helping their professors publish rather than perish. Sincere thanks to Carolyn Augustine, Brett Lindeman, Judy Hatch, Connie Sokol, Karen Paradise, Julie Thwaits, Janet Lomax, and Jacob Gehring.

Herbert Bloom, recently retired senior editor at ALA Editions, never doubted that he would see this book completed. Our long years of association permitted a warm friendship to develop and afforded me the chance to learn additional writing skills from a talented editor. I thank him for the pivotal role he played in bringing this book to the public.

In the final editorial and production stages, Joan A. Grygel earned my appreciation for key suggestions that made the book easier to use and understand.

In September 1990 I was invited to join the faculty of Brigham Young University to teach courses in family history and genealogy. I am grateful for the university's generous support of this project. Colleagues, students, and university leaders provided much-appreciated encouragement and suggestions.

Introduction

The Genealogist's Handbook presents ideas and ideals relating to the roles of ancestors in our lives. They spring from my experiences as a historian, librarian, and genealogist. After years of studying and teaching genealogy and history, helping genealogists as a librarian, and tracing my own and others' ancestors, I awoke to the vision of what genealogy really is—or could be: not endless pedigrees but a story that details people's lives. It can become family history.

There is *something*—more profound than a feeling—at the center of our being that craves to know who we are. Perhaps it is a passion for our purpose. It could be a yearning to know what lies ahead. Whatever it is, it leaves us with a restless, lost feeling during periods of introspection or meditation.

Our world, and the universe in which it is but a speck, seems so large and we in comparison so impotent and minuscule. Do we count for anything? Are we simply flotsam in a great river of life that pushes us along toward death, oblivious of our attempts to influence its direction? Learning about our family's past dispels these uncomfortable feelings and provides answers to many of the questions that we ask about ourselves.

Knowing our ancestors and the turning points and other events in their lives links us to our familial past and provides models for our lives. Knowledge of family history reminds us that the world was and is made up of people and institutions that influence each other. The decisions of forebears affected their world and ours. In some ways progenitors become prophets to their descendants. Their lives warn us away from disaster and point the direction to success and even happiness. We learn from their successes and failures, and we are inspired by their courage. Our ancestors assure us of the continuity of human existence—that it does

not end when lungs, heart, and brain cease working. Whether you believe human immortality is realized in each new generation or in a life after this one, knowledge of generations past provides a solid foundation for our present and future.

Our identity forms in our mind as we see, feel, and hear how other people respond to us. We see ourselves as others see us and treat us. Sometimes we do not like the reflection in the "people mirror" that surrounds us. We doubt that the image is really us—or we hope it is not. Historians teach that as time moves us away from an event, we are better able to see what really happened. How do we step back from our own lives to gain a truer perspective? Studying ancestors' lives helps. Maybe we can see our ancestors' lives better than they could close up. Perhaps by comparing our lives with theirs we see more clearly who we are and what we may become.

This is not simply a handbook on genealogical and family history research methods; it is a guide to discovering as much as resources can reveal about who ancestors were and how they lived. This book's purpose is twofold: to teach researchers how to discover the lives of ancestors in original and other records and then to place ancestors in the context of time, place, and society as they write about those ancestors. If we can extract from the life experiences of the past the values that should guide us today and share them, we can influence events and the people who cause them.

This volume brings together the methods and tools used by genealogists, librarians, historians, demographers, and other researchers that will help you find out who your ancestors were and what their lives were like. You will learn how to set research goals, gather information, and interpret ancestors' lives. Sharing what you discover becomes easier as you develop the writing and computer skills taught here.

The Genealogist's Handbook may be used as a reference tool or as a textbook. Newcomers to the fields of genealogy and family history may want to read each chapter in sequence and apply the suggestions within to their own activities. More-experienced researchers may wish to refer to those chapters that deal with the specific questions raised by their family sleuthing.

As a text, the book is appropriate for introductory college-level courses in genealogy or family history research and writing. It will also strengthen courses designed to train historians in research methods and source evaluation and interpretation. The chapters explain research methods—including computer applications—before introducing family, local, and national sources. The approach used here teaches you how to integrate the vital events of ancestors' lives into a story that presents forebears as whole people. Case studies often demonstrate how this is accomplished. Once you have mastered the basics of finding and interpreting sources, the book demonstrates how these skills can be applied to learning about ancestors' ethnic origins. The last chapter of the book helps you use the information you have gathered to write a family history.

This is not intended to be a comprehensive treatment of all the resources that describe your ancestors or their lives. The methods you learn as you read will guide you to a wide variety of documents and books— some of which are not covered in this book. Experience has taught that family historians who know *how* to look for and interpret records will find needed information about their family with a minimum of outside help.

Chapter 1 describes the differences and similarities between genealogy and family history and the terminology that is used in these fields. The chapter will help you communicate with the librarians, historians, archivists, and others who help you learn about progenitors.

Chapter 2 is a discussion of the methods you use to discover your genealogy or family history. You will learn how to get started and how to organize research findings for easy retrieval and analysis.

Chapter 3 explains the advantages of computer genealogy and family history and introduces you to the roles computers play in modern research.

In chapters 4, 5, and 6, you will learn how events in your ancestors' lives spawned documents and even books that can provide essential information about your family's history.

If you are curious about your ethnic heritage, chapter 7 will be important to your research. It is filled with suggestions for finding facts about Native American ancestors as well as ancestors who came here from other nations and cultures.

Chapter 8 ties everything together by showing you how to share what you have learned about your family by writing a family history.

You will be introduced to a large number of published resources in the following pages. In each case only the author's or publisher's name and a short title are used to identify each work. More information about each book can be found in the list of works cited at the end of the book. The appendixes include addresses and telephone numbers of research centers that may assist you in your quest for information about ancestors.

CHAPTER 1

⊂(⊙ ⊚)⊃

Genealogy and Family History

WHY LEARN ABOUT ANCESTORS?

Since 1976 archivists and librarians have been astonished at the increasing number of researchers who want to trace the histories of their families using the resources of libraries, archives, and historical and genealogical societies. This burst of interest in family origins coincided with the bicentennial celebration of our nation's founding and the publication of Alex Haley's *Roots*. The subsequent presentation of the *Roots* television miniseries added to its impact. We miss the point, however, if we try to explain this fascination with our heritage in terms of media events or celebrations of our history. Our involvement in these events is an expression of the very emotion that drives us to search for our origins.

Who am I? Where did I come from? It is the search for the answers to these questions that makes us participants in historic celebrations and pushes us to trace our ancestors' footsteps through life. Somehow we feel our own identity is linked to ancestors. We have all seen children dressed in their mom's or dad's clothes—they want to be grownups like their parents. When we were young, our own identities were intimately linked to our parents and to brothers, sisters, grandparents, aunts, and uncles. We could look around and see that our own parents had parents and perhaps brothers and sisters who themselves had children who were our cousins. Much of our security and even sense of family pride depended on our relationships with these people. Curiosity about older generations is but an extension of this search for identity and security.

Events in our lives also sensitize us to family history. As we study national or state history we become curious about our own family's role in the wars, depres-

sions, epidemics, and other events we read about. Sometimes answers come as we sit around picnic tables at family reunions or during visits with relatives. As grandparents, aunts, uncles, and parents reminisce about the past, children begin to learn the folklore or legends of their family. However, often the answers to questions about ancestors' lives and roles come only through digging them out of books and original records.

What we read as children and adults also incites interest in our family's past. The religious and secular literature of our generation and ages past often uses family relationships as the vehicle to present the book's plot and define its characters and setting. Think of some of the novels you have read that have families at the center of the story. In addition to *Roots*, James Clavell's *Noble House*, William Faulkner's *Absalom, Absalom!*, Harper Lee's *To Kill a Mockingbird*, and James Jakes's *The North and the South* are titles that come to mind.

Our literature, our religions, and the many cultures represented on our pedigrees emphasize family. It is no wonder that the search for our genealogy is so popular. It is more than a hobby—it is about us. Who is not interested in his or her own role in life's story? It takes little to ignite our passion for family history.

Learning about ancestors helps us understand ourselves better. We discover inherited traits that affect our own personality or health. Knowing that our hair or eye color and many other traits were influenced by ancestors helps us recognize how firmly tied we are to past generations. This link to the past provides a measure of stability in a world filled with transient values and heroes. Our research may also benefit us by providing an early warning of health problems we or our children could inherit that might be avoided by taking timely precautions.

GENEALOGY OR FAMILY HISTORY?

Definitions

Since this book is designed for both the genealogist and the family historian, I often use the terms interchangeably. There are no parts of the book that apply only to genealogists or to family historians. My goal is to encourage the production of family histories that are founded on sound genealogical research and that interpret ancestors' lives in terms most readers will understand. Although I use both terms equally in this text, each has its own definition and its own field of study. My view, however, is that we serve our families best when we master the skills of both disciplines, and that is the purpose of this book.

The first step in mastering a subject is to define what it is. The terms *genealogy* and *family history* do not have universally accepted definitions. You need to be aware of how different researchers define these fields, but before discussing this debate, let's define how each term will be used in this book.

Genealogy is the study of a person's lineage. We search out the names of parents, grandparents, and great-grandparents and list them on a chart. We then search for the names of their children as well as the persons these children married. Thorough genealogists also discover the names of each child's own offspring. These names are grouped together on family charts showing each mother and father with their children. Since each new generation names children after people in older generations, we must use more than names to specify forebears. To distinguish between all of the Davids or Anns in a lineage, genealogists identify a person by that person's parents, birth date, marriage date, and death date. To this information we also add the place each event occurred. That is, a genealogy identifies our ancestors or descendants by showing their names; parents; and birth, marriage, and death dates together with the places where these events took place.

Family history, on the other hand, is a study of our ancestors' or descendants' lives. Once the family historian has reconstructed a family using names, dates, and places, he or she then searches for stories, artifacts, records, and other information that describe the activities of family members. Family history explores how people interacted with other family and community members, how they earned a living, and what they believed. Family historians search for any resource that will permit them to reconstruct forebears' lives and the world in which they lived. Within a family history, ancestors become defined not only in terms of names,

dates, and places but also by what they did during their lives.

Both family history and genealogy are subdisciplines in the general field of history. Another field of study that focuses on families present and past is also called family history and is a subdiscipline of both history and sociology. This scientific study of family history is important to both genealogists and historians of *specific* families because scholars in this field write about families *in general* and family life during the times in which our ancestors lived. This type of family history deals with the function and purpose of the family in society. It explores when and why people marry, family size, the ratio of male to female children, and how long family members live. These social-scientist family historians are also curious about the roles each family member plays inside the family unit as well as within the larger community, and they often study groups of families to identify trends that can be shown easily in statistical tables.

This book is for genealogists and family historians interested in learning about specific families. It is not aimed at the social-scientist family historian. Rather, it focuses on how to find records about specific ancestors and use this information to extend lineages as well as to reconstruct forebears' lives.

Beyond Genealogies

The definitions given in the last section are not accepted by everyone researching ancestors. The debate continues over whether genealogy encompasses how people lived as well as the when and where of their lives. Or is the study of how ancestors lived a separate field we should call family history? A 1987 article by Jayare Roberts in the Utah Genealogical Association's *Genealogical Journal* reviewed key issues in the debate. Roberts felt that the terms had become so confused that they had little meaning today and coined his own term: "family biography."[1] His goal was to motivate researchers to go beyond lists of ancestors to tell us how these people lived and how their lives have affected our own. Roberts is right; when researching ancestors and writing about them we must go beyond genealogy. No new term for this effort is needed, however, because *family history* describes it well. Family history incorporates the skills and facts genealogists use as well as skills and information from many other fields.

Most of us think of a genealogy as a list or chart of families or individuals showing from whom we descended. First on the chart are the earliest-known parents. Next, their children are listed along with their spouses. Following this are listed the children's children, and so on until the present generation. Genealogical charts or lists can also move from the present to the past. The first family in this case might be your own; the next, the families in which your parents appear as children, and so on back in time until no more information can be found about ancestor families. Sometimes the charts depicting an ancestry contain dates of birth, marriage, and death for each person plus the places these events occurred.

Such genealogies do little to acquaint us with our ancestors and their worlds. Knowing the facts of birth, marriage, and death seldom satisfies the drive to relate our lives to the experiences of our progenitors. That is where family history comes in: It is the study of how ancestors lived and their relationships with people and institutions. Genealogies serve as a point of departure for learning about the history of ancestors. Compiling our genealogy is the first step in discovering the history of our family.

Until the late 1970s, few genealogies told the story of a family. Most consisted of traditional lineage and ancestor, or descendant, charts. During the last ten or twelve years, more and more books use genealogies as a framework upon which to stretch the fabric of individual and family lives or family history. These latter publications are devoted to describing, interpreting, and comparing ancestors' lives with those of their contemporaries and of their descendants—us. The following unique example demonstrates my point. In 1989 Susan L. Mitchell published a book that is both a genealogy and a family history. *The Hewitts of Athens County, Ohio* is divided into three parts: "The History," "Photographs," and "The Genealogy." The first part introduces the reader to the places family members lived, the events that influenced their lives, and the society and culture in which they lived. The photographs show how the ancestors looked. The genealogies help identify who was who and how the Hewitts are related to their descendants today.

In *The Genealogist's Handbook*, genealogy and family history are defined as separate fields of study, although each depends on the other. Genealogy is discovering relationships and where and when ancestors lived. Family history is identifying family members in the context of their physical and social environment. In genealogy, ancestors are parents, grandparents, aunts, uncles, and cousins. In family history, they are viewed as workers, worshippers, friends, neighbors, consumers, soldiers, mothers or fathers, brothers or sisters, enemies, and lovers.

Family historians find out about ancestors' lives from interviews, family records, and other documents

that teach us how wars, depressions, racial unrest, strikes, riots, and elections changed or did not change the lives of our forebears. Knowing about ancestors' health, the size and structure of their families, and how long they lived or from what they died will also help us understand them. Ancestors were not passive observers; they were involved in local politics, strikes against employers, and controversies over religious or racial issues. Where did they stand and how did they act out their feelings? Answers to these questions will help us understand history from a personal perspective seldom presented in textbooks. To learn even more, we can compare our ancestors' lives to their neighbors and even to contemporaries in other parts of the country. Like us, our progenitors were the products of their own place and time in history. We cannot relate to them unless we understand what it was like in their day.

RESOURCES FOR GENEALOGY AND FAMILY HISTORY RESEARCH

Records

The major obstacle to finding ancestors is knowing where to look for records about their lives. Sometimes records can be found at home or with relatives. Often we need to search books and records preserved in libraries, archives, historical societies, or government offices. The basis for your search will be an understanding of the places your ancestors lived and the roles of local institutions in their lives as revealed through the records of your ancestors' interactions with these local agencies.

Generally speaking, you will search among three types of records to reconstruct your family's history: family records, the research results of others, and original records. Each of these record types is explained in greater detail in subsequent chapters. In this chapter the terms are introduced to help you better understand the process of re-creating ancestors' lives.

Your research begins in the records you and other family members have. Next, you conduct a survey to discover what other family researchers have published or contributed to genealogical indexes or computer databases about your family. Finally, you fill in the remaining gaps in your family's story by using original records such as censuses and birth, marriage, or death records.

Family Records

Family records are the certificates, heirlooms, stories, and other bits of family history found in the homes and memories of relatives. They include the oral histories you can gather by interviewing family members and their friends, neighbors, and coworkers. Although some people may have gaps in their memories of the past, much of what they tell you may be true. Oral records must be evaluated, as must any other sources you use.

Published Records

When researchers take information from original and oral records, evaluate and enhance it, and then publish it, we have another type of resource: published records. Some genealogists have taken all of the names and other personal data from vital records, cemetery records, and other original records and published them as research tools for others to use. Harold B. Gill's *Apprentices of Virginia 1623–1800* is an example of this type of resource. The author used original American and English records to identify about 2,000 early apprentices in Virginia. (Of course, family histories and genealogies are also examples of published sources.)

Such published research may have been contributed to genealogical societies, newsletters, or magazines or published in books. Although the term "research" evokes visions of dusty volumes on library shelves, it can also include computer databases, card indexes, and pedigree and family chart files kept at local genealogical or historical societies and libraries. It is simply the research of other persons that has been made available to the public. If you think that no one else is interested in researching your family, visit a local library to look at the telephone book from a town where your family lived in times past. Look up your family name and notice how many people not only share your surname but also your given name.

There are many other types of published sources that genealogists use: family and local histories, biographies, newspapers, and genealogies are examples. They describe events that generally took place many years before the history or genealogy was written. They may be based upon research in original sources but are a later interpretation of those sources. Some of these family histories, genealogies, or biographies may have been published as books; others may have remained in typescript or manuscript form.

Original Records

Under the term *original records* fall documents created by public (government) or private agencies to describe your ancestors or their activities. Birth certificates, marriage licenses, and wills probably come to mind as

you think about original records. You will learn that churches, businesses, and clubs, as well as national and local government agencies, created many records that detail parts of ancestors' lives.

Discovering the feelings and the life activities of ancestors requires innovative uses of well-known original sources—birth, marriage, and death records—and sources genealogists and family historians sometimes overlook. For example, popular sources such as birth records will help you determine child spacing and family size. Marriage records may help you calculate the ages of the bride and groom. Death records will generally tell you the cause of death. Less often used sources such as court records will inform you of trials or suits that involved your family. Minutes of town or religious councils may name your ancestors as participants in local events. Even if your family is not mentioned, minutes will at least indicate what was going on in their community that may have touched ancestors' lives.

Original records may be created at the time of an event or later. Their purpose is the same no matter when they were created: to witness that an event took place and list those involved. The birth and marriage records to be found at many of the probate courts in the state of Ohio since about 1867 are examples of original sources. Sometimes an agency or institution will create a document that describes contemporary events as well as some that took place many years before the document was created. These are original records, too. For example, a driver's license lists a person's birth date but was created many years after the person's birth. A death certificate describes the date and place of death but contains information about the date and place of the deceased's birth or marriage. A census shows us where a family lived and who was in the household; it also may list the ages and birthplaces of these persons.

By the time you have read the last page of this book you will understand how original records are created and where they are likely to be found today. In addition, you will know how to extract information from them about your family and their neighbors so that a picture of their lives emerges.

Reference Sources

Reference sources such as gazetteers, history books, and encyclopedias are important in researching and writing a family history. These books describe the places ancestors lived and what happened during their stay there. Reference books may also explain where to look for original records or other resources. For example, *The Origin of Certain Place Names in the United*

States by Henry Gannett is a book you might use to learn more about a place your ancestors lived. To locate the nearest historical society you might look in another reference book: Mary B. Wheeler's *Directory of Historical Organizations in the United States and Canada*.

The following chapters will help you find reference books and published resources that will make the search for records easier and their interpretation more precise.

Statistical Sources

You can also use original and published records to create another kind of source: statistical records. Statisticians tell us that focusing on a few people drawn at random from a population will generally reflect what was happening with most people in the community. The size of your sample is determined by the size of the population you are studying. If your family lived in a village with a population of 200 persons, you may want to look at a sample of 20 to 25 persons. If they lived in a town of several thousand persons, you may want to have a sample of about 100 persons. If they lived in a city of one-half million, you could select a sample of 1,000 to 1,500. The larger your sample the more accurate will be its reflection of the real values—averages, etc.—in the whole population.

There is a limit, however, to the time and effort you should spend on this type of study. Your family may have lived in a city of a million people, but there may have been only 2,000 to 3,000 people in the area you define as their neighborhood. The statistics describing their immediate community/neighborhood are the ones of interest to you. Statistics for populations of large cities are often available in published studies. Let local librarians help you find statistical studies about the cities, states, and regions in which your forebears lived. Tell the librarian about the types of studies that interest you: family size, cause of death, income, occupation, etc. Your goal is to develop general measurements for the population in which your family lived so that you can compare these measurements with the ones you discover when you study your family's statistics. For most studies, you will have adequate data for comparison if you select a sample population of between 50 and 100 persons/families.

The types of data you gather—ages, gender, occupations, causes of death, etc.—are easily analyzed using percentages, ratios, averages, medians, and modes. Each of these methods is explained in the following paragraphs.

Percentages. Using the birth and death records of your ancestor's county, how would you calculate the percentage of newborns who did not reach one year of age? To do so, find the total number of births for the year and the total number of deaths for children who died before reaching one year of age. Then, divide the number who died by the number who were born, and you have the percentage of babies who did not survive one year after birth.

Ratio. If your ancestor's community had 2,000 inhabitants and 4 midwives, what is the ratio of inhabitants to midwives? It is 500 to 1 (2,000 divided by 4).

Average. Suppose you want to calculate the average age at marriage for women living in your ancestor's community in 1880. If 21 women applied for marriage licenses during the year, list the age for each woman and add them up. Divide the total by 21 to obtain the average age at marriage for women marrying in 1880.

Median. If the 21 women who married in 1880 are listed by age from the youngest to the oldest, the woman whose age is listed eleventh on the list is the median, or middle, case. If you are dealing with an even number of cases—such as 20—use the case nearest the middle—10—or the two middle cases that would leave an even number of cases on both sides of these numbers—10 and 11.

Mode. Looking at the list of women's ages at marriage in 1880, you notice that the most common age at marriage was 20—7 women were 20 years old when they married. The age 20 years would then be the mode, or most common age at marriage for the 21 women you are studying.

Because averages can be misleading if you have a few cases represented with very high or low figures, use the other measures as appropriate to help you decide how accurately the average portrays the group of people you are studying. For example:

❦ _____

The average age at death for males in your family may be 60 years and the average for other people in the area 65 years. Closer examination of the figures shows that the most common age (mode) at death in your family was 45. The higher average age at death may be due to two or three ancestors who lived to age

80. Perhaps the age at death for the ancestor in the middle of the list was 43 (median). You also note that 35 percent of your ancestors died before reaching 45 years. The conclusion is that although the average age at death was 60, many ancestors died before reaching 46. This evidence may point to an inherited disease that causes a significant number of people in your family to die at a relatively young age.

Colin D. Rogers and John H. Smith's *Local Family History in England* illustrates how you can conduct these kinds of studies. They also advocate using books written by demographers and economic and social historians to enrich your knowledge about the times in which your ancestors lived. Comparing statistics from your family with local, regional, or national statistics allows you to see your historic family in relation to other families. Your family may be unique, or they may fit the profile the statistics paint of most other families in the area. To decide how unique or common their experiences are, conduct some statistical surveys.

Conducting Statistical Surveys

Chapters 4, 5, and 6 focus on the first step in the process of conducting a statistical study of the people in your family's community: identifying the original and published sources at the record offices, libraries, historical societies, and archives for the community in which your ancestors lived. Second, select from these resources materials from the time period your ancestors lived in the community that name individuals or groups of individuals and contain information relevant to your study. If, for example, you are interested in family size, age at marriage, the time between the births of children, and the ratio of male to female children in the community, these sources may come to your mind: religious or civil vital records and post-1850 U.S. censuses (see chapters 4, 5, and 6).

The third step is to select a sample of persons or families from the record you have chosen and make notes describing the content of each entry or statement about these persons or families. Often the records you find are organized along city, town, township, or county lines. Let's use a county as an example.

Pretend you have decided to use the census schedules for the county in which your ances-

tors lived in 1860. There are forty entries on each page and twenty-five pages of census schedules for the county. You are interested in family statistics; therefore, you want a sample population made up of families. If you were studying the population of the county as a whole, your sample would include randomly selected persons whether or not they were part of a family. Assume that there are about 250 families in the county. Therefore, you are satisfied with a sample population of 25 families. Beginning with the first family entry on the first page of the census, count ten families. The tenth family becomes the first in your sample population, the twentieth becomes the second, and so on until you have 25 families.

Begin with measures such as average age at marriage and death, average family size, the ratio of females to males, most-common causes of death, and average size of land holdings. Calculate figures for your ancestral families in each generation and compare them with one another as well as with those of other people who lived at the same time and in the same region or country. As you continue to gather information, you may become curious about other aspects of ancestors' lives, such as how many children followed a father's occupation, how often they married a second time, how many years elapsed between births of children, and how many miles ancestors traveled from their place of birth to find work or a spouse.

EVALUATING THE ACCURACY OF SOURCES

Regardless of the sources you consult, be critical of their accuracy. Were original sources prepared by eyewitnesses? Did persons whom you interviewed have a chance to see the events they describe, or were they close to persons who were eyewitnesses? Do published sources agree with what you know from research in original records or from reading the books of knowledgeable authors? Do you note a bias in any resource that might make it less accurate?

Any source may provide correct or incorrect information. Original sources created by eyewitnesses when the event occurred are preferred because they have a high probability of being accurate. Later sources should not be discounted, however, because they may be more accurate than some contemporary ones. For example, a clerk in a bureau of vital statistics may transpose a birth date while typing a birth certificate. This error may be corrected later on a driver's license or an application for a job. In this case, the researcher would prefer to use a later source to verify the birth date.

A person's recollection of an event may be more accurate than an official record. Even though the person was not present or was too young to recall an event, that person's version may be more accurate than contemporary documents because he or she grew up in the presence of eyewitnesses who may have told about the event. My mother's story about her birth is an example.

Ruth Bingham believed that she was born in Rockford, Idaho, at the family home. Since no official record of the birth could be found, family members relied on what was listed in the records of the church the Binghams attended in Thomas, Idaho. This source stated that Ruth was born at Thomas, Idaho, on April 10, 1918; therefore, everyone assumed that the Binghams lived in Thomas when Ruth was born. During a family reunion in Idaho, an expedition was formed to find the old Bingham home. Not only was the home still standing, but the present owner had copies of all of the deeds from the time the property was purchased by William and Christiane Bingham until the present. The legal description of the property clearly stated that it was and is in the town of Rockford, not Thomas. Ruth's information turned out to be better than the source created at the time.

Does the preceding example prove that you should prefer the testimony of living witnesses over contemporary written sources? That depends on the accuracy of your informant's recollections. The key to success in using oral history is verification of testimony. People's memories only contain what they have observed, heard, or felt. Sometimes they have been given false information by others. On some occasions they may not have observed an event accurately, storing incorrect data in their memories. Then, too, there is always the danger that they have simply forgotten the facts, and attempts to recall them have created a less-than-accurate image of the past. At the same time, remember that most official documents are simply the observations of human beings recorded for future use; therefore, documents can be erroneous also. Through careful interviewing and subsequent verification, recollections of living witnesses become essential elements in discovering a family's story.

Verifying Evidence You Gather

To verify any record, written or oral, you should compare it with at least two other sources. If you are interviewing someone, have the person comment on events surrounding the incident of interest to you and compare the description with what you can find in local newspapers or other sources. Interviews with other witnesses to the events can also be used to verify what the first informant said.

What do you do if none of the sources agree? If you were called to jury duty in your community, you would face a similar challenge. The defense and prosecution would present the jury with their views of events and outcomes. Often each side's story conflicts with the other's. Whom do you believe? It generally boils down to witnesses and evidence. The issues are the same in genealogical and historical research.

When all of the evidence gives conflicting information, researchers generally prefer the sources created nearest the event in question and have more confidence in records based on testimony from eyewitnesses. If you do not have eyewitness testimony, then you must consider how close the relationship was between your informant and an eyewitness to the event. It is likely that a son's information about his parents' marriage would be more accurate than a great-grandson's. Suppose you find an obituary that gives a birth date different from the one on a death certificate. You note that the person who was listed as the informant for the death certificate was the person's spouse. You may not know who was the informant for the obituary, but you know it went through the hands of a clerk who could have made a mistake. Therefore, the death certificate would be the choice for the most accurate source. What if you later find a birth certificate for the deceased that gave a birth date different from the one on the death certificate? This is a tough call. Considering the stress informants experience at the death of a loved one, the birth certificate created near the time of birth is probably the best source to use.

Identifying Biases in Records

How many income tax returns reflect a person's actual financial status? Have you ever postdated a check or letter? The scribes of the past were subject to many influences and sometimes did not accurately record the facts. As you write a family history, consider the conditions under which sources were created and the biases that could have affected their content. As you seek to interpret the sources you find, remember the following guidelines and questions.

Why was a document created? Considering how careless we often are with them, why did the one we are using survive? For whom was the document intended? Are there other documents from the same locality and time period to help you interpret events in ancestors' lives? The answers to these questions may reveal biases in records or in the minds of those who created and preserved them. These biases directly affect the meaning of the information contained in documents. For example, a will is seldom an unbiased description of the testator and his or her family. In the first place, the will may not list all family members because some may have died, received an inheritance early, or been disinherited. Some wills make a point of explaining why persons are left out. Such explanations are often uncomplimentary and always colored by personal prejudices; they should not be accepted as the final word on someone's character. Furthermore, most people dictated their wills to clerks, attorneys, or notaries who were familiar with what was generally accepted as the appropriate format and wording, and testators often chose phrases that would make them appear as they wished to be seen: benevolent, religious, and virtuous. Leaving a token bequest to a church, religious group, or charity was often expected and became customary, whether or not the testator was a churchgoer or regular donor to such causes. If you examine local church records, you may be able to determine how active your ancestor was in a local church.

People, causes, and events may be left out of a record. Search to see if you can find other contemporary sources to clarify the situation. For example, a local land record describing a sale of land or property normally includes the purchase price, a description of the property, and the names of the buyer and seller; but it would not include a description of the negotiations that led to the land transfer. Consequently, the real story of the transaction remains a mystery unless you search further, as in the following example.

Early Connecticut land records show one of my ancestors bought a large piece of land from another person in the community. The transaction appeared normal enough but was, in reality, the cause of great dissension in the community. My progenitor was called into court by local officials over the matter. The court ruled he was not fit to manage such large holdings, and he was told not to consummate the transaction. My ancestor appealed the ruling and, although he lost, went ahead with the purchase. As a result, he was sentenced to be flogged publicly for contempt of court. He took the flogging, kept the land, and went on to establish a family business on the property that survived for three hundred years. This story would have remained hidden in the pages of local court records had not researchers decided to check these records for cases involving my ancestor. Researchers not only identified facts about my ancestor but also uncovered the names and testimonies of others who became involved on both sides of the controversy.[2]

This story leaves several questions requiring further research: Why did the justices not confiscate the property and return it to the original owner? Why was the original owner willing to accept payment and transfer title for the land in the face of the court's decision? Why was the seller not punished? One place to look for answers would be in local government records or in published local histories. There I may find a description of the laws and ordinances that regulated the transfer of real estate and, perhaps, reasons for the outcome of this case.

The lesson to be learned from this example is that you should not be content to find your ancestors in one or two sources. Try to uncover all of the sources that were created during the period they lived in a locality. The more witnesses you have of your ancestors' lives, the more accurate your family history will be.

Interpreting Dates in Ancestors' Records

One of the most important facts a document reveals is the date of an event in a forebear's life. In some records, the way dates are recorded may confuse you. Following are a few factors to keep in mind as you consider dates in the records you discover.

Over time, calendars get inaccurate because the days, months, and years that have been used to keep track of time's passing do not correspond exactly to the amount of time it takes Earth to follow its course around the sun. In the sixteenth century, Pope Gregory XIII (1572–1585) employed scholars to help him create a new calendar that would solve the inaccuracies in the old Roman and Julian calendars. Since the first century A.D. the calendar developed under Julius Caesar had been used by much of what became the Christian world. By Pope Gregory's time, however, the calendar was off by ten days. To make the needed correction, the Pope decreed that the day after October 4, 1582, would become October 15, 1582. He also decided that the year 1583 would begin January 1. Prior to this time the beginning of the year varied from December to September, depending on local practices.

Many Protestant and Orthodox areas of the world refused to comply with the Gregorian calendar. Among those keeping the old Julian calendar were England and those lands subject to it. From the middle of the eleventh century until September 2, 1752, England celebrated the beginning of the new year on March 25. On September 2, 1752, England and all of its colonies converted to the Gregorian calendar. In Germany—or what was the German-speaking world in 1582—the matter was not so simple. Many Catholic princes permitted their churches to use the new Gregorian calendar in 1582 and 1583. Protestant nobles and royalty waited until as late as 1700. Parts of Graubünden in Switzerland did not accept the Gregorian calendar until 1812. By 1700 the difference between the two calendars had increased to eleven days instead of the ten calculated in 1582. It was not until the first part of the twentieth century that the Orthodox Christian world accepted the new calendar. By 1900 the new calendar was twelve days ahead of Julian dates.

In England and its colonies, including America, the day after September 2, 1752, became September 14. At the same time, King George II (1727–1760) decreed that the year 1753 would begin January 1 instead of March 25 as was the practice formerly. Because of these changes, you may find records that show two dates: April 12/23, 1753. Often records may give the Gregorian calendar date with the abbreviation N.S. (New Style) following it. If the abbreviation O.S. (Old Style) is given, the date refers to the Julian calendar date for the event being recorded. Of course, events that occurred in the latter third of a month would carry a date in the following month as the new style date (June 25/July 6, 1753).

Because of the confusion that was caused in the eighteenth century by differing dating practices, some scribes wrote years thus: March 10, 1749/50. This meant that in some areas the new year (1750) had come on January 1, while in other areas the new year would

not come until March 25. Among Quakers, who often noted dates only by numerals, the problem was compounded. For these early settlers in America, the first month was March and the tenth was December. A person married in the eleventh month of 1749 on the thirtieth day of the month would have been married January 30, 1749/50, not November 30 as some might guess when finding a marriage date of 11/30/49.[3]

When reading dates, remember also that some documents are dated using the feast days of the Christian calendar. Your local librarian can help you find reference books listing these dates. Another oddity is that some records use the Latin notation for the month symbolized by an Arabic or Roman numeral: 7 bris or VII bris for September, 8 bris or VIII bris for October, 9 bris or IX bris for November, 10 bris or X bris for December.

Being sensitive to the fact that record keepers used varying methods to record dates will help you be more accurate in recording dates from ancestors' lives. When calculating a progenitor's age at marriage or death, knowing when the year began or when new or old style dates were used becomes important.

USING RESEARCH FROM OTHER FIELDS

The history of the family is one area of study that has produced a wealth of valuable interpretive data about people from the past. In this discipline are historians, anthropologists, sociologists, and demographers. Each is interested in how families were formed in different cultures, how they have evolved, and what roles families and family members played in local society and in each other's lives. The National Council on Family Relations' *Journal of Family History* is one of the chief forums for research in this field. Book reviews and articles in this journal will keep you in touch with the latest research.

Local historians, social historians, economic historians, political historians—historians of all kinds—play important roles in the effort to understand ancestors. For example, to get an idea of what interests social-scientist family historians, you may wish to look at *Family History at the Crossroads: A Journal of Family History Reader,* edited by Tamara Hareven and Andrejs Plakans. It contains articles from several leading scholars in the field. The bibliographies included in the articles will guide you to some of the key literature in the history of the family.

In articles and books on family history research you learn about courtship and the marriage market—how eligible marriage partners are linked together. Family size, contraception, and abortion and their impact on family life are also examined. The roles of mothers, fathers, and other relatives are explored as are the impact of diet and health on the family. These scholars explore an amazing range of topics including the types of homes families build, the roles relatives play in the selection of a person's profession, and the effects of death on family members. The characteristics these scholars have discovered about historical families also describe your own. Their efforts will help you interpret what you find out about your specific family.

It is from historians that we learn about the events and issues that affected our ancestors' daily lives. Historians describe wars, depressions, riots, culture, education, famines, trade, religion, government, and society in times past. Their studies often compare different countries and time periods with one another. They examine the growth of population, migration, and the rise and fall of countries and institutions. Historians help us put the lives of our forebears in the context of regional, national, and world communities and their workings.

Local-history researchers provide genealogists and family historians with essential facts about ancestors' lives. Local histories let us view relatives as laborers, blacksmiths, farmers, tavern keepers, and in other roles in a community. These historians can tell us what the economy was like, how our ancestors earned a living, and how they dressed. We can learn how people were educated, how they worshipped, and what they did for recreation.

Use the resources of local libraries to understand your ancestors' worlds by searching out relevant histories. In fact, your interpretations of documentary evidence will be lacking if you do not prepare yourself through studying the history of the time and place that produced the records you are using.

You will also want to consult the works of geographers: atlases, gazetteers, maps, and geographical dictionaries. Modern ones are helpful, but most important are publications that show the world and the community during the times of ancestors. These sources often report the population figures for communities. Older atlases also outline railroads and canals and other possible transportation lines of the times. Historical geographies delve into weather, landforms, agriculture, and vegetation of the past. They help us understand famines and the reasons for migration when weather conditions changed or the soil stopped yielding enough to support the population. These studies can help reconstruct the environment in which families lived.

Demographers want to learn about the makeup and movement of populations. They are interested in population growth and decline and its causes. They are interested in how the movements of people in and out of an area affected its growth, the size of households, and the ratio between the sexes or between different age groups. All of these factors affected the decisions our progenitors made and the type of life they led. Understanding the factors behind these phenomena will help clarify ancestors' lives. For example, knowing the ratio of men to women or the breakdown of the population by age group can provide insights into why ancestors married when they did or remained single.

Sometimes original sources will fail us in our search for facts about ancestors. The studies of scholars from the fields just described can help us fill the gaps in our knowledge about a specific family. Through their research we learn about the neighbors of ancestors. We can compare what we know about our ancestors with the people described in these studies and learn how typical our families were.

Robert M. Taylor and Ralph J. Crandall have collected a number of studies to demonstrate how genealogists benefit from the work of researchers in many fields and how these same researchers depend on genealogists for information to validate their studies. Taylor and Crandall's *Generations and Change* is worthwhile reading not only because it shows how genealogists and other scholars benefit from each other's work but also because its articles have something to teach about the lives ancestors led. Several chapters show how information compiled by genealogists is used by historians to learn about past populations and communities. Other sections explain how historical studies have led family researchers to information about their families or helped clarify what the researchers had already discovered.

In a landmark series of articles, Samuel P. Hays outlined the prospects for cooperation between genealogists and other scholars—especially historians.[4] He had great hope that both groups of researchers would become more aware of each other's needs and produce material that would be mutually beneficial. Since the publication of these articles, there, indeed, has been greater use of genealogies and family histories in historical research. Historians, for their part, have produced a wealth of research on historical families and communities and other subjects that benefit the genealogist and family historian. To encourage continued and even increased cooperation between genealogists and scholars from other disciplines, we must produce family histories and genealogies that are accurate and interpretive studies. In the pages that follow you will learn how to benefit from the work of researchers in other fields and to contribute through your own research to their endeavors.

Notes

1. Jayare Roberts, "Beyond the Begat Books," *Genealogical Journal* 16 (spring/summer 1987 Part 1): 1–112.

2. Bernard Christian Steiner, *History of Guilford and Madison, Connecticut* (1897; reprint, Guilford, Connecticut: The Guilford Free Public Library, 1975), 82–87.

3. If you wish more detail about calendars and the dating of documents, see if your local library has any of these: H. Grotefend, *Taschenbuch der Zeitrechnung des Deutschen Mittelalters und der Neuzeit,* 11th ed. (Hannover, Ger.: Verlag Hahnsche Buchhandlung, 1971), 1–28; Donald Lines Jacobus, *Genealogy as Pastime and Profession,* 2d rev. ed. (Baltimore: Genealogical Publishing, 1968), 109–113; William Wade Hinshaw and Thomas Worth Marshall, *Encyclopedia of American Quaker Genealogy,* vol. 2, Repr. (Baltimore: Genealogical Publishing, 1991), 8–10.

4. Samuel P. Hays, "History and Genealogy: Patterns for Change and Prospects for Cooperation," *Prologue* 7 (spring, summer, fall 1975): 39–43;81–84;187–191.

CHAPTER 2

⟅⟆ ⟆⟅

Getting Started

Getting started with your genealogy or family history is a simple process. You begin by identifying family members you already know. At the bottom of a sheet of paper, write down your name and when and where you were born. Above and to the left and right of your name, write the names of your parents, when and where they were born, and the date and place of their marriage. Above, on either side of each parent's name write the names of each parent's mother and father (your grandparents). Do you also know when and where your grandparents were born and when and where they were married? If not, ask your parents or one of their brothers or sisters. If there is no one to ask, a little research will be needed to find birth and marriage certificates.

Now you are doing genealogy, but there is still more to learn about the people listed on the sheet before you. The dates and places you listed tell little about these people and why they are important to you. However, we cannot trace your family's history without starting at the beginning—with dates and places.

Accurate genealogical research is based upon the principles illustrated in the steps you have just taken. Always begin with yourself and work from the present to the past. Use sources that are reliable. Eyewitness accounts are best. In this case, you have direct access to eyewitnesses like yourself and your parents. Suppose you find your surname in a history book or on a plaque at a historical monument and want to prove a connection to that namesake. It might seem logical to start with the famous person and work down to the present generation looking for common relatives, but if you do, you will enter a quagmire that will leave you discouraged and convinced that genealogy is no fun at all. It is far easier to move from now to then. It is also the most

effective way to prove whether you are related to that famous person.

DEVELOPING FAMILY-GROUP RECORDS

What exactly does it mean to start with yourself? First, fill out a family-group record (an example is shown in figure 1). Your local bookstore, stationer, or genealogy shop may have similar forms for purchase.

Fill in the names of your father and your mother on the appropriate lines. Note that there are also spaces for dates and places of birth, marriage, and death and spaces for their parents' names. Under the place in which you recorded this information are spaces for facts about their children. In birth order starting with the oldest child in the family, write your name and the names of any brothers or sisters. In the spaces provided fill in dates and places of birth. For marriages, note the dates and names of spouses. If family members have died, record the death dates.

How do you fill out family-group records when ancestors were married more than once? There could be a record for each marriage listing the spouse who was the father or mother of the children described on the sheet. For example, if your grandmother and her first husband had three children together, fill out a sheet showing the first husband and the three children from that marriage. If the second marriage produced two children—or none—fill out a record showing your grandmother and her second husband and any children from this marriage. Some researchers prefer to fill out records for the marriage that produced their ancestor and list the name(s) of other spouses in the "comments/clarifications" portion of the family-group record.

FIGURE 1 *Family-Group Record*

HUSBAND _____   WIFE _____
Birth Date _____   _____
Birthplace _____   _____
Marriage Date _____   Place _____
Death Date _____   _____
Place _____   _____
Father _____   _____
Mother _____   _____

CHILDREN
(1) NAME _____   SPOUSE _____
Birth Date _____   _____
Birthplace _____   _____
Marriage Date _____   Place _____
Death Date _____   _____
Place _____   _____

(2) NAME _____   SPOUSE _____
Birth Date _____   _____
Birthplace _____   _____
Marriage Date _____   Place _____
Death Date _____   _____
Place _____   _____

(3) NAME _____   SPOUSE _____
Birth Date _____   _____
Birthplace _____   _____
Marriage Date _____   Place _____
Death Date _____   _____
Place _____   _____

(4) NAME _____   SPOUSE _____
Birth Date _____   _____
Birthplace _____   _____
Marriage Date _____   Place _____
Death Date _____   _____
Place _____   _____

(5) NAME _____   SPOUSE _____
Birth Date _____   _____
Birthplace _____   _____
Marriage Date _____   Place _____
Death Date _____   _____
Place _____   _____

SOURCES:

COMMENTS/CLARIFICATIONS/OTHER MARRIAGES:

Research begins with an analysis of what is already known. By starting with the living generation and working backward, you will learn how much is already known about members of ancestral families in each generation. A generation begins when a couple marries and has children. The next generation begins when those children marry and have their own families.

Whenever data for individuals is lacking, the discovery of the life events for those people becomes the research objective: Where and when were they born and to whom and when were they married? What were their lives like? Who were their parents? By making the discovery of information about a specific person your research goal, you define the scope of your efforts in terms of the time period and locality.

Make it a habit to note where you found the information for each entry in the space provided for sources at the bottom of the family-group record. If there is insufficient space, continue your notes on the reverse. A brief entry—a footnote—is all that is needed. For example:

ᨑ_____

Suppose your parents are deceased and you obtained information about them from certificates received through the mail. One of the source notes at the bottom of your family-group record might read: "Information about father from certificates of birth, marriage, and death received from South Dakota Department of Health, February 12, 1994." Knowing the date the information was received or found and the name of the information provider will guide others to the source you used.

_____ᨐ

THE EXTENDED FAMILY

Some researchers prefer to concentrate on direct ancestors. That means they are interested in learning about only parents, grandparents, great-grandparents, great-great-grandparents, and so on into the past. However, a broader approach to family research is preferable because we need to know the kinship networks in which our ancestors lived. How did brothers, sisters, cousins, aunts, uncles, grandparents, and those who married into the family influence each other? Did they share the same household? Did they help one another find employment? Did they move to localities in which relatives had already established themselves? Answers to these questions and the details about why and how

these things influenced family members will be an important part of your family history. Kinship networks are a constant influence in our lives, and to ignore them eliminates a central element in both past and present family life. You can demonstrate this by looking at the guest list you prepared for a wedding reception or a mailing list for graduation announcements. Note the aunts, uncles, cousins, and friends that play a role in your life. To find records tracing activities and movements of ancestors requires a knowledge of their interactions with the extended family and others.

After completing a family-group record in which you are listed as a child, fill out other family-group records for the families of your grandparents, great-grandparents, and so on, as far back in your family's history as information permits. Also complete a record for each child in these families (your aunt/uncle, great-aunt/uncle, etc.) who married. If your mother had four brothers and sisters who married, for example, fill out four family-group records for your research files—one for each of your mother's siblings. Your research will be more productive and accurate if you expand it to cover at least the families of your aunts' and uncles' children in each generation. You will then have a record of several families that connect with your own through marriage to one of your cousins. Their descendants will have records about your ancestors. Knowing who your cousins are, or at least which names are found in cousins' families, may someday guide you to information about your family that was uncovered by an avid researcher who is your second or third cousin. You would be surprised at the number of cousins unknown to you who are searching for information about the same ancestors you are seeking.

Sometimes knowing the names of extended family members is essential to proving relationships. You may encounter families with the same given names as the ones found on an ancestor's family-group record. Only when you determine who the children married and who their offspring were can you identify which family is yours. This approach is essential if, as many researchers do, you extract data on all persons with your family name in each record you search.[1]

Describing Kinship Ties

As you write or telephone family members whom you have never met, you will want to explain how you are related to them. Are they your great-grandparents, aunts, uncles, or cousins? Any degree of a parent, grandparent, or great-grandparent is a direct-line ancestor.

Aunts, uncles, and cousins of whatever degree are collateral ancestors—they were not directly involved in relationships that eventually produced you.

The relationship chart in figure 2 will help you understand your kinship ties to direct and collateral relatives. Kinship is normally understood to be a relationship of blood; your kin share common ancestors with you—common parents, grandparents, or great-grandparents. If you and a kinsman/woman share the same father and mother, you are siblings (brothers/sisters). If you share common grandparents but not parents, you are first cousins. Second cousins share common great-grandparents, third cousins share common great-great grandparents (2 G G parents), and so on. The same system works for your descendants. Your children are siblings to one another. Your grandchildren are first cousins to one another and their children—your great-grandchildren—are second cousins to one another.

You will notice in figure 2, however, that there are some cousins who are "removed." This occurs when the person whose relationship to you is being defined is not in your same generation. Your granduncle's/aunt's children are your father's or mother's first cousins and your first cousins once removed (1c 1r). You are one generation removed from the first cousin relationship that would exist between them and one of your parents. Notice that the children of your great-granduncle/aunt are your first cousins twice removed (1c 2r); you are two generations removed from the first cousin relationship they would have with one of your granduncles/aunts.

Of course you have other relatives. If you marry, you become an in-law in your spouse's family and your spouse has the same status in your family. A spouse's grandparents, aunts, uncles, and cousins become your relatives by marriage. You share no blood relationship with them, but if you have children, they will share a blood relationship with all of your spouse's ancestors and descendants. If you would like more details about how people are related to one another, you may enjoy Jackie Smith Arnold's *Kinship: It's All Relative*. She discusses the different ways we pick up relatives and also provides guidance about tracing hereditary diseases.

PEDIGREE CHARTS

Soon your file of family-group records will grow so large that it will be hard to determine which family fits where in the history you are uncovering. To solve the problem you need to use pedigree charts, as shown in figure 3. Write your name on line 1 at the left of the pedigree chart. The parallel lines above and below (lines 2 and 3) provide space to write in the names of your parents, your grandparents (lines 4–7), great-grandparents (lines 8–15), great-great-grandparents (or 2nd great-grandparents) (lines 16–31).

Pedigree charts help to track research progress and serve as an index to family-group records (figure 1) by using the numbers assigned to each person on the chart. (You can buy some charts prenumbered.) The first person on the chart at the left, the principal, is given the number 1. It is this person's ancestry that will be recorded on the chart. The principal's father will be number 2 and his or her mother number 3. The principal's father's father will be number 4 and the father's mother number 5. The principal's grandfather on the mother's side is number 6 and his grandmother number 7.

As you continue to fill in the names of grandparents in each generation, they are numbered consecutively. Note that all of the male forebears have even numbers and females odd. The number given a father is always double the number on the line on which his son or daughter is recorded. At the end of each line on the right of the page is a space to write the pedigree chart numbers upon which the last person (numbers 16–31) shown is number 1. In the upper left corner of each chart is a space for the number of the chart. The chart on which you appear as number 1 would be chart 1, the chart on which the last grandparent ancestor (number 16) on your dad's side appears as number 1 could be chart 2, and the chart on which his wife (number 17) appears as the principal could be chart 3, and so on.

Instead of starting with the number 1 on each new chart, some researchers prefer to give every ancestor a consecutive number. In such a system, the ancestor's number is determined by his or her place in the ancestry of the person who is number 1 on chart 1. Using the chart in figure 3 as an example, ancestor number 16 would become the first person on chart 2. The father of number 16 would receive the number 32 because the last number on chart 1 was 31 and also because the pedigree chart number of a father is twice the number of his son or daughter.

As you get into research more deeply, you will discover there are many types of charts and many ways to identify the ancestors recorded on them. What you should remember is that pedigree charts depict research progress and allow you to organize your family-group records generation by generation. If you wish, you can give each family-group record the number the husband has on the pedigree chart. This will help you arrange sheets for easy retrieval and filing.

FIGURE 2 *Chart of Your Relationships*

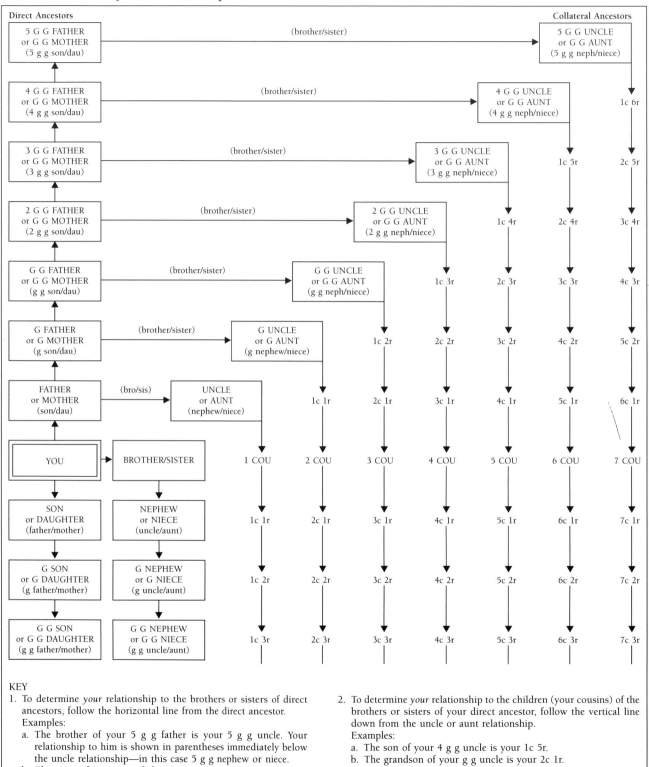

KEY

1. To determine *your* relationship to the brothers or sisters of direct ancestors, follow the horizontal line from the direct ancestor.
   Examples:
   a. The brother of your 5 g g father is your 5 g g uncle. Your relationship to him is shown in parentheses immediately below the uncle relationship—in this case 5 g g nephew or niece.
   b. The sister of your 5 g g father is your 5 g g aunt.

2. To determine *your* relationship to the children (your cousins) of the brothers or sisters of your direct ancestor, follow the vertical line down from the uncle or aunt relationship.
   Examples:
   a. The son of your 4 g g uncle is your 1c 5r.
   b. The grandson of your g g uncle is your 2c 1r.

FIGURE 3 *Pedigree Chart*

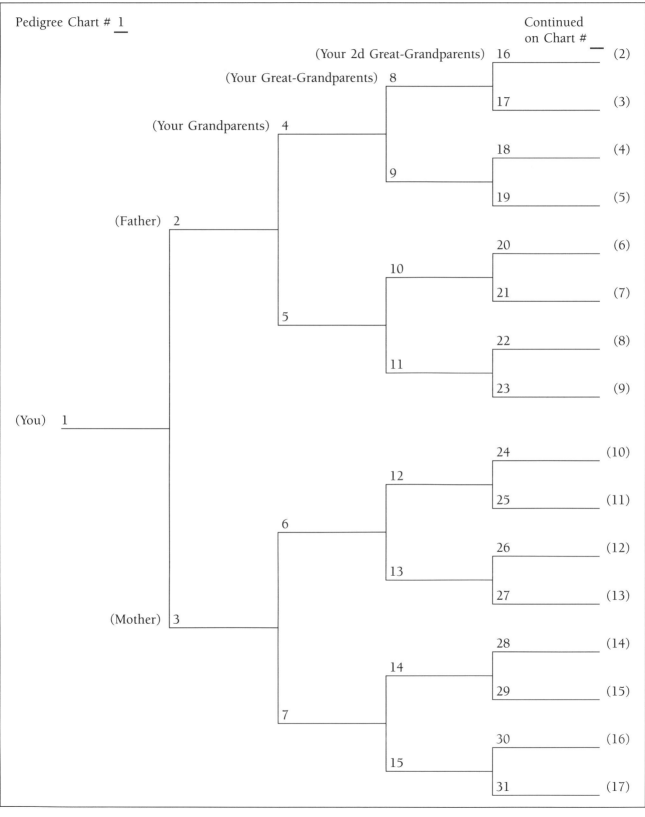

Pedigree Chart # 1

Continued on Chart # —

(Your 2d Great-Grandparents) 16 — (2)

(Your Great-Grandparents) 8

17 (3)

(Your Grandparents) 4

18 (4)

9

19 (5)

(Father) 2

20 (6)

10

21 (7)

5

22 (8)

11

23 (9)

(You) 1

24 (10)

12

25 (11)

6

26 (12)

13

27 (13)

(Mother) 3

28 (14)

14

29 (15)

7

30 (16)

15

31 (17)

DEVELOPING A RESEARCH PLAN AND FILING SYSTEM

So far you have learned that genealogical research requires gathering what is known about your family and writing it down on family-group records and pedigree charts. The second step in the research process is to analyze your family-group records to see where information is missing. Perhaps your pedigree charts show that you have complete information on several generations of grandparents. As you analyze the family-group records for each of these, however, you find that there are missing birth dates, unnamed spouses, or perhaps unnamed children. There will usually be several ancestral lines for which you know nothing about the parents of the last-named persons on the pedigree chart. The goal is to find complete data for each generation and then move on to the next. To keep things simple, work on one family group at a time, identifying the parents, their children, and their children's spouses.

Next you need to decide where to look for the facts to complete your record. Detailed help with this step is given in chapters 4 through 7. Remember that family-group records and pedigree charts are the schematic diagrams or outlines of ancestor's lives. They really do not tell you *how* the ancestors lived or what they did. Later chapters show you how to look for sources that reveal this type of information.

Let me use the example of a neighbor of mine and his family, to show you how the steps outlined lead to records about ancestors. Noel Ballstaedt could be a member of any community in the nation. He has developed an interest in finding out more about the origins of his family.

Noel decides a local library is the place to start his search. He has never felt comfortable in libraries, so when he arrives he wanders through the stacks hoping to see a title about genealogy. Finally, he decides to try the reference desk for help. The librarian responds to his questions about how to trace genealogy by telling him to look in the catalog under the subject heading *Genealogy*. This guides him to the few handbooks the library has on the subject and to some local genealogies. He is not interested in reading a thick volume on genealogy, especially when the index shows him that his ancestors are not in the book. His visit to the library is premature. There are some things he must do at home before returning to the library.

To better identify the kind of help he needs, Noel fills out a family-group record with himself as husband. Next he fills in family-group records for the families of his parents, grandparents, and great-grandparents.

With these charts in hand, Noel has a better idea of where to begin. He knows he will have to search for information to complete the blanks on the charts. Following is a list of missing facts from his family-group records. Each of them becomes a research objective.

1. Grandfather Ballstaedt's birthplace?
2. Grandfather Ballstaedt's birth date?
3. Grandfather Ballstaedt's parents' names?
4. Grandmother Ballstaedt's maiden name?
5. Grandmother Ballstaedt's birthplace?
6. Grandmother Ballstaedt's birth date?
7. Grandmother Ballstaedt's parents' names?

By now Noel knows that finding where his family came from requires learning first about his parents and grandparents. Dates, places, and events in their lives will provide clues about where to search for information about other ancestors. If, for example, Noel finds a marriage certificate for his grandparents, he can determine where to write for a copy of a marriage license that may tell him their ages. Knowing this, he can write to the city in which his grandparents were married to see if a search of the birth records will yield birth certificates. Even if his grandparents were not born in that city, they may have lived there before or after marriage and, therefore, could be found in a census. Knowing their ages will help him identify his grandparents and perhaps their families in the census. The census may in turn tell him the names of his grandparents' parents and siblings as well as the state or country in which each family member was born.

Noel Ballstaedt first goes through his personal papers and those of his parents to determine if information can be found to fill in some of the gaps on his forms. Scrapbooks, birth certificates, marriage licenses, letters, diaries, photos, and anything else from or about family members help. When he has exhausted this resource, he talks with other relatives and even friends of parents, grandparents, uncles, or aunts.

We mistakenly think that the most-accurate records are those kept by some agency or institution. Often the records a family keeps are just as valuable and, in some instances, more factual. Even the remembrances of family members and friends can provide details that official records often miss. Generally, this process will uncover the information needed for the initial research goals Noel Ballstaedt set for himself. Now, he can set new research goals based on what he does not know about ancestors in the next older generation.

Before we go on, let's review what my neighbor has learned about the research process.

1. Fill out family-group records for himself, his parents, grandparents, and, if possible, great-grandparents.
2. Fill out a pedigree chart with himself as number 1 and including the parents identified on the family-group records.
3. Note where information is missing about ancestors.
4. Make a list of research objectives that will provide needed facts:
   Where and when did ancestors live?
   Whom did they marry?
   Who were their children?
   Who were their parents?
5. Research one family at a time.

6. Search through personal records such as photo albums, home movies, slides, letters, certificates, school records, memberships, insurance policies, wills, diaries, newspaper clippings, programs from funerals and graduations, and wedding announcements.
7. Ask family members to search their homes for sources.
8. Contact friends of parents, grandparents, and other family members to gain access to their records and remembrances.

In the course of research, you, like Mr. Ballstaedt, will gather documents and take notes about important facts that will become lost if they are not incorporated into some sort of filing system. There are many systems for genealogical note keeping and filing. Although you probably want to develop your own system, following are some guidelines to consider when setting it up.

The most important part of any filing or note-keeping system is a research calendar or log. A simple research calendar, shown in figure 4, contains columns for the date, a description of the source searched, and the information found in the document. Most researchers identify which individual or family-group record is verified by the information recorded on the calendar sheet. Another column could be added to indicate where a copy or abstract of the source is filed. It is

FIGURE 4 *Sample Research Calendar*

Ancestor/Family: Friedrich Carl Ballstaedt

Date	Source/Activity	Results	File
21 May 94	Visit Dad, search his records	Found following records: Dad's birth certificate F. C. Ballstaedt cert. of naturalization Letters from Germany when F. C. Ballstaedt died	Fr. Ballstaedt Doc. file
05 Jul 94	Interview with Dad	Dad remembers family came to New York from Hamburg Dad's German hometown was Herne F. C. Ballstaedt said his family came from Posen After arriving in U.S., family moved to Decatur, Illinois	Ditto

best to use separate sheets for each ancestral family (husband, wife, and children). If you record facts about several families on one sheet, it becomes hard to keep track of research progress. If you are gathering extensive data about a single ancestor, keep his or her information on separate calendar sheets. By recording which sources were searched and the results, you will not search the same records again in the future.

You may also wish to develop a research plan. Without it time can be wasted reanalyzing research goals each time you return to your project. To make a research plan, write the name of a person you want more information about at the top of a sheet of paper and list the facts missing about this person. These are your research goals. Finally, list the steps to be taken to find the missing information. Figure 5 illustrates a research plan for Mr. Ballstaedt.

Since there are often lapses of weeks or months between research efforts, you may want to keep a research journal. In it you can record thoughts about the facts you have found, ideas for future research, places searched, families documented, and things you should remember the next time you do research.

Every researcher needs to decide in advance what will be done with the documents produced by research efforts. The certificates, extracts, copies of documents, and letters must be filed to make sure they can be found later. Perhaps the simplest approach is to file each document with the family-group record reflecting the information the source provides. If the document provides facts about individuals described on other forms, a cross-reference sheet should be placed with the other forms.

Some researchers keep separate logs for correspondence; others treat letters like any other document received. In the latter case, a reply is recorded on the research log under the date it was received. The sender is listed in the "source" column, and a summary of the facts contained in the letter is written in the "results" column. A copy of the letter remains in the appropriate document file as a reminder; the reply sent is filed with the letter.

SEARCHING BEYOND FAMILY SOURCES

At some point your research will take you beyond the information found in family sources. You will need published resources and original records to help fill in the blanks on your family-group records and pedigree charts. How do you find records that describe an ancestor's activities? The answer lies in understanding the concept of jurisdictions and how records are created and preserved.

Everyone who has ever lived has had vital information recorded in some way: on a piece of paper, in someone's memory, on a stone, and in some cultures—such as Sri Lanka—even on the leaves of plants. In

FIGURE 5   *Sample Research Plan*

Ancestor: Friedrich Carl Ballstaedt (b. abt. 1874—d. 27 Jun 1955)

Missing Facts	Plan

Birthplace
Birth date
Parents' names
	Search Dad's records for:
	    birth certificate
	    obituary
	    letters
	    family Bible
	    photographs
	    diaries
	
	Interview Dad to learn what he knows about grandfather F. C. Ballstaedt's birth and parents
	
	Interview Dad's brothers and sisters to discover what they know and the records they have

every community there are and have been persons responsible for recording information about members. These recorders generally represent some agency or institution in the community, province, or nation. Their responsibility or authority is usually limited to a specific area or group of people. Perhaps some examples will clarify this point.

The United States Bureau of the Census has a nationwide responsibility to record people's names and other personal information. On the regional and local levels, the city or state office of vital statistics records births and deaths, and the county clerk or a similar agent records the issuance of marriage licenses and deeds. Local courts record divorces, wills, and other life events. Insurance companies, fraternal organizations, trade unions, and churches also keep records of members' activities. Local religious records describe a family's participation in a local congregation as well as events such as birth, marriage, and death.

Representatives of these jurisdictions or institutions record data about individuals who live within that area of authority. Sometimes these boundaries are political, such as national, state, and county boundaries; in other instances the boundaries of an institution or organization are described in terms of membership, such as membership in churches and social and fraternal groups. Sometimes jurisdictions have changed over time. In many states, for example, birth, marriage, and death certificates were originally recorded at the county courthouse; by the beginning of the twentieth century, however, most states had established an office of vital statistics to take over most of these functions from the various county offices.

You will encounter roadblocks when the records you seek are not in their expected places. For example, perhaps the county boundaries have changed since your family lived there, and the older records are at the former county seat while more-recent records are at the new county seat. A company, church, or other organization with which your family associated may no longer exist. In such cases, you must find out who assumed responsibility for the records you seek. Often staff members at state archives or historical societies in the area can give you some clues about where these records are today.

Another obstacle is encountered when you cannot find ancestors in records from the area in which you know they lived. Sometimes you may think your forebears left an area because their names do not appear in indexes or abstracts of local records. Indexes and abstracts allow you to search through large numbers of records quickly to see if your ancestors are recorded

there. An *index* is simply an alphabetical list of the surnames and given names of people recorded in a document. Accompanying each name is the page number on which the name appears in the document. An *abstract,* on the other hand, lists not only the person's name and the page on which the name appears but also a brief summary of the information in the document about this person. Abstracts can be arranged alphabetically or chronologically. In the latter case, the abstracts of entries about persons from a given year or series of years are arranged either alphabetically or by the date of the entry.

There are several reasons why you may not be able to find ancestors in indexes or abstracts. Perhaps they are not listed under the names you associate with them because a local scribe may have misspelled the name. Maybe an indexer had difficulty reading the handwriting in a document describing a forebear and, for example, indexed the ancestor William Frey as William Trey or Brey or even Matthew Gray. Furthermore, ancestors may have used several different spellings of their names.

On the other hand, a cursory search of unindexed records that yields no familiar names may make you think your ancestors are not accounted for when they really are. Records without indexes must be analyzed to learn how best to approach them. If they are chronologically arranged, you should search during the span of time that your ancestor was likely to be recorded. If the records are arranged according to some geographic scheme, you should determine what portion of the record contains entries from the locality in which your family lived.

If you are searching an unindexed census, for example, search in the township, county, town, or neighborhood (street) in which local directories, tax lists, or other indexed sources show the family residing. Staff members at local historical societies or libraries may be able to show you how to find your family in an unindexed census. As part of the census activities, communities were divided into enumeration districts. Some communities were already divided into wards, usually an election district, that may be substituted for enumeration districts. In other cases, there may be census enumeration-district or ward maps keyed to local censuses. (See chapters 5 and 6 for further information.)

Discovering the names and activities of people your ancestors associated with will also help you in your search for family information. Sometimes ancestors disappear from the records of a community. For example, they may be there in one census and gone the next. By learning what the records tell us about their neighbors, friends, and relatives, you may learn what happened to your family. Death or other circumstances may have caused your ancestors to move in with cousins, nephews, nieces, friends, or even former neighbors, and thus be counted as part of another household by the census taker.

There will also be cases in which cousins, nephews, nieces, or neighbors were more prominent in the records than your direct ancestors. Reconstructing the lives of these people may give important clues to what was happening with the people you are seeking. There is a lot you can learn about your family by searching for your ancestor's relatives and neighbors in censuses, tax lists, land records, probate records, and other sources as explained in chapters 5 and 6.

Following is a list of steps that lead to records. Some records will be available only in local libraries, archives, or government offices; others may be obtained through interlibrary loan or by requesting a copy of the original. More information about how to find and use these records is provided in chapters 4–7. For the present, take a look at how finding records fits into the research process.

1. List events and dates in a person's life that indicate where information about them might be found.

    Was the person an immigrant, in the military, an heir to property, a landowner?

    Where were parents, brothers, sisters, or children born?

    Where did the person attend school or work?

    Were there other events or activities in his or her life that are recorded in some kind of document (school, employment, government)?

2. List localities (cities, counties, states) in which you would expect to find records about your progenitor's activities in archives, courthouses, historical societies, bureaus of vital statistics, etc.

3. Visit or contact local libraries, historical societies, or archives that have genealogies, local histories, biographies, personal name indexes, or similar materials that may contain data about your ancestor. (See chapters 4–6 and the appendixes.)

4. Write for copies of birth, marriage, or death records from the agent for the locality in which the person lived.

5. Determine if federal or state censuses exist that might have recorded the ancestor.

6. Ask your local librarian to help you obtain the appropriate census indexes as well as microfilms or copies of the census pages showing your family. (See chapter 6.)

7. Determine if the institutions you contact will search their records for you or recommend professional genealogists in the area.

8. If you need help from a local genealogist or researcher, write to the local genealogical society, historical society, public library, or history department of the local high school or college for a recommendation of someone to search the records of the area for you. (See Appendix A for a list of genealogical research centers.)

Researching Local History Sources

In the initial stages of research you will spend most of your time learning about births, marriages, deaths, and movements of the family from one place to another. You soon learn that the pedigree charts and family-group records produced by these efforts are of little interest to most other family members because there is no storyline. The facts on the charts and forms you fill out need to be woven into the daily lives of the people described on them. You want to share in the successes of these ancestors and observe how they handled failures. To help tell this story, you need to exchange your genealogist's or family historian's cap for that of the local historian.

Historians of communities are interested in identifying individuals as a means of illuminating local life and society in the past. They are interested in sources such as newspapers, town council minutes, court records, land records, and other records of local institutions that describe the community itself rather than the genealogies of its families. It is interesting to note, however, that modern local historians often look for clues about the community by examining local families. In this effort they use the same methods as genealogists.

Local historians look for information in sources that describe local architecture, politics, population growth, the economy, professions, climate, and even geography. They examine school records to learn about local education. Local government and church records provide clues about how communities have cared for the needy. Newspaper and business records reveal developments in communication and transportation. Land development, the laying out of streets, and provisions for local services such as natural gas, water, and electricity are studied with the help of records created by local government.

The methods of local historians provide genealogists and family historians with information that makes ancestors come alive within the context of the community. For example, reading microfilm copies of the local newspaper gives new dimension to the story surrounding the death of an ancestor during an epidemic or other local disaster. Reports and histories found at local or state boards of education will help you learn about the role of local schools in your family's history.

Sometimes examining the local histories of ancestors means finding out about various countries. For example, my researcher friend, Noel Ballstaedt, needs to examine local sources on both sides of the Atlantic.

_____

Noel's father was born in Germany and immigrated with his family to Salt Lake City, Utah, about 1910. Shortly after their arrival, the family moved to Decatur, Illinois. Noel Ballstaedt knows that they moved back to Salt Lake City because one of his aunts was born there in 1921.

Noel could use public and academic libraries in Salt Lake City and Decatur that have original or microfilm copies of local newspapers from the late nineteenth and early twentieth century. Reading these newpapers will help transport him back into the world of his father and grandfather. Libraries from these areas could also have local histories, directories, and collective biographies to help him learn about people and institutions in both Illinois and Utah.

Local city or county clerks have land records, tax records, naturalization records, voter registration lists, or local censuses that could tell him about the role an ancestor played in community life. City council minutes and records of the water department, police department, and fire department should provide additional facts about the communities in which the Ballstaedts lived.

Noel knows that the Ballstaedts immigrated from a town named Herne, near the western border of Germany. It is in the heart of the industrial area on the east side of the Rhine known as the Ruhrgebiet. Learning about this locality will be more difficult. Unless he can travel to the area, Noel will probably have to rely on the sources he can find in nearby libraries and information obtained through the mail.

Noel Ballstaedt can find information about his ancestral home in German gazetteers and encyclopedias. Some are available locally, but most will only be found through computer searches of bibliographic utilities such as On-line Computer Library Center (OCLC) and Research Libraries Information Network (RLIN) at his local library. (See chapter 3 for a description of these databases.) These utilities provide access to the collections of thousands of libraries in the United States and Canada. By searching under the subject heading *Germany*, Noel will find encyclopedias, histories, atlases, and other types of books that contain information about Germany and its people.

He can also find local or regional histories by seeking this town or larger cities in the area (Herne, Dortmund) as subject headings in library catalogs or the bibliographic utilities noted previously. Road atlases will help Noel learn about the location and surroundings of ancestral homes. Since the United States is a nation of immigrants, many libraries have collected materials relating to the ancestral homes of local residents. Local interlibrary loan departments or reference librarians can introduce Noel to the tools they use to find these materials at other libraries.

With the help of one of the consulates or the embassy of the Federal Republic of Germany, Noel should be able to obtain information about modern-day Herne. The same offices will also furnish addresses of city offices, local libraries, or historical societies that may provide further information. Once communication with these agencies is established, Noel can obtain copies of contemporary newspapers and other materials to help him learn about the lives of family members before immigration. The materials he finds written in German may require the assistance of someone who reads the language.

_____

Learning to integrate the sources and methods of local historians into genealogical research enriches a family's story. Using this approach, you will spend time learning about the ancestors' community, the jobs they held, and the roles they played in local society. How they earned a living, where they went to school, how they voted in elections, where they served in the military, and who their friends were are all valid questions for the family historian to pursue. You will learn what kind of illnesses and other hardships they faced, how they kept warm in the winter and avoided the heat of the summer, and why they moved from one place to another. Local records may even provide clues about courtship and married life.

In chapters 4 through 7 you will become acquainted with the sources that contain the answers to questions about ancestors' lives. Some are well known, such as civil and religious registers of birth, marriage, or burial. Newspapers, magazines, mail-order catalogs, contemporary photographs, and postcards are also commonly used resources. Although few researchers delve into minutes and reports from local agencies, such sources can tell you how regulations and the actions of local leaders influenced your family. Employment records and the records of fraternal or social groups, where they exist, may tell you a lot about your ancestors' interests and who their friends and acquaintances were. The journals, letters, papers, and biographies of prominent community members are generally overlooked by genealogists bent on narrowly pursuing their ancestors, yet they provide a glimpse of your ancestors' lives through the eyes of contemporaries who may have left records your ancestors did not.

Knowing about local crop failures, fires, political controversies, and other events in your ancestor's community will allow you to interpret the actions of family members. What do you know about the role your ancestor played in the Civil War? That role may have been tied to membership in a local unit of volunteer militia. What happened while these men were away? Who planted and reaped and served and taught? Do newspapers, letters, and birth and marriage records tell you about the impact of that war (or others) on the lives and homes of those left behind?

Sometimes researchers fail to ask questions of the sources they find; they simply take the facts the records offer. Documents often have more information in them than you think at first. When you read census information or deed indexes, are you sensitive to declining or expanding property holdings? Are there tax lists that allow you to monitor the local economy by measuring how much inhabitants paid and whether or not the amount changed over time? Note the prices in catalogs and local newspapers that fluctuate as signals of what local consumers were doing. As you dig through local records, family papers, and materials available on other families in the area, you will develop a family history that people will want to read because it not only describes the statistics of your ancestors' lives but also teaches lessons that have application to your own.

Note

1. Val D. Greenwood, *The Researcher's Guide to American Genealogy*, 2d ed. (Baltimore: Genealogical Publishing, 1990), 52.

CHAPTER 3

❦

Computers and Genealogy

Although America's bicentennial and the *Roots* phenomenon produced unheard-of interest in genealogy during the 1970s and early 1980s, the nature of research remained as it had always been. To be successful, you had to learn what seemed to be complicated research skills. Travel to the localities in which ancestors lived was a must unless the needed records were on microfilms at the Church of Jesus Christ of Latter-day Saints (LDS) Family History Library in Salt Lake City or in the collections of other libraries, archives, or historical societies. Only a few research centers could provide help in finding your ancestors. Many of those who wrote, called, or visited one of these repositories seeking help in uncovering their heritage abandoned the search because it seemed too complicated. Those who persevered in their search for ancestors saw that the birth of the computer age in the mid-1980s changed the basic nature of genealogical and family history research.

The search for ancestors became simpler because of the computer revolution, the growth of research centers in every region of the United States, and the development of genealogical collections at local public and college libraries. You can see from Appendix A that researchers in every region of the United States are now served by one or more major genealogical research centers. These centers have done two things to make genealogical materials more accessible: They have acquired large numbers of microfilmed and published genealogical resources, and they have installed computers. Although computers at local libraries and societies are visible monuments to this new age, it is the computer behind the scenes that has increased the amount of resource material available to researchers.

Many who were caught up in the genealogical excitement caused by events in 1976 developed into family historians who published their findings. These publications, in turn, inspired others to do the same. A growing number of these researchers use computers to share their findings in books, pamphlets, and newsletters.

Computers behind the scenes at agencies producing microfilms and other genealogical publications were used in various ways to increase production. Today, there are thousands of titles produced each year that contain family histories, transcriptions or indexes of original records, or historical studies of the places our families lived. Each year more microfilmed records are made available. Now, personal information about our ancestors is extracted from original records, placed on standard computer disks, and made available in homes and libraries across the country.

Computers help you find information about ancestors, organize it, and share it with other family members. Computer databases available at local public and college libraries, as well as interlibrary computer networks, open the whole world to your queries. The term *database* normally refers to large amounts of data stored electronically and retrieved using a computer. A genealogical database contains information about persons who are linked to families and includes the names, dates, events, and places in each person's life.

The vital facts of ancestors' lives can be preserved in your home computer. Their lives become more meaningful as you arrange dates and places in your computer's family records and reports. As you type in the information, there is no need to have a correctable typewriter or a bottle of correction fluid handy; you can correct errors with a keystroke or go back and insert information you neglected to include in earlier entries. Once you have entered the information, your computer makes it a simple task to write a family history or compile a genealogy to share in printed form with other relatives. If visiting family members want copies of ancestors' family-group records or pedigree charts, it takes only a moment to turn on your computer and printer to make copies.

Today, the bulky books and files containing family records and pedigree charts have been reduced to a few computer disks. Unfortunately, many family historians are either unaware of how computers can help them or apprehensive about making the switch from paper to computer. As a result, many do not use personal computers to make their research easier and more fun. This chapter will help you understand the role computers can play in family history research and writing. The goal is to motivate you to experiment with a computer as a tool to advance your efforts to discover and then share the history of your family.

COMPUTER BASICS

Most of the computer systems you see will have at least four basic components: a keyboard made up of what looks like typical typewriter keys; a monitor that looks like a small television; a printer that may appear to be just a box with a slot for paper to come out or that actually resembles a typewriter because you can see where sheets of paper enter it, pass around a roller, and come out with typewritten characters on them; and finally, the CPU (central processing unit). The brain of the computer—the CPU—works much like your brain. Two things that keep it from being more like humans are that it cannot reason for itself and it has no will of its own. The following paragraphs describe how these computer components work together to produce a pedigree chart or family-group record—or a printed page.

You tell the CPU what to do through a keyboard or a mouse. Using a keyboard to instruct the computer requires only that you type a word or a series of letters—commands—so the computer knows what you expect. As you type the message, it appears on the monitor screen. A mouse, a small box that is no larger than your hand with a roller ball usually on the bottom and some buttons on the top, is another method to "talk" with the CPU—give it commands. A computer controlled by a mouse usually displays small pictures (called icons) on the computer monitor to represent the many things the computer can do. As you move the mouse, an arrow or mark on the screen moves to the image that represents the function you wish the computer to perform. By pressing the buttons on the top of the mouse you tell the CPU which command you are selecting.

A newly acquired computer is useless until it is loaded with instructions (programs) that direct it to perform the tasks you desire of it. These instructions are written in computer language on disks. A computer is programmed to follow commands you give it by placing disks with needed instructions into a slot (a disk drive) in the computer where the computer's electronic eyes or sensors read these instructions. Some computers have a permanent disk inside—called a hard disk/hard drive—that can store instructions as well as data you place there. Other computers work only when an external disk, called a *floppy disk,* is placed in the computer's disk drive where the computer reads instructions needed to perform tasks for you. Floppy disks are similar in some ways to the old 78 and 45 rpm records many of us collected in years past. Information is inscribed electronically on these disks, which can be read and understood by the computer. Before a floppy disk will accept data, however, it must be formatted. Your local computer or office supply store may sell preformatted disks. If you are using a disk that has not been formatted, do not be concerned: the formatting procedure is included in the program (instructions) you will install on your computer when you first use it. Refer to the program handbook for help in formatting floppy disks.

A third type of disk your computer may use is a compact disc, or CD. A CD can accommodate much more information than a floppy disk and requires a special drive, or reader, to transmit the information on the CD to the screen of your monitor.

If you purchase a genealogy program, you will find several disks filled with computer instructions. Once your computer has read (loaded) these instructions, it will help you organize your family records. Using the instructions from the genealogy program disks, the computer will create messages that will appear on your computer monitor asking what you want to do. If you wish to type in (enter) the names and facts you have found, you can select an option that provides a form on the screen where you can type ancestors' names, birth dates, and birthplaces along with other information. The form that appears on your monitor is called a *screen* or a *template.* It has spaces designated for names, dates, places, source notes, etc. You fill in the spaces with information from your research. Your computer can also provide reports—sheets printed by your computer to show pedigrees, family groups, or a person's lineage based on the information you have placed in your computer. You can have the computer show you this information on the monitor or print a paper copy.

The computers you see for sale at your local computer store may be advertised as personal computers—

PCs. You can take a PC home, set it up on a table or desk, and have your own home-computer center. Banks, libraries, businesses, and other agencies often have so many employees and customers who need information from computers that they hook dozens of keyboards and monitors to a huge CPU that can manage much more information than your personal computer can handle. Several keyboards and monitors attached to a central computer make up a computer network. Your local libraries may be connected to a nationwide library network, for example, that allows them to use a giant computer to search library catalogs from libraries in many parts of the country.

Your computer can also connect with networks or other computers through modems—devices that connect computers to telephone lines over which they transmit information. Modems can be purchased at your local computer store. They are described in terms of how fast they transport information over a telephone line, the baud rate. The faster a modem can transmit, the more expensive it is. If you buy a slower modem, however, your telephone charges go up because you spend more time on the telephone transmitting or receiving data.

ORGANIZING YOUR RECORDS WITH A COMPUTER

A personal computer can make organizing and maintaining family records a relatively simple activity. Using a genealogy program, your computer organizes your forebears and descendants into families and links them from one generation to the next by showing from whom you and your direct ancestors descended. Attached to each person are facts you gathered about them and their life: birth date and place, marriage date and place, spouse's name, childrens' names, and personal data. There may be additional facts about some ancestors such as their employment history, military service, health, religious life, and other aspects that make our relatives real people. As you continue to learn more about your family and discover additional ancestors through research, you can add those names and life stories to the records on your computer. Computers also allow you to include references to the sources in which you found information about relatives.

Of course, before you start to use a new genealogy program, you will read the manual from cover to cover. If you do this, the first screen that appears on your computer monitor will not be a mystery. Some programs start by showing you a menu on the computer monitor that allows you to choose an activity (see fig-

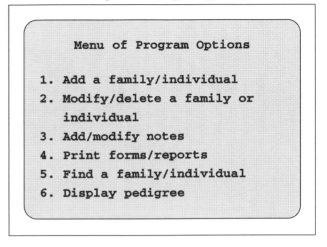

FIGURE 6 *Sample Genealogy Program Menu Screen*

Menu of Program Options

1. **Add a family/individual**
2. **Modify/delete a family or individual**
3. **Add/modify notes**
4. **Print forms/reports**
5. **Find a family/individual**
6. **Display pedigree**

ure 6). From the menu you select the activity you wish to perform: add, modify, or delete individual or family records; add or modify notes; print reports (family-group records, pedigree charts, etc.); find records for individuals or families; or find a pedigree. After you select the functions you wish, a screen appears with places for you to add information or request an action—such as printing a report of every person with the same surname in your computer files.

Other programs show you a pedigree first. As shown in figure 7, you can type in your name or the name of an ancestor on the line marked "principal." By selecting an option at the bottom of the screen you can add, delete, or modify information about this person. You can select a printout of the people or families in your computer files, and you can add notes to any person's record. Another program may show a screen with blanks for you to fill in the name of a person to add to your computer files or whose record you wish to review. A data-entry screen like the one in figure 8 allows you to enter information about a person. Words at the bottom of the screen move you to other functions in the program when highlighted by using your keyboard or a mouse.

Normally the first step in creating a genealogical file is to enter yourself with your birth date, birthplace, and other vital data. Most genealogy programs assign each person a unique number as that name is entered. Since you were the first person entered, you receive the first record number. Your name and personal data can now be retrieved by name or number.

As you enter information about yourself, most programs will ask you to create notes or footnotes with details about where the information entered about a person can be verified—the source of the data. The

FIGURE 7   *Computerized Pedigree Chart*

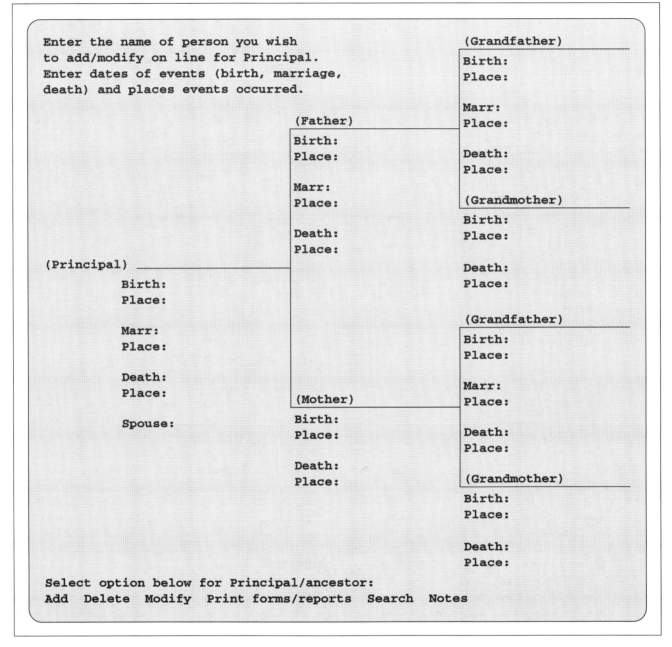

option to add notes may be part of your program's menu or it may be an option listed right on the screen where you enter information about yourself or an ancestor. If there are other facts about a person that you want to preserve, they can also be entered on the notes screen. Information for notes is taken from your research log and document files. You should describe the source—will, cemetery record, birth certificate—and where it is to be found. Sources should be identified so

clearly that another researcher would be able to obtain the same document or data that you did. If the information came from a letter, describe it in terms of its date, the sender, and where it is preserved. If you gained facts from an interview, identify whom you interviewed, the date, place, and where a transcript or copy of the interview is preserved. For materials from family archives, your address or the address of the person who contributed the source you used is also

FIGURE 8 *Computerized Individual Record*

```
                                    Record #: _____

  Name: _____    Male/Female: _____


  Birth Date: _____
           (Day, Month, Year)
  Birthplace:
   Town/Parish: _____    County/District: _____


   State/Province: _____    Nation: _____


  Marriage Date: _____
               (Day, Month, Year)
  Marriage Place:
   Town/Parish: _____    County/District: _____


   State/Province: _____    Nation: _____


  Spouse: _____    Spouse Record # _____


  Death Date: _____
           (Day, Month, Year)
  Death Place:
   Town/Parish: _____    County/District: _____


   State/Province: _____    Nation: _____


  Add   Delete   Modify   Print forms/reports   Search   Notes
```

important. Figure 9 shows an example of how a program might keep track of this type of information.

After you have entered facts about yourself, the computer will instruct you to press a specific key to save what you have entered. This action causes the facts you entered to be stored on the hard disk of your computer or on the disk you inserted into your computer as you began your work. Once you have saved the information about yourself, enter your spouse and children or your parents and brothers and sisters. After saving the information about them, you can do the same for your parents' families, grandparents, and great-grandparents. As these names are entered, the computer keeps track of who among the children of your grandparents became your parent, and who among the children of your great-

grandparents became your grandparent. At the touch of a key, all of these relationships become clear as they are shown on the screen or printed as reports.

Computer genealogy programs allow you to print out your family files in several forms. You can print a pedigree chart or ancestor list demonstrating how comprehensive your research has been. If you wanted one of your children or a brother or sister to have the same family records you do, the computer could print out family-group records and pedigree charts that he or she could keep in a book. If the person has a computer, you could copy the family records onto a floppy disk for his or her use. Programs will also print reports that index all of the names in your files, describe the sources you have used, or describe which persons lack identifying

FIGURE 9 *Computerized Notes for an Ancestor*

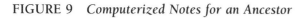

```
                         William Anthon Jones
   30 July 1994                                              Page 1
   SOURCES
      BIRTH: Certificate of birth, Kansas State Department of Health and
         Environmental, Office of Vital Statistics
      MARRIAGE: License issued by Adams County, Ohio, Clerk's Office
      DEATH: Certificate of death, Nevada State Dept. of Human Resources, State
         Health Division, Section of Vital Statistics
      PERSONAL HISTORY:
```

information. Most will calculate your relationship to specific persons in your files. Some programs also print blank forms such as family-group records, pedigree charts, and research calendars. Compare the reports and options available on several programs before buying one.

Many programs today are designed to accept the GEDCOM—Genealogical Data Communication— format. That means you can swap family records with other researchers or send your information to relatives who also keep their family records on computer disks. If you wish, GEDCOM allows you to connect your computer to that of another person and transfer data directly through a modem. At a command from you— typed into the computer from your keyboard—your computer sends or receives family-group records and pedigree charts to or from the other computer using the language and symbols of GEDCOM.

CHOOSING A COMPUTER PROGRAM

Literally dozens of genealogical computer programs are on the market. They differ from one another in the amount of flexibility you exercise in designing the way your forms, charts, lists, and reports will look when printed. Other variables are the amount of information the program allows you to attach to each person's record and whether you can design your own individual and family records. Some provide only spaces for names, dates, and places, while others provide spaces for your sources of information. Another difference is the sophistication of the computer skills you must have to use all of the program's features.

At a recent conference of the National Genealogical Society, several vendors of genealogical software pre-

sented demonstrations of their products. Following are a few examples of these products showing the range in prices that currently exists: Family Origins (Parsons Technology) $49, Roots IV (Commsoft) $195, Everyone's Family Tree (Dollarhide Systems) $169, Family Roots (Quinsept) $240, Brother's Keeper (John Steed) $45, and Personal Ancestral File 2.3 (Church of Jesus Christ of Latter-day Saints) $35.

Computer novices and those who want their computer programs to provide them with standard screens, forms, and reports will feel most comfortable with Family Origins and Personal Ancestral File. These programs provide you with everything you need to organize your data to share with others; there is no need to do anything except follow the instructions. Both programs permit you limited flexibility in designing reports according to criteria you establish—localities, dates, names, etc.—and Personal Ancestral File lets you print blank forms to use in your research—pedigree charts, census-extraction forms, research-log sheets, etc. Family Origins and Personal Ancestral File provide separate files for notes on each individual. Family Origins allows you to alter the screens you use to input information about individuals or families.

Brother's Keeper is a program that more-experienced computer users, who wish to have screens and reports standardized for them, will enjoy. The program permits you to design special reports. It is more flexible than Personal Ancestral File because you can design the screens you use for ancestors' information. You may include space not only for names, dates, and places but also for personal-history facts and source notes.

For those who feel comfortable with computers, Roots IV, Everyone's Family Tree, and Family Roots will be of interest. All of these programs permit you to design your own screens for individual and marriage information. They print out the contents of your files in pedigree format as well as the formats used in two well-known genealogical journals, the *National Genealogical Society Quarterly* and the *New England Historical and Genealogical Register.* These programs allow you to design reports in several different ways and are flexible enough to permit you to produce a genealogy complete with table of contents, bibliography of sources, and index.

Your local computer software store will probably carry most of the programs discussed here. The Personal Ancestral File is available only from:

LDS Distribution Center
1999 W. 1700 South
Salt Lake City, UT 84104

If your local computer software dealer does not have any genealogy programs, contact one of the genealogy program publishers mentioned previously, or check the fall issue of Ancestry Publishing's *Genealogical Computing* at your local library. This issue lists most of the programs available, their cost, and publishers' addresses.

For a more-complete listing of genealogy computer programs, refer to a recently published guide to 155 genealogy software programs by two computer genealogists, Donna Przecha and Joan Lowrey's *Guide to Genealogy Software.* The authors tell you their views on the programs reviewed, include examples of the reports the programs produce, and explain how each program can be used. Addresses for the publishers of the programs as well as a list of genealogical software publishers whose programs were not treated in the book are included. With this book in hand, you can decide which program fits your needs and then write to its publisher for more information.

COMPUTER BULLETIN BOARDS AND NETWORKS

As discussed earlier in this chapter, you may communicate with genealogists and family historians around the United States with the use of a modem. One means is through computer bulletin boards. Persons with interests in specific families or genealogical topics send queries via their computer modems to a central computer that serves as an electronic bulletin board. At the central computer the messages are sorted and filed. You can connect your computer by modem to the central computer and see a list on your computer monitor of the queries sent to the bulletin board. When you see some-

thing of interest, you send a command to the central computer that lets you receive the full text of the query.

Several companies and nonprofit organizations make information sharing between computers easy. CompuServe's Genealogy Forum and Prodigy's Genealogy Bulletin Board are two commercial computer networks. By paying a membership fee you can link your computer to a large central computer network and search several databases—among them one containing genealogical information and queries from other subscribers to this service. In addition to learning about genealogy programs and information, you can find out who else is interested in your family. By using your computer and modem to communicate with these people, you are able to learn the status of their research and share what you have found. If you decide to try a computer service such as the two mentioned here, ask for information about their genealogical features before joining and paying any fees. Since these services rely on your telephone, your telephone bill will increase after you join.

The National Genealogical Society's Computer Interest Group also sponsors a genealogical bulletin board. Through it you can learn about the research of others as well as new developments in computer genealogy. For more information check a current issue of the *NGS Newsletter.* Inside each issue the Computer Interest Group publishes the *NGS/CIG Digest* with information about its bulletin board and genealogy computer programs. For a contemporary look at genealogical bulletin boards, read Steven Hayes article "Hooked on Bulletin Boards."

For those of French ancestry, the French national telephone system has developed a computer network for any person with a telephone, a computer, and a modem. Called Minitel, it not only permits you to search for living persons' names and addresses but also provides access to a number of genealogical databases created by local genealogical societies in France. For further information write to:

Minitel Services Company
888 Seventh Avenue, 28th Floor
New York, NY 10106
212-399-0080

Today there are many national and international computer networks. Perhaps you have access to one or more of them at work or at a nearby library. One of the largest is the Internet. Talk to your computer specialist at work or the computer services librarians at your local libraries. Ask them if there are genealogical services or bulletin boards available on the national or international networks they use.

GENEALOGICAL DATABASES ON DISK OR CD

Several agencies have made information about millions of individuals available through publications on compact discs (CDs) as well as floppy disks. The most widely known of these is FamilySearch, developed and published by the LDS Church. It provides access to information about some 250 million deceased persons. FamilySearch is available at the LDS Family History Library in Salt Lake City and at its branches, which are called LDS Family History Centers, in more than 1,000 locations in the United States and Canada. Recently it became available for lease to libraries and other research centers through:

GeneSys
400 Dynix Drive
Provo, UT 84605-9010

FamilySearch provides computer access to compact discs containing the International Genealogical Index, with events, dates, and places for more than 200 million names; the Ancestral File, with 15 million individuals linked in families; the Social Security Death Index, documenting about 39 million persons registered with the Social Security Administration who died before 1988; and the Military Index, describing thousands of military personnel who lost their lives in Korea and Vietnam. Also included is the Family History Library Catalog with a surname-search feature that permits you to search the Family History Library's large collection of genealogies and family histories for your ancestors' surnames. Two of these databases, International Genealogical Index and Family History Library Catalog, are also available in microfiche editions.

Two other Utah-based organizations publish genealogical data on compact discs and floppy disks. Gene-Sys of Provo provides every-word indexes to selected published family histories and censuses and the death records of the Social Security Administration. The American Genealogical Lending Library (AGLL) of Bountiful provides census and other indexes on floppy disks. See Appendix A for the address of the AGLL.

INTERLIBRARY COMPUTER NETWORKS

As a graduate student studying medieval German families and communities, I needed materials that were not found on the campus where I studied. Before going to see the interlibrary loan librarian, I consulted the many volumes of the *National Union Catalog* published by the Library of Congress. These volumes contained author entries for the books in the Library of Congress. Under each title some of the libraries in the United States were listed in which the materials I sought could be found. I was surprised to learn that there were books about the towns I was studying at various libraries around the country. Today, most of the major research libraries in the United States, as well as most colleges and universities, are part of interactive computer networks that allow any researcher access to thousands of library catalogs across the nation. A rapidly growing number of public libraries are also joining these catalog networks. As new materials—books, journals, microfilms—are processed in cataloging departments of member libraries, they are added to the library's own computer catalog. Because member libraries' catalogs are accessible to searchers at any other member library, all new materials added to the catalog of one library are automatically accessible to researchers anywhere there is a computer attached to the network.

Libraries in the United States generally use the Library of Congress subject headings and the Anglo-American Cataloging Rules when describing books and manuscripts in their catalogs. This means that you can search the subject catalogs of thousands of libraries using your family name or the town or county where your ancestors lived as the subject.

If you wanted to see what could be found in these libraries for your surname, you would do a search using your surname as the subject. A subject search for each might turn up some records or books that would help you better understand an early ancestor's life.

The best way to begin using the computer resources at your library is to talk to a librarian about what is available. Local librarians can help you learn how to use computers to search for information about your family in books in their library and other libraries. Remember that you are looking for books about your family name or books about the place your ancestors lived.

Most colleges or universities have a librarian who is responsible for computer resources at the library. At Brigham Young University, for example, it is the computer-assisted-research services librarian. A visit with that person will provide you with an overview of the computer resources available at your local college or university library. Let me use the university library where I teach as an example to illustrate, because I believe it is typical of most large- or medium-sized universities.

❦ _____

The computer research services librarian at Brigham Young University is also an experienced genealogist who long ago became addicted to computers as a tool in his research. He is always willing to help researchers use the many networks available in the library. He can provide them with access to Research Libraries Information Network (RLIN), Online Computer Library Center (OCLC—Dublin, Ohio), and to a "gateway" network that is connected to many libraries not affiliated with OCLC or RLIN. If we count only libraries affiliated with OCLC and RLIN, our university library has access through its computers to the catalogs of more than 1,000 university, college, public, and private libraries.

The Brigham Young University library and other major research centers and libraries are attached to several information networks that provide searches of huge periodical and newspaper computer indexes. Added to these resources is a local area network (LAN) within the library. This LAN permits access to a number of databases including one that lists most of the residents in each community in the United States, their addresses, and their telephone numbers. This is a great tool when you are trying to identify cousins in other cities who have the same surnames as your ancestors.

In college, public, and private libraries that do not have an electronic-media specialist, the interlibrary loan librarian or the general reference librarian will know about the computer assets in local libraries. For a list of library networks and catalogs, see Michael Schuyler's *Dial In: An Annual Guide to Online Public Access Catalogs.*

KEEPING UP TO DATE

By now you are asking how you can learn more about computer genealogy and stay current with the changes that take place almost weekly in this rapidly expanding field. To satisfy the first question, read *Computer Genealogy: A Guide to Research through High Technology,* a book edited by Paul Andereck and Richard Pence, which provides an in-depth discussion of the role of computers in genealogy and family history.

The journal *Genealogical Computing,* published by Ancestry, provides the most-comprehensive coverage of new developments in this field. The fall issue of this journal includes a list of genealogy computer programs currently available. In addition, joining the Computer Interest Group of the National Genealogical Society will bring you the *NGS Newsletter,* each issue of which includes the *NGS/CIG Digest.* The *Digest* provides reviews of new genealogy computer programs, hints on how to better use the program you may have, and other information about genealogists around the country who are involved in making genealogy easier and more productive through the use of computers.

CHAPTER 4

◖◗ ❦ ◖◗

Family and Neighborhood Records

In learning about ancestors, first study people and their relationships with each other: family, neighbors, friends, employers, and representatives of local and regional agencies or institutions. Next, examine the place they called home. Analyze buildings, geography, weather patterns, transportation, health, recreation, clothing, technology, the economy, communication, local culture, and even diet. Collect statistical data from sources that permit this type of analysis following the guidelines you learned in chapter 1. This approach allows each piece of the puzzle to "come to the witness stand" to give its "view" of what happened. In this chapter you will look at descriptions from the family circle and then at records from the ancestral neighborhood.

The sources cited in this and later chapters are not exhaustive. With a little brainstorming you could make a more-complete list of potential document types for your family. The procedure requires only a pencil, pad, and one or two family members or friends—although it can be done alone. Using what you already know about your ancestors, imagine what their life was like. List records that might have been created as a result of interaction with family, friends, neighbors, community members, or institutions. First on any list should be the sources in your own home and the homes of other relatives.

THE FAMILY ARCHIVES

Some of the most-accurate information about ancestors is in the homes and minds of living relatives. As with family-group records and pedigree charts (see chapter 2) the place to start is with yourself. What have you collected over the years? Most of us have photo albums,

slide collections, home movies, and videos. Have you also saved letters and postcards? Do you have a special place in which you keep track of births, weddings, or deaths—perhaps in a family Bible? Do you keep a journal or diary? Have you inherited heirlooms or family records from parents, grandparents, aunts, or uncles? Perhaps you collect newspaper clippings and other kinds of memories.

All written and remembered data as well as all artifacts held by family members are part of the family archives. We could also call it the family's collected memories and stories. In your family archives you will find letters, journals, family photo albums, paintings, jewelry, clothing, certificates, and a hundred other things that are hard to describe but invaluable in piecing together your family's history.

After you have searched the closets, attic, and basement, collect the material in one place and keep it together in storage boxes or a filing cabinet. Arrange your material into groups of like documents or objects. Next, rearrange your collection of records and artifacts according to which family owned or produced them. Materials that relate to your mom and dad and their children would constitute a single file. Other files would be created for the families of your grandparents. Make a list of what you have in each file with a brief description of the items. If items apply to more than one family group, file them in the file you feel is best and put a card or piece of paper in other files noting where the materials can be found.

Next, check the archives of other family members. Remember that cousins, aunts, and uncles are interested in the same persons you call grandfather and grandmother. All of you are collecting memories of the same family. Call or write to find out how much family history material your other relatives have. Let me illustrate with an example from my own family.

◖◕ _____

My mother, born Ruth Bingham, was orphaned a few weeks before her second birthday. I knew very little about her parents, William and Christiane Bingham, or her brothers and sister. What I have learned in recent years came from records and memories she had and from the remembrances and documents of my cousins, the children of her brothers and sister.

Ruth is the only member of her immediate family alive today. One of her stepmothers prepared a genealogical record describing her family as well as families of grandparents and aunts and uncles. Much of what Ruth knows about her history comes from this record. She also has several old photographs of her parents and grandparents and eyeglasses that her mother wore clipped on the bridge of her nose.

For many years I felt that my mother's family had left few traces. Then I was discovered by some cousins who, like me, had been trying to reconstruct the lives of their orphaned parents. We exchanged copies of the materials each of us had gathered and, thus, filled in some of the gaps in our family's story.

Among these items was a letter my mother had written to her 16-year-old sister, Athlyn. Dated December 4, 1926, it describes Christmas hopes for an 8-year-old in Ogden, Utah. The family Ruth lived with had little money for Christmas; she anticipated no gifts, just a chance to borrow a sister's doll. It had been nearly seven years since Ruth's parents died of influenza. She was living with her father's sister, Aunt Louisa Bingham McDonald, and her husband, Uncle Walter McDonald. (Aunt Louisa died just six months after the date of the letter.) This letter gave me a chance to peek at a moment in my mother's life that even she had forgotten—until she saw the letter.

Ogden
Dec 4, 1926

Dear Sister,
How are yow getting a long I have ben witing for a letter from yow wright and tell me if yow will send your doll to me for chirmisas wile you. We have snow now have yow? I wish yow a happy crimes. and I hope yow will send your doll for me this crimes if yow wont I will cry so yow better send it so yow send it wont you

your Ruth

this hachpe is for athlyn

After Athlyn's death, her children found the letter among her papers. They also found a photograph of the five orphaned children taken shortly after their parents died—Christiane on February 28 and William on March 12, 1920. In it the children are on the front porch of a comfortable-looking stone farmhouse. They are all dressed in warm winter clothing. (The home still stands today.)

Did you figure out that "chirmisas" and "crimes" both were Ruth's spelling of Christmas? How about "hachpe" for hankie or handkerchief? The letter and photograph found in a cousin's family papers gave me insight into my mother's childhood that even she could not provide.

_____ *◕◗*

The point is that the family archives include the documents, artifacts, memories, and experiences of all family members. These witnesses are essential to your research. Assembling your copies of the family archives or at least a list of what is available is the first step in documenting the activities of progenitors.

Once cousins, aunts, uncles, parents, grandparents, brothers, and sisters discover you are gathering family facts, they may begin sending materials to you. Some will send original records, others will send copies, and still others will simply let you know what they have. This may be a good opportunity to see if there is interest in selecting a family record keeper. Even if there is no desire to collect family records and artifacts in one place, you can copy as much as possible or at least list it in your own inventory of family sources. Make a habit of listing what you receive and noting where you filed it.

You may want to get advice on storing the various types of materials you receive. The conservator at the local university library, state archives, or historical society may be able to help. In addition, local libraries may have books on preserving documents and photographs.

USING INTERVIEWS AND LETTERS AS SOURCES

Information from grandparents, aunts, uncles, or friends of family can take you back several generations in your family's history. They may have known your great-grandparents personally and may have access to oral traditions from your second great-grandparents and even earlier generations. Through the stories of my grandfather, who recently died at age 97, I know the history of his ancestors back to the beginning of the nineteenth century. My grandfather grew up listening to the stories of his father, who was born in 1862. His father in turn listened to the family's history as told by his own grandfather, who was born in 1805. You can see how easily oral sources can take you back two, three, or even four generations. Just a reminder—know enough about your informant and the events being described to verify the traditions and history the person shares with you.

Interviews with relatives, friends, neighbors, co-workers, and others are the best means of identifying the thoughts and feelings that existed in your family and their community. In some cases they can give you firsthand accounts. Often they are passing on what they heard from parents, grandparents, or others of earlier generations. Opinions, biases, and preferences are seldom expressed in official records.

Interviews may be conducted in person or over the telephone. Sometimes letters are a preferable tool because they provide a better opportunity to verify what is being shared. Letters also allow the respondents time to do a little research before they reply to your questions. In either case, the most important part of gathering memories is the preparation for the oral or written interview.

Preparing for an Interview

First, decide the goals of the interview. Which facts are central to your research? What do you hope to know after the exchange is over? For example, you may be missing some birth, marriage, or death dates. Family members may have dropped from sight in the records you have searched, and you need some clues about those members during that time. Interviews can allow a glimpse into personal lives and give you more facts—or opinions—about family legends. Witnesses can help you learn what life was like in the past.

With your goals clearly in mind, you can now do some background study to make the interview as productive as possible. Read a little about what was happening around the world and on the home front during the life of the witness. If you can, look at some of the local newspapers from the time period to help isolate the events that were on people's minds then. Back issues of newspapers are often on microfilm at a local public library. If you live a great distance from your ancestor's locality, your own public library can request the microfilmed newspapers you need from a library in the area in which ancestors lived. The events you read about can be mentioned during interviews to give your informant a point of reference or to jog his or her memory.

Next, learn as much as possible about the person you will be questioning. Make note of events in the witness's life and in the life of his or her community—birthdays, marriages, illness, military service, employment, local elections, economic and natural disasters—anything you can find that will help the person focus on the people and happenings of interest to you. How old is the interviewee, and what is the state of his or her present health? What is the individual's occupation? What was the person's relationship with the ancestor you are studying? What are the informant's hobbies or special interests? Where and when did the person attend school? If the informant attended school with your relative, you can gain insight into a part of your forebear's life that often escapes notice. Even if they attended different schools, you can learn what school life was like back then. Gathering facts about informants may require telephone calls or letters to their family, friends, and neighbors. The work it requires to prepare for an interview will pay off in the quality of the information you uncover.

An example may help demonstrate how you can use interviews in your research.

Pretend you want to learn more about your great-grandfather, your dad's grandfather. Your great-grandfather and great-grandmother have been dead for many years. In fact, only their youngest child is still living. She is 80 years old and is your grandaunt. You decide to pay her a visit for an interview about your great-grandfather. Among your goals are these: find out the date and place of your great-grandfather's birth and marriage and details about his wife and children, and learn the names of his parents, when and where they were born and married, and the names and vital data for each of their children. You are also curious about what family life was like in your great-grandparent's home.

You will want to learn about the period in which your great-grandfather's family lived to help you better understand what your grandaunt will tell you. She was born in 1913 and her parents probably about 1873–1878, if they were 35–40 when she was born. Dig out your American history book or check out one at your local library. Read through the sections that cover the period from 1870 to the present. While at the library, ask about local newspapers and local histories. If you can, find the newspaper printed on the day your grandaunt was born and make a copy of the front page. Do the same for the years she would have been 16, 18, or 21. If she was married and you know the date of this event, get a copy of the front page for that day. A local-history book will also have descriptions of events in these years. Use this information to get a feel for the times in which your grandaunt and her family lived. Take copies of pages from the books or newspaper articles you find relating to important local, national, or international events during her life. You can show these to her during your interview and assist her efforts to recall personal and family events that occurred at or near the same time. These questions require your grandaunt to give the dates and places you need but also provide her with an opportunity to tell you more about her family's home life.

Talk to your parents and to your grandaunt's children, grandchildren, nieces, and nephews. Ask them to tell you their impressions of your aunt. Learn her hobbies, where she attended school, and what some of her favorite things are.

Most people store memories in chronological order. Plan your interview to begin at a particular time in the person's life and move forward or backward from that point. It may help to start with the present and move backward in time. Jumping from 1930 to the present and then back to 1920, for example, will make it more difficult for the subject to string events together and remember important details.

Several books are available on the subject of oral history. Two titles you may want to explore are Cullom Davis, Katherine Back, and Kay MacLean's *Oral His-*

tory: From Tape to Type and William Fletcher's *Recording Your Family History*. Most local libraries will have these and other titles on the subject. Ask your public or college reference librarian to help you.

Outlining an Interview

Finally, write an outline of the interview. Under each of the goals you have established for the interview, list a few questions you think will produce the facts you need. Again, remember to ask questions that will get you beyond vital statistics. Make a note to be sure to allow the person you are interviewing to give his or her opinion about family relationships and your ancestor's role in local society and politics. You also want to learn about religious views and the roles of ancestors in the workplace. Plan to ask the persons you interview to point out local sites of interest such as family homes, farms, local buildings, and even geographic features—mountains, rivers, and fields—that played a role in the family's history. (If you have the opportunity, visit and photograph some of these to add color and texture to your family's story.) Include a note about asking the person being interviewed to refer you to other witnesses. Always be sure to ask about photographs, heirlooms, journals, diaries, and letters they or other family members have.

Returning to the example of interviewing your grandaunt, after preparing for the interview you are now ready to write down some questions.

To get facts about your great-grandfather and his family, ask some questions similar to these:

1. What names did your family use for each other, or were they generally known only by their full names (first, middle, last names)?
2. What role did birthdays have in your family's traditions?
3. What are the birth dates of everyone in your family? What birthday celebrations stick out in your memory?
4. Did your parents ever visit their birthplaces, and did they take you or the other children along? What do you remember about it?
5. What family stories about your birth or the births of your brothers and sisters do you remember?

6. What do you remember about your parents' anniversaries? Did they ever go back to the place where they married?

━━━━━━━━━━━━━━━━━━━━━━━ ☺⟩⟩

Now write some questions on your own. Remember that the goal is to avoid questions people can answer yes or no or only with a name, a date, or a place. You want to know the memories, or oral history, your respondent connects with these names, dates, and places.

Conducting and Transcribing Interviews in Person

Some of us prefer to record interviews on tape; others just use a pad and pencil. It is probably wise to use both unless the subject objects. The pencil and pad will serve as a backup to your recorder if it malfunctions during the interview. You can also note the interviewee's facial expressions or body language. As the interview progresses, new questions or ideas will come to mind that you can jot down for use later in the interview. After you turn on the recorder, visit with the person for a few minutes; do not plunge immediately into the interview. Let the person get accustomed to chatting with you while the recorder is on, and make a few notes on your pad to help him or her adjust to that also. After you sense that the subject is relaxed, proceed to follow the outline you prepared.

Many people become uneasy when cross-examined by an interviewer who keeps firing questions from a prepared outline. Experienced interviewers try to glance at their outlines while working questions into the conversation. It is best to memorize key points in the interview beforehand. You want your subject to reminisce over the past with you, not feel pressured to be a good witness.

Take along a camera or a video recorder. Take pictures of the person you are interviewing as well as his or her home. If your subject is reluctant to loan photographs or documents, take photos of them. When taking pictures, try to place the objects in a well-lighted area—lit by natural light if possible. At night, use your flash. Use film designed for taking photo portraits. Ask at your local camera shop for advice.

After the interview, transcribe it using your notes to help with passages that are difficult to understand. Send or take a copy of the transcript to the subject and ask the person to make any corrections or additions he or she feels are necessary before returning the typescript to you.

These recordings and transcripts become part of your family archives. Include them on your list of family documents with a note about their contents.

USING DIARIES, JOURNALS, LETTERS, AND BIOGRAPHIES AS SOURCES

Without oral sources, your family's story would be incomplete. How can you find this type of information for ancestors who lived so long ago that you no longer have access to their firsthand accounts of your family history?

You do have access to original records—some of them published—that serve as substitutes for a personal interview. That is, journals, diaries, letters, and autobiographies are examples of personal accounts about people, places, and events in the past. If some of your ancestors left these types of records, you can use them to cross-examine forebears much as you would living informants. Interpreting these writings requires an understanding of the period in which they were written. You must also know something about the person who produced the record. Remember that anything written is colored by the writer's experiences and opinions. Therefore, your ancestors' writings must be interpreted using your knowledge of the attitudes and prejudices affecting them.

In addition, don't overlook the papers of other families in your ancestors' neighborhood or community that may help your research efforts. Some of these families may have left papers describing family and community activities that also apply to your family.

FINDING BIOGRAPHICAL MATERIAL IN LIBRARIES AND ARCHIVES

Your ancestors may have left materials that found their way to a local library, historical society, or archive. If so, you will need the help of staff to learn how such materials can be found in catalogs or inventories.

When we seek a book in a library and we know its author or title, it is easiest to look up the title or the author's name in the library's catalog. If we want a book about a specific topic we look up a subject heading. For genealogists this means that family histories are cataloged under the name of the family as both a title and a subject. The book *The Smith Family in America* would be filed under its title and author but also under the subject *Smith Family*.

Many of the records we need relate to a specific locality. Here again, localities are treated as subjects in most catalogs. *Connecticut* is a subject. Under this subject heading are subheadings relating to the history of Connecticut, biography in Connecticut, and genealogy in Connecticut. A town or a city could also be a subject heading. The key to understanding the subject scheme in catalogs of large libraries is found in *Library of Congress Subject Headings*, 15th edition, 3 volumes. Smaller libraries may use *Sears List of Subject Headings* edited by Joseph Miller. Most libraries have a copy of these books at the reference desk or in the cataloging department that reflects their cataloging organization. Ask to look through their pages to get an idea of how to search the subject headings in your library's catalog for books about your family or the locality in which they lived.

Today, computers have simplified searches in library catalogs. Many college and public libraries use online catalogs or compact disc copies of their catalogs. The software associated with these computer catalogs can guide you to books about almost any subject. You can enter the standard Library of Congress subject heading or—in most libraries—select a keyword for the computer to use in its search for the books you want. As discussed in chapter 3, this same electronic miracle will let you search the catalogs of libraries that are many miles away with the aid of library utilities such as OCLC and RLIN. You can do subject, author, title, or keyword searches in the collections of many public, private, and academic libraries with large genealogical, biographical, or local-history collections. Let me show you how using OCLC or RLIN can help you learn more about your family.

《C _____

The university library where I teach has access to both OCLC and RLIN systems, so I decided to see what I could find out about the Wright family. A subject search of RLIN turned up fifty-six entries. I tried the same approach for a locality that no longer exists—Saybrook, Connecticut—where some of my ancestors lived. (It was known by that name when my ancestors lived there in the seventeenth century. Today it is named Deep River.) In RLIN I found eighteen entries for Saybrook, Connecticut. An OCLC search turned up eight entries for Wright and six entries for Saybrook. Interestingly, there were few duplicate entries in the two systems.

_____ *》*

In libraries, biographical material can be found under the subject heading *Biography*. It may also show up under a locality as a subject heading—*Vermont, Biography,* for example. Using your surname as a subject will usually lead you to biographies and genealogies. In archives, material is arranged under the agency or individual that created it. In each instance, you are interested in personal papers, minutes, descriptions, journals, and diaries from persons who lived near ancestral hometowns at the time family members were there.

Perhaps you can find a copy of Patricia Pate Havlice's *And So to Bed: A Bibliography of Diaries Published in English* or *New England Diaries, 1602–1800: A Descriptive Catalog of Diaries, Orderly Books, and Sea Journals* compiled by Harriette M. Forbes. You may find other similar books in your local library or by asking local interlibrary loan librarians to search the catalogs under the subject headings *Social Life and Customs, Diaries,* or *Biography.* Your search may turn up a few bibliographies compiled by William Mathews such as *American Diaries: An Annotated Bibliography of American Diaries Written Prior to the Year 1861* or *American Diaries in Manuscript, 1580–1954: A Descriptive Bibliography.* Another title you may find is Louis Kaplan's *A Bibliography of American Autobiographies.*

Using Biographical Materials from Other Families in Your Research

Perhaps you wonder how biographical materials like those discussed in the previous section apply to your family history. A couple of examples will show you their content can add value to your own research.

《C _____

Many people trace their families to seventeenth-century New England. One of the most well-known personal records from this period is *The Diary of Michael Wigglesworth 1653–1657,* edited by Edmund S. Morgan. Michael Wigglesworth was born in England on October 18, 1631. In 1638 his family emigrated to America and settled in New Haven in modern-day Connecticut. A 1651 Harvard graduate, Wigglesworth became one of New England's best-known Puritan clergymen. He taught at Harvard from 1656 until his death in 1705. During the same period he served as pastor in Malden, Massachusetts. He is still best remembered for his poem *The Day of Doom.* It warns of the horrible future that awaits the unrepentant after death. This same gloomy spirit is also found in his diary. His life seemed an uphill battle to overcome his wicked nature, cope with health problems, and survive rejections from women he had hoped to marry. His students were also subjects in this personal narrative. They were prone to sinful thoughts and behavior and easily distracted from their scholarly pursuits. (That sounds like some of us during our college years.) For the family historian, that is an important point. Even though Michael Wigglesworth may not be your New England ancestor, his thoughts came from your ancestor's world, his students were like some of your ancestors, and the women who rejected him were like women in your own family. That is how the personal writings and other records made by people in the past help us imagine what life was like for our kin.

_____ ☙

The current interest in social history has generated a number of books that describe people and their relatives. *America's Families: A Documentary History*, edited by Donald M. Scott and Bernard Wishy, is an example. The remembrances and other documents in this book give us eyewitness accounts of life in American families from the seventeenth century to the present. Excerpts from the Wigglesworth diary are included and several of his letters.

❧ _____

Another person we meet in *America's Families* is William Byrd II (1674–1744). The lives of Michael Wigglesworth and William Byrd II are a study in contrasts. The former was an austere, often guilt-ridden Puritan minister and teacher; the latter was a wealthy, well-educated Virginia gentleman. The one viewed life as a test; the other saw it as an adventure. Byrd spent most of his young-adult years—until 1705—in England. It was in that year that his father died in America. Young Byrd returned home to Virginia to oversee the family's estate. His diary gives us the feeling that he is sharing not only his daily routine but also intimate moments in his life. The editors of *America's Families* have also included some of Mr. Byrd's personal correspondence. These documents allow us to test the impressions we have from

reading his diary. Are similar topics covered in both his diary and letters? In cases where the answer is yes, is Mr. Byrd consistent in his treatment of these topics? If not, what do these differences tell you about the purpose of the letters or the diary? All of us present some parts of our lives differently to the public than to our closest family or friends.

You may not be related to the Byrds; nevertheless, William Byrd's feelings about his wife and children and his thoughts about religion, politics, and earning a living reflect values and interests prevalent at the time your ancestors lived. Learning about Byrd's life through his letters and diary will introduce you to feelings and ideas that reflect a portion of your ancestor's world.

_____ ☙

If the only facts you can discover about ancestors are dates and places of birth, marriage, and death, examine the published and manuscript materials that depict the lives of contemporaries. Consider the issues, relationships, and events in the lives of these ancestral neighbors to help you put the lives of your forebears in perspective. Although your family may have belonged to a different social or economic strata than those whose writings or records you have found, consider the issue of differences and similarities between your progenitors and their contemporaries. Can you identify social, political, or economic issues in the writings and records of nonfamily members that likely were of importance to most persons living in that time and place?

In addition to journals and diaries, autobiographies can provide valuable information. Few of my ancestors or yours left autobiographies; fewer still left published ones. Some of them may have written or dictated a short life sketch that has been handed down with other family documents. If so, these will be of help in telling your family's story. If you have no autobiographical sources in your family, you must turn to the published and manuscript biographies of people who lived at the same time and in the same region as your family.

A natural extension of this line of research is the inclusion of biographies written by authors who were contemporaries of the persons about whom they wrote. Local libraries and historical societies collect biographies of persons from the area. These may be obtained through your own public library or from the libraries in the localities in which your family lived through interlibrary loan.

FINDING AND USING NEIGHBORHOOD RECORDS

The next step in your brainstorming effort to find records takes you into the neighborhoods in which your ancestors lived. Each of the thousands of neighborhoods in our nation has its unique characteristics. Researchers should always look for activities on the neighborhood level that would create records. The following examples are aimed at making you conscious of the possibilities, but they are not a complete list of neighborhood sources.

What is a neighborhood? It is the street you live on, adjacent streets, shopping centers, schools, and houses of worship. It even includes voting districts, water districts, and other groups or institutions that exist within the area in which you spend most of your time. The definition of your neighborhood can also be expanded to include your place of work or to encompass clubs and organizations with which you spend time, such as the Veterans of Foreign Wars, chapters of fraternal organizations, or labor union locals. A neighborhood can be visualized as the next level of social interaction outside the family. To people living in a rural setting, distances may be greater, but the definition is the same.

What kinds of neighborhood activities produce records you can use? The people in your ancestors' neighborhood attended religious services together, sent their children to the same schools, traded at the same stores, and belonged to the same clubs. These organizations kept records that may yet be accessible through local record offices, libraries, historical societies, and archives.

Oral sources also play an important role in reconstructing historic neighborhoods. If neighbors of your family are still living in the area, plan to interview them or write them a letter. The guidelines given previously in this chapter for interviewing family members can be used here also. If the time period you are studying is too remote to permit interviews with living contemporaries, turn again to journals, diaries, and biographies.

The content of neighborhood records varies. Sometimes they can provide birth dates and addresses. They may include names and addresses of other relatives. Business records, for example, give you a glimpse into the economic life of ancestors through details about loans, credit extended, and income. The diaries and other papers of local midwives and physicians are another important type of neighborhood record. If these records exist, they are found in the hands of family members or deposited at local libraries, historical societies, or archives.

School Records

School records are another important neighborhood source; however, local regulations may limit their use. Usually, former students and their descendants are permitted access to these records. Student records reveal more than the grades students earned: You can learn how old students were in a given grade, who the parents were, where they lived, and which classes they took. Sometimes a place of birth is recorded, and a health record may also be included. Names of teachers and classmates, awards earned, extracurricular activities, and test scores are all there. How well your ancestor got along with peers and teachers may also be a part of the record. Perhaps some of these teachers or classmates became prominent enough locally to have biographies written about them, and members of your family may be mentioned in the biography. If not, the biography may provide background by describing activities in your family's neighborhood. The comments noted on school records by teachers and administrators can help you understand your ancestors from a perspective that is seldom considered in most family history writing. Remember, too, that yearbooks can contain not only pictures but written comments from fellow students. Most high schools have copies of the yearbooks published in the past.

Finding school records for the twentieth century is fairly easy. If the school is still in operation, a letter, telephone call, or visit may lead to the information you need. If the school is no longer in existence or you do not know how to find it or its records, a call to the local school board office may help. Sometimes you will need help from the state school board office or the office of the state archivist. Your local library may have a directory of schools and school districts similar to the U.S. Department of Education's *Directory of Public Elementary and Secondary Education Agencies.* You can also check the local telephone directory.

For schools that were in operation in the eighteenth or nineteenth centuries, you first must find a local history that tells about early schools in the area. Once you have identified the school, you can seek the records at the state archives or historical society, state board of education offices, or perhaps even the local public library, university library, or historical society.

Religious Records

One neighborhood institution that created a number of important records is the religious congregation your ancestors may have belonged to. Most of us think congregation leaders kept only records of religious events in members' lives; however, many congregations kept histories, minutes, financial, and other records. Perhaps ancestors played a role in a youth group or adult auxiliary that is documented in rolls and minutes. Your ancestors' roles in their local religious communities and the impact of religion in their lives can often be traced in records such as these. Some congregations have published histories that will contain information about your family and their friends.

Finding religious records is much like looking for school documents. If the congregation that family members belonged to is still in existence, the records can be sought there. If the congregation in the area belongs to a state or regional organization (synod, diocese, conference, etc.), information can be sought from these offices. Again, local histories help by giving information about churches in the community. These clues may point to the location of records today. Local and state archives, historical societies, libraries, universities, and genealogical societies may also be able to help. Many religious groups have published directories that will help you find the church records needed. For example, the Reformed Church in America Commission on History produced a *Historical Directory of the Reformed Church in America, 1628–1992.* For the Roman Catholic Church there is P. J. Kennedy and Sons' *The Official Catholic Directory.*

Several guides to church records are available. Examples are E. Kay Kirkham's *A Survey of American Church Records* and August Robert Suelflow's *A Preliminary Guide to Church Records' Repositories.* Let your local public or college reference librarian help you find these and similar titles.

Other Neighborhood Resources

Finding out about neighborhood organizations and their records is not as difficult as it may seem. Many communities have directories. Although coverage of some eastern seaboard areas in such publications began as early as 1784, directories did not become widespread until the period 1830–1860.[1] You will learn more about the use of directories in research in chapter 5.

Local histories, local newspapers, and old telephone books are also sources of information about neighborhoods and the businesses and other organizations that were part of the local scene. Remember that newspapers, directories, and telephone books are most easily found at local libraries, historical societies, and ar-

chives. The genealogical research centers described in Appendix A have major collections of directories from many localities.

Perhaps an example will help illustrate how you can find and what you can learn from sources created by businesses, churches, and other institutions in the neighborhood in which your family lived.

∎@ ————————————————

Suppose that your ancestors came from Poland in 1910 and settled in Cleveland, Ohio. You would like to learn where they came from and the names of relatives or friends from Poland already in Cleveland. With the help of a local reference librarian you find some histories of Cleveland and a 1910 Cleveland city directory. Next, you request these resources through interlibrary loan. As you study these resources you learn that a certain Michael P. Kniola operated a travel agency that served many of the Polish immigrants to Cleveland. How do you find out if the records of this neighborhood company still exist and whether or not they include your family? Remember that nearby historical societies and libraries often collect local records.

At your local library you talk to the reference librarian again. This time you need help learning about historical societies and libraries in Cleveland. The librarian can help you use Mary B. Wheeler's *Directory of Historical Organizations in the United States and Canada;* R. R. Bowker's *American Library Directory;* or P. William Filby's *Directory of American Libraries with Genealogy or Local History Collections.* From these books you learn that the Western Reserve Historical Society in Cleveland is a key repository for records from the area. That is where you will find the files of the Kniola Travel Agency.

You learn that Michael P. Kniola, a Polish immigrant, provided for himself and his family through operating a grocery store in a Cleveland neighborhood. From time to time he became involved in helping other Poles immigrate to the United States by loaning money or serving as a sponsor. Finally, in 1890, he decided to set up a travel bureau in his store. In 1900, he sold his grocery stocks to devote full time to the travel business. From the files of this nineteenth-century travel agency comes information on hundreds of Polish immigrants, complete with passport applications, photographs, and information on friends and relatives in this country.[2] Now you can search these records to see if your family used the services of Mr. Kniola.

—————————————————— ☙

Using records and interviews from the family archives and neighborhoods in which your ancestors lived is the best way to begin learning about your family's history. After you have exhausted these records, it is time to start looking for records created by

agencies in the cities, counties, and states in which your family lived.

Notes

1. Arlene Eakle and Johni Cerny, *The Source: A Guidebook of American Genealogy* (Salt Lake City: Ancestry Publishing Company, 1984), 390–393.

2. Gregory S. Plunges, Lynn M. Siller, and John J. Grabowski, "Register: Kniola Travel Bureau," Manuscript 3678 (Western Reserve Historical Society, Manuscript Collection, Cleveland, Ohio, 1977).

CHAPTER 5

⦗⦘

Town, County, and State Records

To be successful in your search for information about your family you must know how to find and interpret the records that describe ancestors' lives. This method requires that you first try to find out where ancestors lived and then identify the records created in that community during the time your ancestors lived there. Next, you must discover where these records are likely to be found today. The real value of this method is that it requires you to view your predecessors' lives much as *they* did: within the context of the town, county, and state they called home.

Vital records testify about births, marriages, and deaths. Cemetery records and court records reveal additional information about the people in the community and their relationships with each other. Minutes of local government meetings, police records, and tax and voter lists present still another view. Newspapers, local histories, and biographies share community and family life from their authors' perspectives. You want to find as many contemporary witnesses of your ancestor's life as possible so that your view of the past will be through the eyes of scribes who lived there when your family did.

If you limit your search to the few sources described in research manuals as being the most desirable to use, for example, birth, marriage, and death records, you ignore the fact that clerks and recorders created many kinds of records that, if given a chance, will reveal a picture of local life and how your family fit into it. The records you will learn about in this chapter are only examples of the many kinds of records you can discover on your own.

LEARNING WHAT OTHERS KNOW ABOUT YOUR ANCESTORS

The first step in discovering and interpreting local records is to survey secondary sources to determine whether or not other researchers have compiled published or unpublished descriptions of your forebears and their hometowns. *Secondary sources* are writings based upon facts found in primary sources—original documents. Someone else may have written about your ancestors—including where they lived. You will discover these facts in the many books, articles, and indexes that contain the research of other genealogists and family historians.

The thousands of genealogical societies founded in this country during the past 150 years provide researchers many opportunities to publish their findings in genealogical journals, newsletters, and indexes. Some persons are so excited about their family histories that they publish them as books. Other book-length family histories remain as manuscripts in libraries and archives around the country. Thousands of family histories and genealogies are available to you that may provide clues about names, places, dates, and relationships that had earlier eluded you. A logical place to begin looking for works about your family is the community in which your family lived.

Libraries and historical or genealogical societies in the area in which your ancestors lived will have genealogies and family histories in their collections about local families. Always ask if they have developed genealogical or biographical indexes that may include your ancestors. Also ask if the library or society maintains files of researchers working on specific families so that you can coordinate your work with them.

The staff at your local college or public library may be able to search the computer catalogs or the published catalogs of other libraries for books about your family. The branches of the Family History Library of the Church of Jesus Christ of Latter-day Saints in Salt Lake City (LDS Family History Centers) have the library's catalog in microfiche or compact disc versions. The LDS Family History Library has one of the largest collections of family histories and genealogies in the world. Many are on film and can be ordered for use at the nearest LDS Family History Center. In addition, the libraries listed in Appendix A have large family history and genealogy collections. If you are able to visit one of them, your first goal should be to dig through the library's catalog to determine if there are genealogies or family histories for the families on your pedigree chart. Researchers planning a trip to the Family History Library will want to consult J. Carlyle Parker's *Going to Salt Lake City to Do Family History Research.* This book helps you identify the library's resources and provides guidance on their use.

One of the most important libraries listed in Appendix A is the Library of Congress. Your local library may have a copy of James Neagles's *The Library of Congress: A Guide to Genealogical and Historical Research.* Reading it will help you visualize the large number of bibliographies, indexes, local histories, genealogies, and biographies that are available to help you learn more about your family. You may live a great distance from the Library of Congress, but many of the materials Neagles discusses will be available at libraries and research centers near you. Much of the material at the Library of Congress describes individuals and families in the cities, counties, and states of this nation. Unlike the National Archives, which will be discussed in chapter 6 and which preserves only materials created by the United States government, the Library of Congress houses in its many divisions some of the most valuable biographical, genealogical, and local history materials in this country. In fact, the Library of Congress genealogical collection ranks as one of the largest in the world. Although you cannot borrow books from the Library of Congress, knowing the titles of books it has about your family will permit you to borrow them from other libraries.

Bibliographies

One way to become acquainted with the vast number of genealogical publications is through a bibliography

such as P. William Filby's *American & British Genealogy and Heraldry.* Filby covers national, state, and regional indexes, bibliographies, guides, and handbooks. You may not find your family's name in Filby's volumes, but you will find references to indexes and bibliographies that will include it and other names on your pedigree chart. For example, Filby lists Marion Kaminkow's 1972 two-volume *Genealogies in the Library of Congress: A Bibliography* and her *Supplement, 1972–1976.* Kaminkow produced a *Second Supplement, 1976–1986,* which has been updated by a Library of Congress publication, *Genealogies Cataloged by the Library of Congress Since 1986.*

Kaminkow has also edited a bibliography of family histories found in libraries other than the Library of Congress, *A Complement to Genealogies in the Library of Congress.* Nettie Schreiner-Yantis's *Genealogy and Local History Books in Print* will also help you identify publications about your family and the communities in which they lived.

Indexes to Periodicals

Most of the genealogical societies and family organizations in the nation publish newsletters or journals that carry short genealogies, family histories, and biographies. It may be to your advantage to join a genealogical society or family organization that deals with your family or focuses on the area in which some of your ancestors lived. Many of the genealogies and articles such organizations have published are included in Anne Budd, Michael Clegg, and Curt Witcher's *Periodical Source Index: 1847–1985.* Articles appearing in print since 1985 are indexed in annual volumes. The latest volume—Clegg and Witcher's *Periodical Source Index: 1986–1992*—includes material published through 1992. *Periodical Source Index* volumes provide subject, locality, and surname indexes to the large collection of current and discontinued genealogical and local history periodicals at Allen County Public Library, Fort Wayne, Indiana. About 2,000 periodicals have been indexed. To help you find which major libraries have the titles referenced in these volumes, Clegg has edited a bibliography titled *Bibliography of Genealogy and Local History Periodicals with Union List of Major U.S. Collections.* With the information provided in this book, you can write or visit libraries that have periodicals containing articles about your family.

If your library does not have these indexes, perhaps it will have *Index to Genealogical Periodicals* edited by Donald Jacobus. It covers many of the best-known periodicals from 1859 through 1952. A new edition of the Jacobus *Index* is edited by Carl Boyer. Boyer's edition provides a single set of name and place indexes plus new, simpler codes for the periodicals. (In the original work there were separate indexes for each of the three volumes, and the codes used in the index entries to guide the reader to the desired articles were difficult to understand.) Both are listed here because libraries generally have one or the other but seldom both.[1]

Another popular index, the *Genealogical Periodical Annual Index (GPAI)*, has been published since 1962 with several editors and publishers. The latest edition, edited by Laird C. Towle and published in 1992, covers some 308 periodicals to the year 1990 with a surname, subject, and locality index. For the period from 1956 to 1962 there is an index to selected periodicals in Inez P. Waldenmaier's *Annual Index to Genealogical Periodicals and Family Histories*.

Your local library may subscribe to several genealogical periodicals with a national scope that provide annual indexes to the articles and reviews they publish. Check to see if the library has the New England Historic Genealogical Society's *New England Historical and Genealogical Register,* the National Genealogical Society's *National Genealogical Society Quarterly,* New York Biographical and Genealogical Society's *New York Genealogical and Biographical Record,* David Greene's *The American Genealogist,* Everton Publishers' *The Genealogical Helper,* Ancestry Publishing's *Ancestry,* or the American Genealogical Lending Library and Historical Resources' *Heritage Quest.* These will help you keep abreast of new developments in the field as well as find articles and books about your family. Your local reference librarian can show you how to find these periodicals and use their index volumes.

Throughout this book you will be reminded that you learn more about ancestors if you compare their lives with the lives of others who lived at the same time in the same region of the country. You can talk to your local public or college librarian for help in finding books that describe families and communities in the past. *America: History and Life,* edited by Peter Quimby, indexes articles in periodicals and reviews of books and dissertations that describe life in America. Appearing in five issues each year, its issues 1 through 4 contain abstracts from periodicals and citations from reviews and dissertations, and issue 5 contains cumulative subject, author, and title indexes. You will find it at large public libraries and most university libraries. Before consulting this index, make a list of areas that interest you: marriage patterns (When do people marry? Where do spouses come from? etc.), family life, sex roles (wom-

en's and men's roles in the community and the family), mortality (ages at death, causes of death, etc.) are a few examples. When you go to the library to use *America: History and Life,* search under the topics you have listed. The articles, books, and dissertations you find will seldom be in your local library. Ask the interlibrary loan librarian to help you borrow them from other libraries.

Local Histories and Directories

Around the beginning of the twentieth century and again at the bicentennial anniversary of our nation, there was great interest in local history and genealogy and a large number of local histories were produced. Marion J. Kaminkow's *United States Local Histories in the Library of Congress: A Bibliography* is the best place to start looking for histories of the localities where your ancestors lived. Follow up with a search of P. William Filby's compilation *A Bibliography of American County Histories,* which describes some 5,000 county histories.

Local libraries in your family's community may also have city or county directories from the time your ancestors lived there. If not, try contacting one of the libraries listed in Appendix A. Directories are published locally as well as by large national publishers specializing in this kind of publication. Local directories were designed to list everyone living or doing business in the community. Normally each family is represented by the head of the household, unless other adult family members were employed in local businesses. Many directories were microfilmed by Research Publications of Woodbridge, Connecticut, and are listed in a series of guides under the title Research Publications' *City Directories of the United States, 1860–1901: A Guide to the Microfilm Collection.* A new segment of this publication, describing microfilmed directories from 1902 to 1935, was published in 1993. The same publisher is continuing efforts to preserve pre-1860 and post-1901 directories on microfiche. In local libraries look for these collections in the catalog under the name of your ancestor's town or county. Sometimes libraries have separate catalogs or registers for this collection. Check at the reference desk if you find no entries in the catalog.

Another local and family history survey source is the Library of Congress *National Union Catalog of Manuscript Collections (NUCMUC).* Begun in 1959, it is an attempt to register the manuscript collections in various repositories in the United States. Its volumes are issued annually and cover the period from 1959 to 1991. The 1959–1961 volumes were published by J. W. Edwards of Ann Arbor, Michigan. The 1962 edition came from Shoe String Press, Hamden, Connecticut. Since then, annual volumes have been published by the Library of Congress. Starting with 1986, new entries in each year's volume also have been entered into RLIN, a national network of research libraries (see chapter 3). Each published volume has its own index; periodically a cumulative index for several volumes will be issued—for example, *National Union Catalog of Manuscript Collections: Index 1980–1983*. The indexes include a name index (place names, personal names, surnames, corporate names), a subject index, and a repository index. An invaluable aid to this collection is Chadwyck-Healey's *Index to Personal Names in the National Union Catalog of Manuscript Collections, 1959–1984*. To use this resource, simply look up the family name you are seeking in the alphabetical index. If you find a reference to your family, a brief description will guide you to the *NUCMUC* entry.

If you are interested in manuscript collections from a specific town or county, use the name indexes in *NUCMUC* volumes. The name index might also list local companies or other organizations whose records may name your ancestors as members or employees. If you know the name of a company for whom an ancestor worked, for example, check to see if it shows up in the name index. For example:

During my family history research I checked the name of an international mining company with operations in Utah, Kennicott Copper, and found a couple of entries referring to personal papers of Kennicott executives that are now available to researchers. These papers will help me understand the impact of this large employer on the local economy.

Historical Maps

Historical maps are an important source of information about the communities in which your ancestors lived. The city fire insurance maps produced by the Sanborn Map Company show where individual structures were located and provide structural details of some of the buildings shown on the maps. A good description of this collection is the Library of Congress *Fire Insurance Maps of North American Cities and Towns Produced by the Sanborn Map Company*. The Library of Congress has one of the most complete collections of these maps. In many counties mapmakers also produced plats of

landownership in the county. These are maps showing property boundaries as well as the names of individual landowners. Fire insurance maps and county landownership maps provide you with a bird's-eye view of your ancestors' community. Richard Stephenson's *Land Ownership Maps: A Checklist of Nineteenth Century United States County Maps in the Library of Congress* is an important guide to one of the best county map collections in existence. Copies of the maps you find in this checklist may also be available at local county clerks' offices or historical societies.

Surname Indexes

Several state and local genealogical societies, for example, the Ohio Genealogical Society and the St. Louis Genealogical Society, have developed surname indexes to genealogies researched by their members. Perhaps a society or library for the area in which you are searching has prepared a similar index. Look up the societies listed for your state in Elizabeth Bentley's *The Genealogist's Address Book*.

The LDS Family History Library has developed several indexes to genealogical information. The surname segment of the library's catalog lists the approximately 80,000 family histories in the collection. The Family-Search International Genealogical Index (1993 edition) on compact disc contains some 200 million names showing birth dates, birthplaces, marriage dates and places, and names of spouse or parents. The Library's FamilySearch Ancestral File (1993 edition) on compact disc contains more than 12 million individuals linked into families over several generations. All of these resources are accessible at LDS Family History Centers and other research centers (see Appendix A). The compact disc versions of the International Genealogical Index, Ancestral File, and Family History Library Catalog are retrieved using the FamilySearch program discussed in chapter 3. Microfiche editions of the International Genealogical Index and Family History Library Catalog are available at the Family History Library in Salt Lake City and at LDS Family History Centers.

Genealogies and Biographies

We often look only for recent publications about an ancestor. Experienced genealogists know that earlier writers often had access to living witnesses and to manuscript sources that no longer exist or that have become lost in large collections. Therefore, older compendiums of genealogy or biography—on both the national and the local level—can be of value. In my own research, for example, books such as James T. White Company's *The National Cyclopedia of American Biography,* volume 4, and J. H. Beers' *Commemorative Biographical Record of Middlesex County Connecticut* have given me valuable data on my Connecticut ancestry. These two titles are good examples of the type of publication so popular from about 1880 to 1920. Community biographies and genealogies such as these were often done with financial support from families whose members appeared in their pages. Publishers would contact members of the community and solicit contributions and information for these publications. Some of them are poorly done; others are quite accurate. Although these older sources may contain some inaccuracies, they could reveal information no longer available elsewhere. You may find valuable information about an ancestor in one of them. Some collective biographies cite the sources upon which the articles are based; others do not.

Biographies and genealogies are generally cataloged first under the locality and then under the subject heading *Biography* or *Genealogy.* An example might be *Chicago—Genealogy.* There are also numerous county and state biographical directories or compendiums. To see what your library has, substitute the name of the county or state for the city shown in the example; that is, you must look for *Kansas—Genealogy* or *Chippewa Co., Minnesota—Biography.*

You may be able to verify information found in genealogical or biographical compendiums by using the books and articles published by local, regional, and national genealogical societies. Most well-trained genealogists and family historians cite the sources they use and verify the information they present in several original sources. A prominent example is New England Historical Genealogical Society's *New England Historical and Genealogical Register* that has been published since 1847. Volume 58 (1904) gave me important data I used to evaluate the validity of the entries I had found in the two compendiums previously noted. For older genealogies and family histories, consult Joel Munsell's Sons' *Index to American Genealogies* fifth edition; its *Supplement, 1900–1908;* and Joel Munsell's *The American Genealogist, Being a Catalogue of Family Histories,* fifth edition.

One of your local libraries should have a copy of an important and well-known compilation edited by Fremont Rider, *The American Genealogical Index,* or the revision and replacement of this work, *American Genealogical-Biographical Index,* new series from the Godfrey Memorial Library. The latest volume (1993) covers alphabetized names between Taylor, Shadrick, and Thatcher, Theophilus. The volumes in both series provide access to thousands of genealogies written about American families. You will find more books of this type at the research centers listed in Appendix A. The purpose here is simply to alert you to this type of publication. Remember that you do not need to have specific titles in mind to find published indexes or other genealogical or family history materials; you only need to learn *how* to find this kind of resource in the catalog of the libraries available to you. Local reference librarians can help you quickly narrow your search to relevant materials.

FINDING WHERE ANCESTORS LIVED

Knowledge of where and when events occurred in your ancestors' lives is essential to your research. Realizing where someone lived on a given date helps you decide which records to search and where to look for them. Most of the dead-ends family historians and genealogists have on their pedigree charts exist because they do not know where an ancestor was born or lived. Following are some questions that, when answered, will show where a forebear lived.

1. Where did the person die? Perhaps he or she lived there long enough to be described in several local records. Many records are created when we die that explain important facts about our lives. Some of these will be discussed later in the chapter.
2. If the person was a parent, where were the children born? Records in children's birth communities may provide important details about both parents' lives.
3. If the person was married, where was the spouse from? Perhaps both spouses lived in the same town before marriage.
4. Where were the person's siblings born? These localities may also be the birthplace of your lost ancestor.
5. Can you find your ancestor in a statewide or nationwide census index (see chapter 6)? The index will show you where your ancestor lived at the time censuses were taken.
6. Are there other people in your ancestor's neighborhood with the same surname as your ancestor? These persons could be relatives who came

from the same locality where your ancestor was born or lived.

7. Was your ancestor involved in a migration movement? Consult local and U.S. history books for the time period in which your ancestor lived. Identify whether or not your ancestor and his or her neighbors were part of migration movements entering or leaving the area in which you last found your ancestor. The localities where these movements originated or ended may have records about your ancestors. Not all persons who left with a migrant group continued with them to their destination. Look for ancestors in the records of communities located along migration routes.

Many of the records covered later in this chapter contain notations about an ancestor's previous residence. When you or I move into a new community, there is a period of time when our former residence is listed on many documents. It was the same in the past. Land records, religious records, employment records, school records, voter registration lists, and other records we will discuss shortly may have a note about your relatives' last place of residence—especially records created near the time they moved in.

PUBLIC AND PRIVATE JURISDICTIONS

After you have traced your family as far as possible using the research of others, it is time to seek out original records and make your own contribution to family history. First, you must know where your ancestors lived. Next, you must learn where the records are kept that were created by record keepers. In chapter 2 you were introduced to the idea that ancestors lived within nongovernment (private) and government (public) jurisdictions in which their activities were recorded by local clerks. Remember that a jurisdiction is an imaginary line drawn on a map or around a group of people by officers of public and private institutions. Within the city limits, the mayor and city police have jurisdictions, for example. Within your county—but excluding the incorporated cities—the county board or commission and the county sheriff have authority. Some of your life activities may fall under the jurisdiction of state officers. For example, in Utah, I pay state income taxes, and it is the state that issues my automobile license plates and my personal driver's license. These are public, or governmental, jurisdictions. A church, an employer, an insurance company, or a fraternity are private agencies,

and each documents the activities of members or clients. The local newspaper, private hospitals, and businesses are also nongovernment agencies whose records may describe members of your family.

Because the search for both government and non-government records generally leads to the same community, county, or state, they will be discussed together here.

LOCAL AND STATE RECORDS

Records in Cities and Counties

After collecting the family and neighborhood records described in chapter 4, your search should focus on information in the towns, cities, and counties in which your ancestors lived. Begin by making a list of records you think these jurisdictions may have created. You may be wrong, but your list of potential records will help you devise questions to ask local officials. For example, in New England, town government was more important than county administration; therefore, at local New England town offices you may find birth, marriage, death, probate, land, tax, court, and school records.

Outside New England, cities and towns tended to let the county courts and county clerks handle probate records, vital-event registration (birth, death), marriage licenses, and tax records. In unincorporated areas, all local government record keeping fell to county officials. For that reason you may find everything from deeds to school records in county courthouses. City clerks outside New England preserved records such as city council minutes, business licenses, building permits, police records, and school records.

Larger cities often took responsibility for registering vital events, and some maintained their own courts. In New York City, for example, old records from various agencies within the city have been turned over to the Municipal Archives Department of Records and Information Services. Among these documents are birth records from 1847 to 1910, some deaths from 1795 to 1949, and some marriages from 1847 to 1938. Another city department, the Division of Vital Records, provides information on births dating from January 1, 1910, and on deaths from January 1, 1949. For marriage records after 1907, this office refers researchers to the city clerk of the borough in which the license was issued. Note that there is an overlap in the years of records preserved in different jurisdictions in New York City. This often happened when the original registration of a birth, marriage, or death was copied for use in another office within the city. Such duplication is a great help to genealogists and family historians when the original record has become lost, damaged, or destroyed.

For most areas in the United States the records created by county officers will be essential to your research. If you do not know which county your ancestor's hometown is in, ask a reference librarian to help you. A book such as *Bullinger's Postal and Shippers' Guide for the United States and Canada,* from Bullinger's Guide Incorporated, will help you find the right county. As an alternative, ask the librarian for an atlas that has an index to cities in the various states. The *Rand-McNally Commercial Atlas & Marketing Guide* is a popular atlas because it indexes smaller communities. By using its maps and index you can determine which county your family lived in and where the county seat is today. If these or similar books are not available, ask for a ZIP code directory. It will list the town, the county it is in, and its post office. In 1991 a new multivolume gazetteer (geographical dictionary) of the United States appeared that may be in one of your local libraries: Frank Abate's *Omni Gazetteer of the United States of America.* Some libraries may have the compact disc version from Silver Platter Information of Arlington, Virginia. These publications make it easy to pinpoint your ancestors' communities.

It is possible that when your ancestors lived in the community you are examining, it was not in the present county. County and court boundaries sometimes changed, and that could affect where you would look for ancestors' records. The following resources report such changes: Elizabeth Bentley's *County Courthouse Book,* Alice Eichholz's *Ancestry's Red Book: State, County, & Town Sources,* and George Everton's *The Handy Book for Genealogists.* In addition, check local libraries or historical societies for old maps or gazetteers that will describe your ancestor's hometown as it was at the time your ancestor lived there. An example of an old gazetteer is Leo de Colange's 1884 *The National Gazetteer: A Geographical Dictionary of the United States.* The following example shows how you would use some of the preceding reference books to learn about an ancestral hometown, Saybrook, Connecticut.

From the *County Courthouse Book* and *Red Book* you would learn that probate records for Saybrook, Connecticut, were kept at different times in the town clerks' offices of Essex, New London, and New Haven, Connecticut. Local histories, gazetteers, and maps show that Say-brook became Deep River in 1947. Therefore, maps of the area do not show Saybrook any longer. Based on such information, town offices in Essex, New London, New Haven, and Deep River would be added to your records survey in a library catalog or to your list of places to write for information.

Both cities and counties have law enforcement records, minutes of official meetings, licensing records, school records, directories of county officials and employees, and records for development and maintenance of roads and utilities. Each of the records kept by county clerks has something to contribute to the picture you are developing of ancestral home communities.

It is in cities, towns, and counties that most non-government sources were created. For example, newspapers, published in America since before the Revolution, are an important source of information about people and the events in their lives. The local directories discussed earlier were published by local and national firms but are considered a local nongovernment source because they list the inhabitants of cities and counties across the nation. Other nongovernmental sources include business and mortuary records. The businesses that served your ancestors also provided employment for many of your forebears. The records of local businesses can be a great help in learning about how people earned a living and in verifying where ancestors lived and when they arrived in a community. Local mortuary records also contain a great deal of information about local inhabitants.

Although usually thought of as neighborhood institutions, as discussed in chapter 4, religious and fraternal organizations may have served a broader area than a neighborhood. Many communities had only one church, and its records covered everyone in the area, but perhaps your ancestors belonged to a religious group in which there was only one congregation for the entire county. Similarly, there were many social and fraternal groups whose members came from a larger city or were scattered throughout a county.

State Records

State governments can provide several records describing your forebears. Some states have conducted censuses in years between federal censuses. They permit you to tune in to ancestors' lives at five-year intervals rather than every ten years using only federal censuses.

The Source: A Guidebook of American Genealogy, edited by Arlene Eakle and Johni Cerny, provides information about which states conducted censuses and when they were taken. Ann Lainhart's book *State Census Records* describes state census records for each state and how to locate them today.

Each state also had the authority to raise military forces that served in the state militia; today, men and women serve in state National Guard units. Many states have kept files on citizens serving in both state and federal military units.

By 1920 most states had assumed responsibility for keeping records of births and deaths in the state. County clerks and county courts had been doing this up to that time.

State departments also create records describing people doing business in the state. Such records may range from registers of marks and brands used by farmers and ranchers on their livestock to documents describing the officers and activities of corporations. Your ancestors were also recorded as taxpayers, automobile drivers, and purchasers of state lands. In some states, state courts handle civil, criminal, and probate cases; in others, state courts primarily hear appeals from lower courts.

Court Records

You may have noticed that some types of records are found on all three levels of government as well as the federal level. Court records illustrate this point. Inside America's patchwork of jurisdictions are various city and county courts with names such as surrogate court, orphans' court, justice of the peace court, and circuit court. Some states have separate probate courts with jurisdictions that coincide with neither city nor county boundaries—Connecticut is an example. There are also federal district courts in each state that keep their own records or turn over older records to the nearest National Archives and Records Administration regional archive. Take time to study the court system for the areas in which your family lived. You will often find records that help to identify progenitors and to explain what happened in their lives. Let your local librarian help you discover local histories or government directories that describe how courts were organized in the places your family lived.

Even though you can find local courts listed in the government section of your telephone book, such listings will not tell you about the types of records these courts keep. The previously mentioned *County Court-house Book* by Bentley includes brief descriptions of each state's court system. The LDS Family History Library in Salt Lake City publishes state-research outlines that provide brief overviews of the court system in each state. You may write the Family History Library for information about this series (see Appendix A). To better understand the role of courts in your ancestors' lives and how to locate court actions involving them, refer to chapter 19, "Court Records," in Val D. Greenwood's *The Researcher's Guide to American Genealogy,* second edition. This information will help you decide which court clerk you need to contact.

Although the names of courts may change from state to state, the types of records created by them are similar. When a person dies, for example, a court with jurisdiction in the matter handles the probate proceeding. Jurisdiction is determined by where the deceased person lived or owned property. If someone dies without a will (intestate), the court decides who will administer the estate and what will be done with property and other possessions. If a will is left behind by the deceased, the court becomes responsible for enforcing its provisions, and a copy of the will becomes part of the court record. In such cases, court documents provide valuable information about family and friends involved in a deceased person's life. Usually a county court or a city court would handle such matters. If the probate proceeding involved property in more than one county, a court with statewide jurisdiction would handle the case.

Another court record of interest deals with adoptees and orphaned children. These records provide facts about the children involved (age, sex, etc.) and about guardians or adoptive parents approved by the court. Which court dealt with the matter was determined by where the children lived or where the adoptive parents lived.

Chapter 7 deals with naturalization records. These, too, were created by local courts. Immigrant ancestors applied to a court of record with jurisdiction in the city or county in which they lived. They could also go to a federal court for assistance. You will learn more about locating federal court records in chapter 6.

Divorce records may also be of interest to you. City, county, and in some instances state courts could grant divorces. Usually the proceedings were in a court with jurisdiction for the area in which the two parties to the divorce lived. Sometimes couples left the area to establish residency in another county or state to file for divorce.

Civil suits about land, business agreements, and other issues may have taken your ancestors into local courtrooms. If family stories or documents point to such activities, follow up by learning if records of your forebears can be found in a local court.

CONTENTS AND USE OF GOVERNMENT AND NONGOVERNMENT RECORDS

You have learned about several public and private records to this point. During your research you will discover many additional record types. The following sections examine the content of some of these records in the context of what they can tell us about ancestors and events in their lives.

Births

Both government and religious birth entries normally contain the names of children and their parents and the date and place of birth. The records of births kept by neighborhood and community religious congregations sometimes add to this information the names and residences of godparents, sponsors, or witnesses who are often relatives or close friends. Knowing their names can help you reconstruct the kinship ties in your family. Newspapers—at least from the last part of the nineteenth century—often publish birth notices naming the child and his or her birth date, parents, and residence and sometimes the name of the hospital where the child was born.

Birth dates, birthplaces, and parents' names can be found in other records. For example, school records may give an age or a birth date. Pupil files may list the parents or guardians and their address in addition to the student's grades. Sometimes a place of birth is recorded. There may also be a health record for the student.

As ancestors go through life, their activities generate other records that describe birth dates and places and name family members. Among these are insurance records, bank records, and employment records. Local and state military records can be a source of family information. They provide the name of the person, date and place of enlistment, and the units in which the person served. They may also give the person's age and birthplace or place of residence. Military pension records are more likely than enlistment records to list dependents. Records for local military units and their members are normally kept at state archives or historical societies. Federal military records are explained in chapter 6.

The same local sources that date events in our ancestors' lives can be analyzed to tell us about what their surroundings were like, the decisions they made, and the people they knew. For example, use birth records to find all of the children in the family and to learn where your ancestor fit into the birth order. A progenitor's place in the birth order of the family may help you explain relationships between siblings or events in your forebear's life. Later in life when maids of honor were chosen, witnesses invited to a christening, or an administrator of an estate selected, the impact of childhood family relationships may become apparent.

Birth records help you analyze the spacing between children and the ages of parents at the birth of the first and last children. These facts can be compared with what you know about present-day families as well as family practices at the time your progenitors were raising their children. Perhaps you can see practices emerging in the families of an ancestor's children that differ from the family they were raised in. Can you explain these differences based on what you have learned from the birth records of your ancestors?

We can also catch a glimpse of health conditions at the time of a person's birth if journals, hospital records, birth records, or newspapers give data about the weight and height of newborns. If you note a decline in weight or health of second, third, fourth, and fifth children, is it related to the mother's age or health or are there inherited traits affecting these children? You will need to look back into the birth and death records of earlier generations to make a judgment about inherited health traits.

Marriages

You need information about when and where ancestors marry and facts about the new spouse's family. Government marriage records list the bride and groom by name, their ages, the date and place the marriage license was issued, the date and place of marriage, and sometimes the places of residence of the bride and groom. Religious marriage records name bride and groom, their ages, and place of residence or home congregation. They may also contain the names of the bride's and groom's parents and the places of residence of the parents.

Employment records, insurance records, and military records may contain facts about a person's marriage(s). Spouses' names and the date and place of marriage may be recorded in them.

Marriage records tell a story, too. As pointed out earlier, many of them give us the ages of both bride and groom. Sometimes they note where each partner came from. There may be an indication of whether or not it is a second marriage. As you look over your pedigree charts, how old were the grooms? Were the brides younger or older as a rule? Which ancestor was the oldest or youngest bride or groom? What was the average age at marriage for each generation, and what was the most common age at marriage? Do these values change from one generation to the next? Remember that averages sometimes hide important facts. For example, the average age at marriage for your male ancestors may have been 25 years. When you look more closely, however, you note that about 25 percent of them were older than that, and more than half that group may have been over thirty. Why did people wait so long to marry, or on the other hand, why did they marry so young?

Did age at marriage affect family size or the prevalence of a second marriage? When a place of birth or residence is given, how close did bride and groom live to one another? Perhaps most spouses came from one or two locations. Why?

With help from birth or marriage records, you can observe the spacing between children and learn a little more about what your ancestors' life was like. Imagine a mother with several small children all under the age of six on a 160-acre farm where only she and her husband provide the labor. Life would be anything but tranquil or easy!

Marriage and birth records help you calculate how soon after or before marriage conception of the first child occurred. What might be the reason for this? In some cultures, for example, it was common to wait until conception before following through with marriage plans. How old were mother and father when the last child was born? Do any of these variables change from one generation to the next? Are any of the sources you have found helpful in explaining what you are observing? If not, read some books in local libraries that discuss marriage and family during the period you are studying. Local reference librarians can help you search for these books under subject headings such as *Marriage—United States, New England—Social Life and Customs, Family—History,* and *Children—History.*

Family historians have always been interested in how strictly families adhered to traditions and customs. How did your family feel about religion or its ethnic heritage? We have seen a great deal of change in these areas in the last fifty years. How prevalent were church weddings versus those solemnized by local judges or justices of the peace? Did your ancestors tend to marry within their own faith? Were ancestors more or less active in a local church after marriage? Tracking spouses in church records before and after marriage may provide clues here. Were they noted as contributors and churchgoers, or was their participation not recorded in minutes, lists of contributors, or those attending services?

Do you find that ancestors married within their ethnic group? Did newlyweds have ancestral origins in the same towns or areas in which their families lived before emigrating to the United States? We often find that the tendency to marry within the same religion or national group diminished over time. Did this happen in your family? If so, how much did this tendency decline in each generation?

Deaths

Another important event you will want to document for your ancestors is the date, place, and cause of death. City, county, and state clerks and health departments are responsible for issuing death certificates copied from official death records. Death records normally state the name of the deceased, the date and place of death, the cause of death, and often a date and place of birth. Sometimes surviving children are mentioned. The names of parents and/or spouse may be noted. Some death certificates show the name of the person who provided the information for the certificate, which helps you evaluate the accuracy of the information. If the information in the death certificate was provided by a neighbor, it may not be accurate. The attending physician normally signed the death certificate; knowing the physician's name may guide you to a biography or journal at a local historical society.

The deaths of ancestors also produced records at the local cemetery. Tombstones and sexton's records provide death dates and sometimes a date and place of birth and a spouse's name. Names of other family members may also be noted in the sexton's records. Since the late Middle Ages, sextons have cared for the vestments, vessels, and the furnishings of churches and dug the graves in church cemeteries. Today, we continue to refer to the persons responsible for local government and private cemetery records as sextons. Their records note in which plot a person is buried and may mention who paid the cost of the burial plot—frequently a family member.

Remember that a person may not be buried where he or she died; the family burial plot may be in another town in which the person was born or married. Burial could also be where the family had lived for a long while or where children or siblings were buried. To find addresses of cemeteries in localities where your ancestors lived, look in Deborah Burek's *Cemeteries of the U.S.—A Guide to Contact Information for U.S. Cemeteries and Their Records*. Check with your local librarian to see if the library has this or similar directories in the collections.

Probate records, including wills and inventories of estates, may have been created because of a relative's death. Often the death date is noted in the probate proceeding. Probate records were created whether or not a will was left by a deceased person, and they often name family members, neighbors, and agencies in other localities in which the deceased lived. Generally the probate proceeding is conducted in the community in which the deceased lived. If the person owned property or was involved in business in another town, the court record of that jurisdiction will also have an entry.

When we die, many types of records find their way into our probate file or packet. In these files are letters, affidavits, decisions of the court relating to the estate, copies of deeds, inventories, and other papers relating to the life of the deceased. Inventories are especially helpful in reconstructing the physical environment in which your progenitor lived. Furnishings, buildings, animals, clothing, tools, utensils, and many other items are mentioned. Wills and inventories also describe the wealth of forebears.

Perhaps local probate records contain a copy of your ancestor's will. Wills often name other family members and help you verify facts you have found in other records. Remember, however, that family members may have been left out of the will because they had already received a share of the estate, passed away, or had a falling out with the testator. Wills may identify property and personal belongings and, thus, give you a glimpse of your ancestor's wealth and lifestyle.

When a person dies, a mortuary or funeral home is often contacted to help with the funeral arrangements. I once had a student who, with his wife, had earned money for school by living at a mortuary as caretakers. Part of their job included cleaning up the basement and organizing old records stored there. They found files detailing local funerals dating from the middle of the nineteenth century. In the area east of the Mississippi, such records may exist for even earlier dates. Local directories published near the time of your ancestor's death will list local undertakers. Local or state historical societies may also have mortuary records that were donated to them. Consult *The Redbook National Direc-*

tory of Morticians, from the publisher of the same name, and Adrian Boylston's *The American Blue Book of Funeral Directors* for addresses of funeral homes.

Newspaper death notices—obituaries—normally name the deceased and often provide information about family members, where the deceased was born, and background on his or her life. The accuracy of an obituary depends on how well the writer knew the deceased person.

Looking through death records where a cause of death is mentioned will also provide facts about local health conditions. How long did the children in your ancestors' families survive? The answer to this question can also provide information about health conditions and the risks of death to children. What were the odds a child would live to 6, 10, 12, or 16 years of age? How many died because of poor health, and how many died due to environmental causes? Most of us think of environmental deaths as a phenomenon of the twentieth century; however, in the past children were especially susceptible to weather conditions and pollution in the air and water. Ancestors who survived to become teenagers often had developed immunities to numerous organisms in food and water. Many of their peers died as children because their bodies could not withstand the infections brought on by poor sanitation and living conditions permeated by rodents, insects, microorganisms, and spoiling food. We sometimes forget, also, that children of the past lived in surroundings that were dangerous. Being trampled by horses or falling into fires or water-filled ditches were daily risks our ancestors faced as children. Death certificates, newspapers, family letters, church records, and personal journals or autobiographies document areas and time periods where there was little understanding of how to prevent illness and disease and the household risks faced by children.

Do you find from ancestors' death certificates that many of them on one line of ascent or another died rather young? What were the causes? Perhaps hereditary illnesses will affect you and your children.

Other Life Activities

A number of additional records describe peoples' dealings with each other and local government and identify family members and their neighbors. The sale or transfer of land from one person to another is often recorded in local records. Deed books register land transfers and may mention spouses and other family members. If the land sale or transfer was due to a death in the family, that fact may be noted, thus enabling you to estimate a death date for an ancestor. By learning when persons in your family first bought property in an area, sometimes you can isolate when they arrived there. When land is sold to a new resident or to someone outside the community, the new owner's former home or current residence may be noted in the record. Such information permits you to track ancestors to previous residences where more records about them and their lives await. Since local officials are often asked for copies of deeds, many of these collections have been indexed by the names of the grantees (buyers) and grantors (sellers).

Local tax records normally list only the name of the taxpayer, the amount of tax, and sometimes his or her address. The appearance of a person on a tax list may be a clue that he or she just arrived in the community or that the person has become eligible to be taxed because of local property and age requirements. When censuses are not available, tax records can help you identify the heads of households in an area at a specific time. The date a person's name disappears from the tax list may signal death or a move to another locality, facts that are essential to your attempts to describe what happened in ancestors' lives.

Adoption cases and civil suits can be followed in court records. In these records you may uncover names of family members, ages, and addresses. Court records also give you a glimpse into ancestors' lives from a perspective few other sources provide. For example, you can uncover relationships between family members and neighbors as well as others who interacted with your family. Researchers often avoid tracing adoption proceedings or civil suits because of restrictions that are designed to protect the privacy of the participants in adoptions. Your position as a descendant or heir may entitle you to access. If you or an ancestor were involved in adoption proceedings, check with the court clerk to discover the specific restrictions covering these records. In some instances you may want to employ an attorney to help you gain access to these materials.

Court records show the names of orphaned children and list administrators of estates and guardians for those children. Who are these administrators and guardians? How do they fit into your ancestor's life? Are they brothers or sisters, friends or neighbors, or relatives or strangers appointed by the court? The answers to these questions will help you re-create the kinship networks and friendship networks within which your ancestors lived and moved.

Learn about neighbors' families, where they came from, and what they left behind when they died. Your ancestors' lives may parallel to some degree the lives of these neighbors. Neighbors of ancestors may appear as witnesses on documents, godparents in religious records, administrators of estates, or guardians of minor children in wills or probate records. If your ancestors were not landowners, records of their landowning neighbors may give you clues about when people moved in and out of the community. Use state censuses, local tax lists, plat maps (see chapter 6), and directories to identify the neighbors of your ancestors, and then watch for their names as you search the records of the locality in which your family lived.

The pre-1850 state census schedules generally name only the head of the household with statistics for the other males and females in the household. These statistics may include school attendance, disabilities, race, and status (slave/free). The occupation of the household head is often noted, as is his or her status as a veteran, a landowner, or a recent immigrant. State censuses often list the value of property owned by the respondent and, thus, provide additional clues about the personal wealth of ancestors. The content varies from state to state and from census to census, but it always provides information helpful in defining our forebears' lives. Many state censuses—especially after 1850—list the entire household by name and provide individual data on each.

Although many state censuses are not indexed, that should not be a barrier if you can find a directory, indexed federal census, or some other list of community members' addresses near the date of the state enumeration. These resources can help you pinpoint where a progenitor lived and narrow your search to a geographic area in a state census—town, county, census enumeration district, etc.

Just as you and I are influenced by our surroundings, so were your ancestors. Try to learn about the physical, emotional, and social environment prevalent in the community in which ancestors lived. Relate these findings to how children followed—or did not follow—patterns established by parents and other adults in the area. If original records provide only scanty information about personal and family life, turn to published sources to fill out the picture of your family's past.

FINDING THE RECORDS YOU NEED

Someone has responsibility for records that describe your ancestors. There are steps you can take to find who that person is and obtain the records you need. There are three places you will find the local and state public and private records you need: at the offices of local and state organizations; in local archives, historical societies, and libraries; and at the LDS Family History Library in Salt Lake City or one of its branch Family History Centers. The first place to check is the Family History Library or your nearest Family History Center, whose services are available to the general public.

In 1938 the Church of Jesus Christ of Latter-day Saints began a program to preserve records from around the world on microfilm that identify individuals and families. Today, the library's microfilm collections number 1.5 million rolls containing more than 3 billion pages of documents that name people who lived in communities around the world. The largest number of microfilms—about 400,000 rolls—are in the Library's United States collections. Each roll of microfilm is described in the Family History Library Catalog available on compact disc as part of FamilySearch or on microfiche at the Family History Library in Salt Lake City and at each of the more than 1,000 local Family History Centers in the United States and Canada. Appendix A lists the address of at least one LDS Family History Center in each state. Write to the LDS Family History Library in Salt Lake City at the address in Appendix A for a complete list of Family History Center addresses. If the records you need are not in the microfilm collection of the Family History Library, you may find them at local or state government offices, historical societies, and libraries.

Finding Town, County, or State Records

There are basically two kinds of towns as far as finding records goes: ghost towns and towns that still exist. If the town your ancestors lived in is still in existence, the place to start looking for records is at the town (city) hall. If the town no longer exists, its records may be in the custody of the nearest neighboring town government, at the county clerk's office, or with the state archives or historical society. If ancestors lived outside of city or town boundaries, their records should be at the county seat of the county in which they lived.

In general, records normally remain close to the jurisdiction that created them. To find government records for towns, ask first at the local government offices. If the records for the period you need are not there, someone in that office should be able to tell you where they are. Whether the records you seek will actually be held by the town, county, or state government depends on local laws and record-management practices. Most states have laws promoting records management and preservation. Archivists and records managers have

been more successful in some states than in others. To the researcher this means that local records may have been transferred to the state historical society or state archives. In states with county records-preservation programs, town records may be with the county historical society or a county record depository. Some records, however, are not in the state archives or local historical society; they may have been donated to a local public or university library.

State archives and historical societies play a role in preserving nongovernment records, too. Many organizations from the private sector donate records to the state archives or historical society because they know the staff there has the skill to catalog and preserve the materials.

If you are looking for vital records kept at state offices of vital statistics—births, marriages, and deaths—check Thomas Kemp's *International Vital Records Handbook*. For early vital records use the aforementioned Bentley's *County Courthouse Book*. It contains the addresses of county courthouses as well as town clerks in New England and adds the independent cities of Virginia—cities outside of a county jurisdiction. For each state there is also a brief overview of the county courts and the records they created.

Another book that will help you find addresses of local agencies is Eichholz's *Ancestry's Red Book*, which outlines local records and record-keeping practices in each state and helps you understand the historical development of each region. The chapters on each state provide addresses of a number of local libraries, archives, and historical societies and help in finding local newspapers, periodicals, and manuscript collections. Both the *County Courthouse Book* and the *Ancestry's Red Book* give the dates counties were formed. Except for New England and Virginia, both books ignore resources that were created by municipal governments, and they provide limited help in finding local nongovernment sources. Be aware, also, that there are a number of local libraries and historical or genealogical societies that are not included in these books. This problem can be overcome by using the following additional titles.

The standard guide to libraries in the United States is R. R. Bowker's *The American Library Directory*. A guide to libraries with genealogical collections was compiled by William Filby titled *Directory of American Libraries with Genealogy or Local History Collections*. Another helpful guide is Lee Ash's *Subject Collections*. In the index to *Subject Collections* you can find addresses of libraries in the United States and Canada that have collections in the areas of interest to you: genealogy, local history, geography, etc.

Universities often have collections devoted to the history of the state and community in which they are located. You should check their collections of newspapers and other media. We sometimes forget that these institutions collect books and manuscripts by and about local residents, families, businesses, and government. These libraries will also be found in *The American Library Directory*.

The staff members at county and state institutions often know whom to contact about city records. If they do not, a letter to the city clerk or city recorder will help you find out about records on that level of government.

The staff or members of local historical and genealogical societies will also be important resources for learning about the records from your ancestors' communities. Finding these organizations is just as easy as it was to find libraries and county courthouses. The *Directory of Historical Organizations in the United States and Canada,* edited by Mary Wheeler, contains the addresses and telephone numbers of historical societies, museums, archives, and some of the genealogical societies in the United States and Canada. If you are interested in a guide to genealogical societies, Mary Meyer has compiled *Directory of Genealogical Societies in the United States and Canada,* listing some 5,000 organizations.

Another directory that may help you is the *Directory of Archives and Manuscript Repositories in the United States,* compiled by the National Historical Publications and Records Commission. It contains addresses of both public and private institutions that collect manuscript materials. At the repositories listed you will find government and business records as well as personal papers, genealogies, journals, and biographies. Many of the institutions listed in this guide are also in the *Directory of Historical Organizations.*

If the records you seek belong to an association, the *Encyclopedia of Associations,* edited by Deborah Burek, Karin Koek, and Annette Novallo, may help you get in touch with the current officers of an association your ancestor joined, who, in turn, may be able to tell you where earlier membership records can be found. In this same vein, your ancestor may have joined a fraternal organization listed in Alvin Schmidt's *The Greenwood Encyclopedia of American Institutions: Fraternal Organizations.*

Libraries with limited collections of reference books will generally have at least the following two titles. Eakle and Cerny's *The Source: A Guidebook of American Genealogy* contains a comprehensive treatment of genealogical resources. In it you will discover additional ideas for finding many published and original records. The second book most libraries are likely to have is Bentley's *The Genealogist's Address Book.* This valuable tool provides addresses for a large number of city, county, state, and federal agencies. Local, county, state, and national genealogical and historical societies are also listed.

Using the Telephone Book to Find Ancestors' Records

Many of the addresses of local record keepers will be found in the books mentioned in the previous sections. If you do not have access to these guides, or if the city or town you need is not listed, there is another way to find the local records you need—find the telephone number and address of local government agencies in the telephone directory for the place your family lived. Your local city, county, or college library may have a collection of telephone directories, and they may subscribe to a service that provides telephone directories for many of the cities of the United States on microfiche or compact disc. If these suggestions fail, call your local telephone company to see if it can help. You can also contact the telephone company for the place in which an ancestor lived to see if it can help you find the addresses and telephone numbers for records offices for the area.

In local telephone directories, you will note that there are several agencies listed under city government. Which one has records about your ancestors? The name of the agency will give you a clue about its records. City departments keep many different types of records: everything from birth and death certificates to utility billing records and various types of licenses and permits. The city recorder, the mayor's office, or the city manager's office can help you find minutes of city council meetings. These offices can also help you determine where to find other records that interest you if their location is not apparent from the telephone book.

The county clerk or recorder will be able to provide help with county records if you cannot figure out which office to call from the telephone book. The county clerk can also help you determine where court records are preserved. The department names you will find in the telephone book will give you an idea of the many areas of community life regulated by county officials. If the county has a directory of departments and personnel, you may be able to get a copy. It will list the functions of the county's government with telephone numbers for each department.

On the state level, an administrative services department may be listed in the telephone book that can give you information about offices that keep records of interest to the family historian. If not, the governor's office should be able to help. You may also find a number listed in a local telephone book for state government general information. Finding the subagencies of state departments may be important to your research. For example, the function of caring for the health of the state's residents is handled through the Health Department, which in turn has an Office of the Medical Examiner whose records may be helpful in learning about the circumstances of an ancestor's death. In some states the Health Department's functions require an Office of Vital Statistics that generates birth and death certificates. Your state may have a separate department of vital statistics whose records are organized in the archives or records center under the various names of the departments in the office. One of these departments may have been responsible for recording births and deaths.

You will often find the state archives listed in the telephone directory with the other state government offices. Archives staff can give you information on records that have been turned over to them. The staff at the state library may also be able to help because they often deal with different departments and may know which ones would have records of interest to you.

Finding Nongovernment Records

The search for local private records starts at the present offices of newspapers, churches, funeral homes, cemeteries, hospitals, and other institutions that you believe may have records of ancestors. Sometimes you will find that the records were destroyed. Hopefully, they still exist and are at a local office or at a local historical society or archives. The directories of libraries, societies, and archives mentioned earlier will help here. A recent telephone directory may also serve to identify current addresses and telephone numbers for the agencies you seek.

Next, you need to determine the names of agencies that functioned during your ancestor's lifetime that may no longer exist. Histories of the cities and counties in which ancestors lived normally name local private institutions and discuss their roles in the community's history. Local directories published during the time your ancestor lived in the community will also list local businesses and other organizations such as churches and social and fraternal organizations. The best place to look for the records of these institutions is in the nearest historical society. Even if the historical society does not have the records, it may know where you can find

them. If there is a college or university in the area, the special collections room at the library may contain local records also. Many public libraries also have local history collections that include records from local private agencies. Many communities have established pioneer or local history museums that include artifacts and exhibits that will help you reconstruct community life when your ancestor lived there. Furthermore, these museums may have received donations of records, photographs, and artifacts that came from local private organizations. Your ancestor may be included in photographs or records in these museums.

In chapter 6 records of nationwide nongovernment institutions are discussed. Some of the suggestions for finding records presented there have application here as well.

Requesting Information from Local Record Keepers

Once you know when and where ancestors lived, you can use the books of addresses cited earlier in the chapter to make a list of offices and agencies that may have records about them. Your list should include local libraries, archives, genealogical and historical societies, local city and county clerks, and local courts. Continuing with the Saybrook, Connecticut, example, your list might look like the following. (The full address of the agency is omitted to save space.)

Archives/Libraries/Societies
Acton Public Library (Old Saybrook)
Connecticut State Library and Archives
Connecticut Historical Society
Connecticut Society of Genealogists
Middlesex County Historical Society
Saybrook Colony Founders Association, Inc.
New Haven Colony Historical Society

Local Government Offices
Deep River Town Clerk (for vital records before July 1, 1897)
Connecticut State Department of Health Services, Vital Records Section (vital records after July 1, 1897)

Your next step is to contact the agencies and request the information you seek. Let's continue to use Saybrook as our example, pretending you have traced your family there about 1840.

In your letter to each agency, explain that you are preparing a history of family members who lived in and around Saybrook and that you need help to consult records created as early as 1840. Ask the staff to fill out the enclosed record survey form (an example is shown in figure 10) and return it to you. Enclose a family-group record naming the mother, father, and children you are searching for in Saybrook, and include any dates or other information you have. Request that agency personnel search their records for documents describing the persons on the family-group record.

On the survey form, provide a sentence or two of instruction, explaining that you are interested in any sources they may have that name residents or members of residents' families. Make the form simple and short. If it seems complicated, most officials will not fill it out because they have limited time for such requests. On the form provide space for answers to questions such as:

What is the name of the source?

What are the general contents of the record?

What is the approximate period covered by the record?

Is there an index to the records?

What are the restrictions for using or copying these records?

FIGURE 10   *Sample Local-Records Survey Form*

Dear Records Custodian: Please list the records you have that identify people in your community by name, address, occupation, status, birthdate, etc. Also note any restrictions relating to their use by researchers. The record types listed are examples. You may have additional record types that should be listed because they describe individuals by name.

Record Type	Contents (Names/Dates)	Time Period in Record	Indexed?	Restrictions
Births				
Marriages				
Deaths				
Probates				
Tax Lists				
Voter Registration				
Land/Property				

A simple form might have abbreviated versions of these questions across the top of the page, forming five columns. To help local officials, fill in a few records you hope to find there as examples.

Now that your letter and forms are ready, address them to the offices on your list. Some of the offices you contact will send back certificates or copies of documents identifying people who match the descriptions on your family-group record. Many offices are not staffed to perform record searches and will simply inform you of the records they have and the rules for using them. Others will refer you to a researcher you can hire to gather information for you.

Organization of Local Records

When you gain access to local or state government records, you must find out how they are organized. If they have time, the office staff may be willing to explain their filing system. Items may be filed topically—correspondence, invoices, receipts, etc. Within a topical file, records will generally be filed chronologically—although some entries may be filed alphabetically by the name of the person(s) on the report, application, or other document.

To conserve space in offices, older or infrequently used records are often retired to a records center or an archive. In these repositories records are filed under the name of the function or agency that created them. The function of regulating state agriculture, for example, requires among other things the registering of brands and identifying of animals owned by individuals and companies. In some areas, records of brands may be the earliest records you can find naming your ancestors. Filed under the functions of each agency or department are the records generated by their daily operations. Files for each unit or department may be further divided into subject categories such as personnel, policies, equipment inventories, etc.

Most records centers or archives have registers that list the agencies whose records they preserve. They also have guides to these records that show how they are organized in the archives.

Historical societies often treat their original records—or manuscripts—much as an archivist would. The holdings of these societies may be organized under broad functional categories such as local business records or documents pertaining to the history of a state or region. Under these broad divisions the records may be arranged in subcategories according to the person or agency that created the record. In some instances his-

torical society collections are organized geographically. If a county historical society collects records about the towns and cities within its jurisdiction, for example, its files may be separated into sections for each of these communities. Within a community's files or record groups you might find categories for business records or records of local clubs or societies. The records of the Kniola Travel Agency mentioned in the last chapter are an example.

In 1976 the papers of the Kniola Travel Agency were donated to the Western Reserve Historical Society. Under the heading *Kniola Travel Agency,* the papers are arranged in six series: correspondence, financial records, legal records, real estate records, personal and miscellaneous records, and oversize records. There is much in this collection that will help those tracing the Kniola family and ancestors who had dealings with the travel bureau. A look at the register to this collection would show which documents would be of greatest use in research.[2]

Always explain your research goals to the staff of the office you visit. They do not need long descriptions, just a brief explanation of what you are looking for. They will know which areas in their collections should be searched first. Use the registers to manuscript collections found in most archives and historical societies to help you narrow the search to the records that seem the most promising. As you scan archive registers, look for dates and places that coincide with events in your family's history.

CREATING A LIST OF POTENTIAL RECORDS FOR YOUR FAMILY

The records presented in this chapter are only examples of the many types you might find in localities in which your ancestors lived. You should prepare your own list of records you hope to find. Prepare this list after learning about the history and institutions of the place in which your ancestor lived. County and state histories will help you get started. Consult W. B. Stephens's *Sources for U.S. History: Nineteenth Century Communities* or Eakle and Cerny's *The Source: A Guidebook of American Genealogy* for ideas about the records found in many communities. Now let's expand the brainstorming technique you learned in the last chapter to produce a list of records and records offices that can provide more information about your ancestral families. Suppose that your ancestors are from Oshkosh, Wisconsin (you may substitute any locality you wish). Your goal is to find records from Oshkosh and the surrounding region that will identify specific members of your family and give information about their lives. Imagine your family lived in and around Oshkosh from about 1845 to 1925. Which public and private agencies would have created records during this time and where are the records today?

Finding the answer is not as hard as you might imagine. Start by comparing your life to that of your ancestors from Oshkosh. What is your family life like? Are you married or single? What is your home like? How do you earn a living? Which local agencies protect you, your family, and property? Are you protected from crime by local police? Name other services you receive from local government. Are there religious organizations to which you belong, or do you prefer to keep your beliefs to yourself? What other organizations do you participate in? Describe banks, stores, or other institutions in the area that play roles in your life. For each life activity, list records you think might have been created and who you think the custodian of the records would be today.

Start at the beginning, with birth. Who was involved with your birth? Did anyone make a record of it? Today hospitals keep records of births, local laws require registration of births at bureaus of vital statistics, and newspapers print local birth announcements. Local churches and synagogues also record births. Now, what about birth in Oshkosh? During the time your ancestors lived there, babies were delivered with the aid of family members, a midwife, or a physician. When were hospitals founded there? Most of your ancestors were probably born at home. In Winnebago County (Oshkosh is the county seat) births were recorded beginning in 1876 by the county clerk. Some midwives and local doctors kept records, if only in a journal, that may have mentioned the birth of some of your ancestors. During the period your family lived in Oshkosh newspapers were published. Perhaps some of the births in your family were reported there.

Next in the life cycle comes childhood. Today, children are recorded on insurance forms, tax returns, social security records, vaccination records, employment records of their parents, and school records. In Oshkosh, children would be found most often in school records, in court records relating to the probate of an estate or guardianship, or in religious records.

As you grew older you started your career and perhaps thought of marriage. You may have bought a car, a house, and other things that brought you in contact with local government officials, banks, and other agencies. You became a taxpayer and voter. Government came to depend upon your participation for financial and moral support. For example, perhaps you served in a local National Guard unit or on a jury. Your ancestors in Oshkosh may have purchased property, including animals for transportation and food. They may have become involved in local government or the militia and supported local government through payment of taxes. Among Winnebago County's records, you will find deeds showing land sales, tax lists, and voter registration lists. The county clerk also recorded marriages beginning in 1848. Minutes were kept of city meetings that can teach you details of local life seldom touched by other sources. Newspapers also carried wedding announcements along with local news and advertisements.

When you pass from this existence, a number of records will be created: death certificates, mortuary records, newspaper obituaries, cemetery records, and probate records are a few of them. The county clerk as well as the local probate court became involved when your ancestors died. There were also cemetery records created and new land records to cover transfers prompted by the death of your relative.

The events covered so far are really just a small part of community and family life. What about records created by your employment? Are there parallel records for your ancestor that came from trade and commerce sources, such as blacksmiths, millwrights, millers, lumber mill owners, or seed merchants? These sources are hard to find without help from the reference staff at local libraries or historical societies, but they may be able to refer you to old directories that list local businesses or know where historic business records might be found. Following is an example.

❧ _____

Several years ago, a good friend at the public library in Oshkosh, Wisconsin, sent me a few pages of employees' records from a local lumber company found in a collection of papers donated to the library. Among them I found an application for employment taken September 6, 1917, that listed a man's name, birth date, and place of residence. The application showed that the man was a native of "Prussia" and that he understood "some" English and spoke German. He was married and had three children at the time. The form also showed that his father was employed by the same firm. The same form tells us that the applicant had been in Oshkosh for a year and that he had lived in New York State prior to moving to Wisconsin.

Look at the many clues found in that application for employment. Did a relative ever help you find a job? Kinship networks are critical to understanding what happened in your family. Perhaps the personnel record of the applicant's father will give more information about the family.

You may want to find out what ancestors ate and how they dressed. Old catalogs, recipe books, and newspaper advertisements will help you learn about these subjects. Local museums may have artifacts that will help answer some of these questions.

Many ancestors were active in local religious organizations and patriotic or social groups. Like you, they also found time for recreation and education. Local organizations often kept membership records and some even kept histories. Local histories and old newspapers often mention these types of organizations and their activities.

What about community services? As today, roads had to be maintained, water allocated fairly, waste disposed of, disputes settled, the needy cared for. Who did it? Were records kept?

Remember, too, that communities had a cultural life. There were local musical groups, writers, artists, and musicians. Sometimes there were local schools that played a prominent role in the community and the region. City, town, or county administrative records will have information about some of these activities. Council meeting minutes may be a good place to start. Newspapers, broadsides (handbills or posters used in political campaigns to advertise local events or present different sides of contemporary issues or ideas), personal diaries, and autobiographies are also good sources to help you learn about community activities.

Now that you have a list of potential sources, use the reference books cited earlier in the chapter to compile a list of government offices, libraries, archives, and historical/genealogical societies that may have these resources.

Accessing the Records You Find

After you have received information about the types and whereabouts of records available for your family's community and state, you must decide how to access these records. Perhaps some of them have been microfilmed or copied and placed in one of the research centers listed in Appendix A. If not, perhaps you can travel to the place in which the records are kept to gather facts about ancestors. You could also hire a local genealogist to do research in local records for you. There may even be history students at the local college or high school who would be willing to search these records for a reasonable fee. If you do travel to local record offices, libraries, archives, or historical societies, be sure to write in advance of your visit to ensure that the materials will be available when you arrive. Sometimes local holidays or unusual office hours will hamper your research.

Notes

1. Kory L. Meyerink, "Genealogical Periodicals," in *Printed Sources* (Salt Lake City: Ancestry, forthcoming 1994).

2. Gregory J. Plunges, Lynn M. Siller, and John J. Grabowski, "Register: Kniola Travel Bureau," Manuscript 3678, Cleveland, Ohio: Western Reserve Historical Society, 1977.

CHAPTER 6

National Sources

In the previous chapter you learned how to find records about your family that were created by local and state agencies—public and private. To find ancestors in these local records, you needed to know the name of a town or a county where your family lived and the dates they lived there. Sometimes ancestors changed their residence several times; in these instances, you would be grateful for inclusive lists of people indexed by surname, covering several or all of the states. Such nationwide records exist; most of them are products of the nineteenth and twentieth centuries. During this time period, private agencies—such as businesses and associations—as well as the United States government generated documents identifying people across the nation.

Private agencies with a regional or national scope of operations may have records about your elusive ancestor. These institutions could have been employers, service agencies such as insurance companies, or fraternal groups such as the Disabled American Veterans. Their records may contain all of the persons in a state or region who are or were associated with the agency. In addition to showing where and when ancestors lived, private records often reveal facts that are not recorded elsewhere.

The word *national* often connotes an association with the federal government. However, in this chapter it means the nationwide jurisdictions of national government and private businesses, associations, or agencies with offices and clients throughout the United States. First, you will learn about the many nongovernment records that contain information about your family. This chapter cannot cover them all, but it gives you an idea of what to look for. Second, you are introduced to examples of records created by the federal government, many of which are accessible through the National Archives. In both instances you will learn how to find these records and use them to discover facts about your family.

NONGOVERNMENT RECORDS

The fifty years following the Civil War saw a new development in commerce as well as other segments of the private sector: the establishment of companies and other types of associations with nationwide constituencies. Employers such as railroad, oil, steel, banking, retail, and mining companies expanded operations to many states and territories. Nationwide businesses that depended on a broad consumer public also kept records on employees and customers. Fraternal organizations often kept records on lodges or local chapters scattered across the country. Among the more-modern records of help to the researcher are the records of national service or professional organizations such as Kiwanis, Rotary, American Library Association, and the many trade unions formed since about 1875.

Which agencies or organizations would have had an interest in your ancestor? To answer this question, you must understand what life was like in the town and time in which ancestors lived and reconstruct the daily life of the family under study. What were their needs? How were these filled? Which institutions existed locally to meet these needs, and were any part of a national network or chain? As you discovered, such information may come from the family archives; from neighborhood, county, or state records; or from newspapers, local directories or histories, or biographies.

Was your ancestor employed by a national company such as a railroad? Did he or she provide for self and family as a farmer and participate in a local chapter of a nationwide farmers' organization on land obtained from the federal government? Were there life insurance policies, loans, investments, or other goods and services obtained from organizations with a nationwide operation?

Many other possibilities could be explored: fraternal groups, alumni organizations of schools and universities, cultural and ethnic associations or societies, and religious or political organizations. Any national organization with chapters or offices near where your family lived might have recruited your ancestor.

Patriotic and Lineage Societies

The records of patriotic and lineage societies such as the Daughters of the American Revolution, Mayflower Society, and Veterans of Foreign Wars can provide helpful information. To join these and similar organizations a person had to prove an association with an event through personal participation—as in the V.F.W.—or through a relationship to a person who was there, such as an ancestor who fought in the Revolutionary War. Application forms and membership files of such organizations contain personal information about the applicant, often including his or her genealogy back to the ancestor whose life or activities qualified the applicant for membership in the association. Some of this information may be fabricated or erroneous, but the bulk of it was compiled with a sincere desire to be accurate. In fact, some societies check the applications for accuracy. In any event, you could quickly determine the accuracy of such an application by taking a random sample of persons from the pedigree chart and comparing their personal data with facts you can assemble from original documents, such as birth records.

If you are interested in Civil War ancestors, several lineage societies exist for descendants of both Union and Confederate soldiers and sailors. Burek, Koek, and Novallo's *Encyclopedia of Associations,* Eakle and Cerny's *The Source: A Guidebook of American Genealogy,* and Bentley's *The Genealogist's Address Book* list addresses for many of these organizations.

For many years the National Society of the Daughters of the American Revolution has published lineage books with brief lineages of NSDAR members. If you find ancestors in one of the lineage books, contact the NSDAR Library in Washington, D.C., and ask for a copy of the member's application in the hope that it will provide clues for your research. Of the 164 *Lineage Book* volumes published, 160 are indexed in *Index of the*

Rolls of Honor (Ancestor's Index) in the Lineage Books of the National Society of the Daughters of the American Revolution. The NSDAR has also published the *DAR Patriot Index,* which lists Revolutionary-soldier ancestors of members and their birth dates, spouses, military rank, and the state from which they served.

Consult *The Hereditary Register of the United States of America,* edited by Jerome F. Beattie, or "Section 12: Veterans', Hereditary, and Patriotic Organizations" in Burek, Koek, and Novallo's *Encyclopedia of Associations* to learn of the many societies created to commemorate the service of American military men and women. Write to those of interest, requesting a search of their member roster for persons whose surnames match those of your ancestors. Find out if they will send you photocopies of applications to the organization from your possible cousins or forward a letter from you to members who have surnames matching the ones on your pedigree chart. (Many institutions are hesitant to give out the home addresses of their members.) Make up a questionnaire to send to those whose names match those of your ancestors. Include a pedigree chart or ancestor list detailing the ancestors and descendants of interest to you.

Searching for Nongovernment Records

As with local records, the maintenance and preservation of records created by the private sector in the United States has had a checkered career. Few large institutions did more than store old records in inexpensive, out-of-the-way places. Often the oldest records were destroyed as space ran out. In the 1960s and 1970s an interest in archival and records-management programs developed as businesses and other private institutions began to pay more attention to their records. Today, most large companies have a records manager. Some even employ archivists to inventory and preserve the files and papers that have accumulated in basements and warehouses.

Sometimes private national records have been donated to libraries or archives. In such cases these manuscripts may be listed in the Library of Congress's *National Union Catalog of Manuscript Collections,* which registers records that have been received at libraries, archives, and societies in the United States. Using this source, you may find that a company, fraternity, or society has preserved its records in a local archive, library, or historical society. Another point of access is through a microfiche collection that provides descriptions of many of these manuscripts: Chadwyck-Healey's

National Inventory of Documentary Sources in the United States.

Nongovernment records are more difficult to find than federal records because there has been no consistent effort to preserve and catalog them for easy access by researchers. Few texts about genealogical research methods cover sources produced by private agencies. Usually, the personnel or accounting department of a company can help trace old employment records or customer files if they still exist. (Note that access to such records is usually restricted to family members or descendants, employees, and scholars.) For agencies with no commercial interests, such as fraternities, societies, clubs, etc., current officers may be able to help you find older records.

One of the few research guides that deals with these records is Eakle and Cerny's *The Source.* Chapter 10, "Business and Employment Records," by Kory Meyerink, Elaine Barton, and Arlene H. Eakle, contains suggestions for pursuing this avenue of research and a bibliography for helping the genealogist get started. This chapter is especially helpful in tracing defunct businesses. *The Source* also presents sections about records from railroads, associations, and hereditary and lineage societies. Information about company museums, historical societies, and other private records agencies is available in Joel Makower's *The American History Sourcebook.*

Once you have decided which agencies you want to question about an ancestor, you need an address or telephone number. If the organization still exists and you know its headquarters or local or regional office, you can use the telephone book or the information operator to get a telephone number. A nearby library may have a collection of telephone directories on microfiche or compact discs for many of the areas of the United States. A look at the telephone directory for Washington, D.C., for example, will provide a large number of addresses for national organizations with headquarters or offices in the nation's capital.

Nationwide directories can help you find businesses and other organizations. Burek, Koek, and Novallo's *Encyclopedia of Associations,* Alvin J. Schmidt's *The Greenwood Encyclopedia of American Institutions: Fraternal Organizations,* and Joel Makower and Alan Green's *Instant Information* will help you identify organizations that may have counted your ancestors as members.

The biggest problem for researchers is finding records from companies or associations that no longer exist. Some have been taken over by other organizations, some have changed their names, and still others have disappeared. If you think the agency had a branch office in your ancestor's hometown, an old city or county directory preserved in a nearby library or historical society may let you verify the organization's name and old address. With this information, you can check if a local historical society has inherited that organization's records.

Since most national companies had to have a business license from the city, county, or state, perhaps you can find a copy of the application at a local city or county clerk's office or at the state archives. Businesses and private organizations that incorporated within a state had to file documents with the state government requesting incorporation. Nonprofit groups often did the same. Copies of these documents will contain the names of the officers of the corporation. Former officers who are still living could be interviewed. Children and grandchildren of corporate officers may also have information about what happened to a company's records. The key to finding licenses and papers of a corporation or other institution is knowing where the home office and its branches were. *The Source,* edited by Eakle and Cerny, lists home offices for some defunct national companies and gives suggestions about finding others by using old business directories. You learned earlier that large cities attracted branches or headquarters of many institutions. Using city directories for New York, Philadelphia, Boston, Chicago, St. Louis, Omaha, Denver, and San Francisco may help you identify regional or national offices for many companies and private organizations. The historical societies in these areas may have information about the records of these agencies even though the company ceased to exist many years ago.

Once you have learned where the present-day offices are for a business or association, write to see if they can furnish a copy of your relative's personnel file or membership. For an insurance company, bank, or other business, ask if they have the applications or transaction files for customers or clients from the time of your ancestor; if they do, request a copy of your relative's file. The following example from my own research demonstrates how records from private agencies provide essential facts on ancestors' lives.

✺ ——————————————

After my father (Raymond Sanford Wright, Jr.) died, we found that he had left few documents behind to help us compile his history. He had never talked much about himself, so my brothers, sisters, and I knew very little about his life. We learned a lot by interviewing family members, but there were parts of his life we had to learn about from other sources. We knew he had worked for the Southern Pacific Railroad. I could remember collecting mail from the family mailbox that included a copy of a magazine from the Brotherhood of Locomotive Engineers and Trainmen. With the help of the telephone directory, some reference books, and with what I knew about his life, I turned up several addresses: headquarters of the Southern Pacific Transportation Company in San Francisco, the Railroad Retirement Board in Chicago, and the United Transportation Union in Cleveland, Ohio, which was formed in 1969 through a union of the Brotherhood of Locomotive Engineers and Trainmen and several other railroad employee unions. I also found an address for a Brotherhood of Locomotive Engineers in Lakewood, Ohio, in which my father may also have had a membership. (The Railroad Retirement Board is the only one that is a federal agency. You will learn more about how it helped me in the section on social security and railroad retirement records at the end of this chapter.) Let me share what I found from writing to the first three agencies.

The first to answer was the Southern Pacific Transportation Company. An assistant vice president for employee relations and his staff had searched the files and come up with a computer printout with a one-line entry covering my father's twenty-two-year career as a railroader. It stated only when he began his service, his last day on the job, and his job title, "engineman." The letter explained that employee files are destroyed three years after the employee's death. Had I acted earlier, I could have received a copy of his complete file. In their search, the staff at Southern Pacific came up with a record of another Raymond Sanford Wright with a different social security number. Since they thought that perhaps he was a relative, they sent me a copy of the record they had found. It was a file card with the heading "Record of a Retired Employee." The person named on the card was my father's father. The record contained a summary of my grandfather's career with the same railroad. At the time of his retirement my grandfather was listed as "office engineer" in the Salt Lake division. His service with the railroad stretched from February 20, 1913, to November 1, 1959—the date of his retirement.

The next letter I received was from the Brotherhood of Locomotive Engineers in Lakewood, Ohio. They could not find any entry for my father as a member.

The records of the United Transportation Union in Cleveland, Ohio, showed that my father first joined the Brotherhood of Locomotive Firemen and Enginemen October 20, 1952. He was a member until his death, which had also been recorded in his membership file. They also gave me his 1952 address and his address at the time of death. Since our family had lived in several homes, these addresses helped me pinpoint the dates our family lived at two of our homes.

FEDERAL GOVERNMENT RECORDS

When you think of federal records, you probably think of censuses, military rolls, land records, naturalization records, passenger lists, and perhaps social security records. However, there are many other types of government records that contain clues for the family historian. Many of these are relatively easy to find and use at the National Archives in Washington, D.C., or at one of the National Archives regional offices in several cities across the nation (see Appendix A). Some of these records may even be available in microfilm at a library near your home. Other records, such as social security files, are not available at the National Archives offices. In the remainder of this chapter you will learn about some of the records and services available through the National Archives and Records Administration, and about some of the records that are available only at the offices of the agency that created them.

The National Archives of the United States

Prior to 1934, there were no archives of the United States. Persons who wanted to look at censuses, military records, government employment records, or other federal records had to go to the agency that created them. Each office was responsible for organizing and storing its own records. Officials within the federal government became concerned about the maintenance and preservation of files that were collecting in offices around the nation. Historians and other researchers joined forces with them to encourage the founding of the National Archives in 1934.

You can easily learn which records in the National Archives will help in your research. The National Archives and Records Administration (NARA) has published a pamphlet entitled *Using Records in the National Archives for Genealogical Research*. This twenty-six page overview lists censuses, land records, records of Native Americans, naturalization records, passenger lists, passport applications, personnel records, claims for pensions and bounty land, military records, Seaman's Protection Certificate applications, and Coast Guard records. It includes a short but helpful description of each source and instructions for getting more information about the records.

NARA publishes a large number of guides, books, and pamphlets that will help you decide which federal records may be of value. Write for a copy of its catalog of publications at National Archives and Records Administration, Publications Services Branch (NEPS) (see Appendix A). If you would like to read about how researchers have used records in the National Archives, read *Our Family, Our Town: Essays on Family and Local History Sources in National Archives*, compiled by Timothy Walch.

Not all records created by federal agencies are at the National Archives in Washington, D.C. Older records from government offices across the nation are preserved and made available at twelve regional National Archives offices (see Appendix A). For example, the National Archives Pacific Southwest Region at Laguna Niguel, California, holds records from federal offices in Arizona, Southern California, and Clark County, Nevada. On the other coast, the National Archives New England Region at Waltham, Massachusetts, handles materials from Connecticut, Maine, Massachusetts, New Hampshire, Rhode Island, and Vermont. As a service to researchers, regional centers maintain collections of microfilms containing popular genealogical sources such as the censuses, passenger lists, and military records held in Washington, D.C.

The best handbook describing the services and holdings of regional archives is Loretto D. Szucs and Sandra H. Luebking's *The Archives: A Guide to the National Archives Field Branches*. The holdings of each regional archive office are also described in a series of guides published by the NARA. You can get a copy of the guides for the archives that interest you by writing to the National Archives Washington office at the Publications Services Branch or the NARA Trust Fund Board (see Appendix A). When you write, request a list of current NARA publications. Among them will be several that relate to your research. You can buy catalogs of National Archives microfilms that describe the cen-

suses, passenger lists, military records, and other popular family history sources available on microfilm.

Since many of the National Archives microfilms have been purchased by public, private, and academic libraries, you can get them through interlibrary loan. You may also rent microfilms from the National Archives Microfilm Rental Program (see Appendix A). The Mid-Continent Public Library in Independence, Missouri (for residents of Missouri only), and the American Genealogical Lending Library of Bountiful, Utah, are examples of libraries that specialize in microfilm loan to researchers. Call your local library or nearest regional National Archives office to see if it has any additional ideas about how to obtain National Archives microfilms on loan.

You can keep track of developments at the National Archives, including new microfilm publications, by reading *Prologue,* the journal of NARA. Ask at your local library to see if it subscribes to this periodical.

Beginning Your Research in National Archives Records

NARA's *Guide to Genealogical Research in the National Archives* is a detailed guidebook you can use to decide which National Archives records you need. Its twenty chapters provide the history and detailed descriptions of many records genealogists can use to learn about their ancestor's contact with the government, such as census, passenger, arrival, naturalization, military, land, and court records and other records of particular groups, such as Native Americans, African Americans, merchant seamen, and civilians during wartime. Researchers who need a detailed summary of the records at the National Archives will also want to use the Archives' *Guide to the National Archives of the United States.*

Keep in mind a few general rules when you prepare to use federal records. You must know how the persons you seek interacted with the government. Were they military service men or women, government employees, or applicants for benefits? Could they have been involved in legal action as a plaintiff or a defendant? Were they members of a minority or other group with a special relationship to a government agency or part of a group regulated by federal law? Soldiers, sailors, immigrants, Native Americans, African Americans, and homesteaders are examples of such groups.

Next, you must know when and where the ancestor had contact with the government. For example, when and where did your ancestor live when a census was taken? When and where was the individual inducted into the military? If the person was an immigrant, when and where did the ancestor arrive and later become naturalized? If the ancestor was a litigant in a federal court, where and when did the court action take place? When and where was the ancestor employed by the government? If you know where your ancestor had contact with a government agency, you can determine where the record of this interaction is found today by contacting the nearest National Archives regional office.

Sometimes you may know that an ancestor was an employee of the government, but you do not know *which* department. The *Official Register of the United States* may provide some help in this regard. Between 1816 and its last edition in 1959 it was published by several different government departments under varying titles.[1] The first issue, under the title of *Register of Officials and Agents,* was published in 1816 by the State Department, and the last comprehensive issue was published in 1921 by the Bureau of the Census. From 1922 to 1959, only government employees in administrative positions were listed. The publisher of the 1959 volume was the U.S. Civil Service Commission. If a family member's federal government employment ended after 1910, the National Personnel Records Center may have his or her employment file. (See Appendix A.)

The holdings of the National Archives are organized into record groups, such as records of a government bureau or similar administrative division. Each record group is assigned a number to facilitate filing and retrieving records stored in the National Archives or its branches. The record group number assigned to an agency's records remains its identifier regardless of where the record is available. For example, to track down information on an ancestor who was an employee of the Department of the Interior from 1865 to 1882, you would examine the documents of Record Group 48 at the National Archives, which contains the records of the Department of the Interior from 1849 to 1907 and includes appointment papers. The appointment papers for Arizona, California, Colorado, Florida, Idaho, Mississippi, Missouri, Nevada, New Mexico, New York, North Carolina, Oregon, and Wyoming have been microfilmed and are available for purchase or through local regional National Archives offices.[2] Record Group 163 at the National Archives Rocky Mountain Region in Denver, Colorado, contains the World War I draft registration records: thirty-three cubic feet of "records dated 1917–1919, including lists of men ordered to report to local boards for military duty and final lists of delinquents and deserters for Colorado, Montana, North Dakota, South Dakota, Utah, and Wyoming."[3] At the National Archives Mid-Atlantic Region in Philadel-

phia you will find the records of local and district draft boards from Pennsylvania, Virginia, West Virginia, Delaware, and Maryland under Record Group 163.[4] The Atlanta, Georgia, National Archives Southeast Region office is the primary repository for Record Group 163 and has records from all of the draft boards in the nation. However, copies are available at other regional archives for the draft boards in their region.[5]

Census Records

The censuses undertaken by the United States government every ten years since 1790 are probably the most popular of the government records used by family researchers. Censuses become available to the public seventy-two years after they are recorded. The latest census open to researchers was taken in 1920. Descendants of persons in post-1920 censuses may request form BC-600, Application for Search of Census Records from the U.S. Department of Commerce (see Appendix A).

A *census return, census form,* or *census schedule* is the original record filled out by enumerators—officials responsible for identifying and recording all persons living in the area assigned them. Examples of census records are shown in figures 11 through 14 and 17. Some people confuse the original census records or schedules with published statistical abstracts taken from censuses. An example of a statistical abstract is the U.S. Bureau of the Census's *Statistical Abstract of the United States—1993: The National Data Book.* Abstracts do not contain names or personal data; they simply profile the nation's population by summarizing personal data into statistics. In the 1990 censuses, for example, you were asked about your ancestry. Your answer, combined with millions of others, is included in table 56, "Population by Selected Ancestry Group and Region: 1990" on page 51 of the above publication. If you had answered that your ancestry was Czech, your response would be represented by the statistic in the table showing that 1,296,000 people gave the same response as you.

Finding an ancestor in a census ties that person to a place and time in history. That information enables you to search other documents from a specific locality and year to learn if your family's activities were recorded by local clerks.

In the censuses from 1790 to and including the 1840 returns, each head of household is listed by name and his or her place of residence is recorded. These returns also include a statistical summary of the other persons in the household by tabulating their age, sex, and race. Census returns for most states have been preserved on microfilm and are available at regional branches of the National Archives. Few original returns exist except those that have been preserved in local archives. Many libraries and historical societies have purchased the filmed censuses for their state or county. Figures 11, 12, and 13 show pages from the 1790, 1820, and 1840 censuses. According to the last page of the 1790 census of Middlesex County, Connecticut (microfilm roll #1), there were 18,855 persons living there in February 1790. Of these, the following totals were given for each of the column headings: 4,730 "Free white males of sixteen years and upwards, including heads of families"; 4,132 "Free white males under sixteen years"; 9,632 "Free white females including heads of families"; 140 listed as "All other free persons"; and 221 "Slaves."

In the 1820 census (figure 12) there are categories for "Free White Males," "Free White Females," "Slaves," and "Free Colored Persons." The latter two categories are divided into "Males" and "Females" with spaces for each age group: "under fourteen," "of fourteen and under twenty," and so on.

The 1840 census (figure 13) tabulated "Free White Persons" and "Free Colored Persons" on the front page of the form and has spaces on the back for statistics about "Slaves." The back page also asks for the names of Revolutionary War or other military pensioners.

The 1850 census enumerated "Free Inhabitants" on Schedule 1 (see figure 14) and asked the census taker to mark in column 6 whether a person was "White," "Black," or "Mulatto." Schedule 2 of the 1850 census counted "Slave Inhabitants." The instructions given enumerators required that they record the name of each slave holder in column 1. A number was recorded in column 2 for each slave instead of his or her name. The numbers were assigned in order as each slave was counted: the first receiving number 1, the second number 2, and so on. Slave numbers began again at 1 for each succeeding slave holder. Each slave's age, sex, and color (black, mulatto) was also recorded. (Note in figure 13 that the enumerator failed to number slaves as required, placing a *1* in column 2 for each slave.)

If you are tracing your African American heritage, knowing how race and status were recorded will help in the search for your family. You may be able to find their household if you know the slave holder's name. Since slaves' ages are listed after 1790, you may be able to identify your ancestor if you can guess his or her approximate age in the year of the census. Make a list of families from the census that meet these criteria, then search local records to learn if one family contains fam-

ily members or slaves with the names and/or ages you seek. A will or a land record may name a head of household you found in the census; it might also list children in the family and slaves. The inventory of a deceased person's estate generally lists slaves along with other property. It was not until the 1870 census that former African American slaves and their households were enumerated by name. (See chapter 7 for more information about tracing African American families.)

Your ancestor would not be named in the censuses taken from 1790 through 1840 unless he or she was a free head of household. If your ancestor was not the household head, how do you identify him or her? Perhaps all you know is your ancestor's name and an approximate age or birth year. If you know the ages of an ancestor's parents and brothers and sisters at the time of the census, look for households in which the head has the same surname as your family with adults and children whose ages and gender match that of your ancestor's family.

Beginning with the census taken in 1850, every free member of the household was listed, and the person's age, sex, race, and state or country of birth were recorded. From that census on, you could also learn how many household members were in school, who spoke English, if your ancestors lived in their own home or rented, and how much land they owned.

From 1850 to 1880 special census schedules were created detailing information on mortality, business, agriculture, industry, manufacturing, and social statistics for the area. If an ancestor died during the twelve-month period before the census, the census form includes the month in which that person died, cause of death, and number of days he or she was ill. In 1918 and 1919 these schedules were offered to state archives and historical societies. Those not claimed were offered to the National Society of the Daughters of the American Revolution.[6] These schedules were returned to the National Archives in 1980 and are available as National Archives microfilm publication T655. The areas involved were Arizona, Colorado, District of Columbia, Georgia, Kentucky, Louisiana, and Tennessee.[7]

Other special census schedules may contain information that will help you describe your ancestors' lives and the community in which they lived. Agricultural schedules listed the names of owners or tenants of farms with gross production of $100 (1850) or $500 (1860 to 1880). The industrial schedules (1850 to 1870) and manufacturing schedules (1880) listed businesses and owners with an annual gross production of $500.[8] The censuses of 1880, 1900, 1910, 1930, 1950, and 1980 include special enumerations of Native Americans.

FIGURE 11 *1790 Census Return*

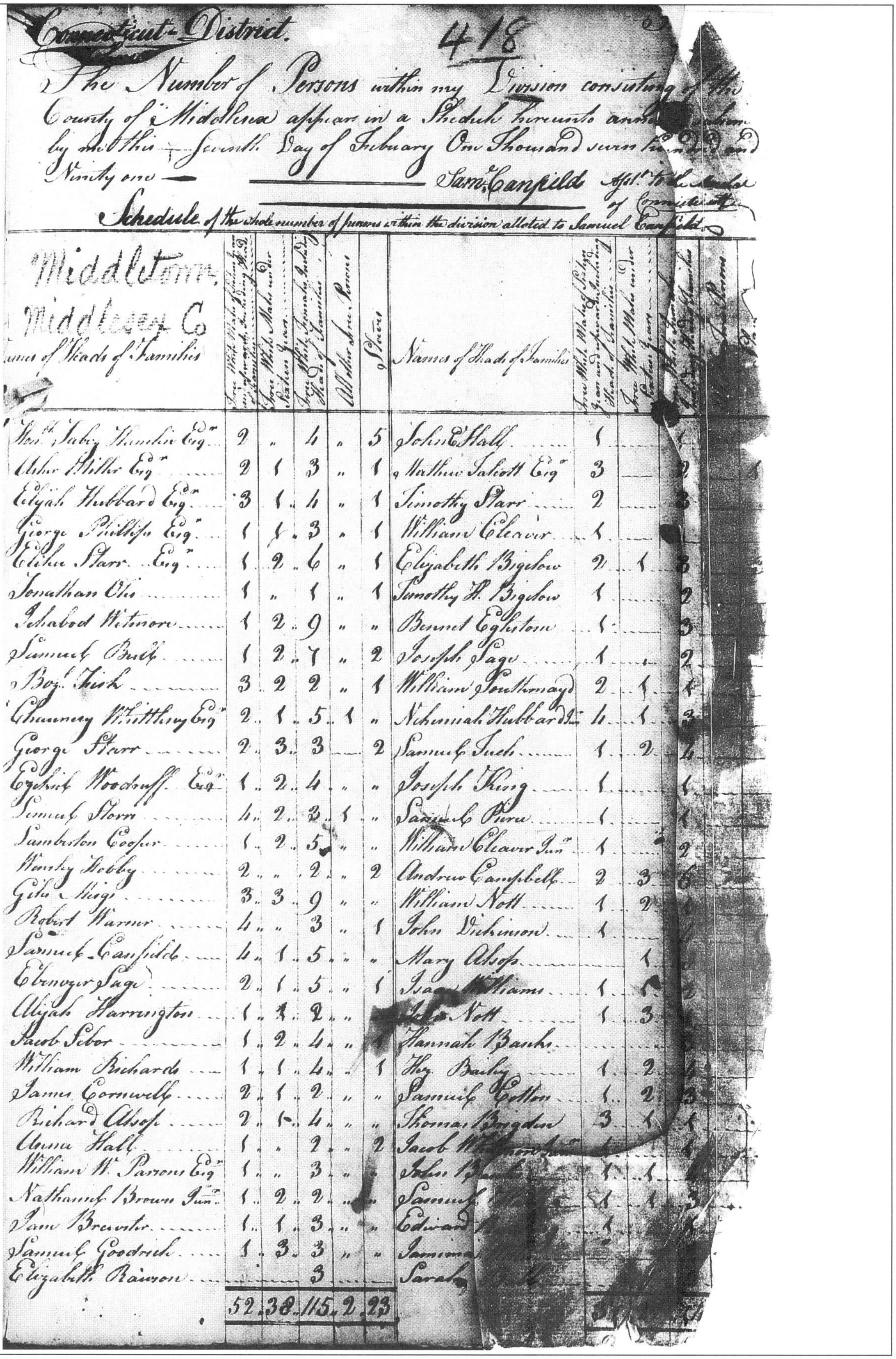

Connecticut District. 418

The Number of Persons within my Division consisting of the County of Middlesex appear in a Schedule hereunto annexed ... by me this ... Seventh Day of February One Thousand seven hundred and Ninety one — Saml. Canfield Asst. to the Marshal of Connecticut

Schedule of the whole number of persons within the division allotted to Samuel Canfield

Middletown, Middlesex Co.

Names of Heads of Families	Free White Males of sixteen years and upwards, including Heads of Families	Free White Males under sixteen years	Free White Females, including Heads of Families	All other Free Persons	Slaves
Honl. Jabez Hamlin Esqr.	2	"	4	"	5
Asher Miller Esqr.	2	1	3	"	1
Elijah Hubbard Esqr.	3	1	4	"	1
George Phillips Esqr.	1	1	3	"	1
Elihu Starr Esqr.	1	2	6	"	1
Jonathan Otis	1	"	1	"	1
Ichabod Wetmore	1	2	9	"	"
Samuel Bull	1	2	7	"	2
Benj. Fish	3	2	2	"	1
Chauncey Whittlesey Esqr.	2	1	5	1	"
George Starr	2	3	3	—	2
Ezekiel Woodruff Esqr.	1	2	4	"	"
Samuel Storr	4	2	3	1	"
Lamberton Cooper	1	2	5	"	"
Wensley Hobby	2	"	2	"	2
Giles Meigs	3	3	9	"	"
Robert Warner	4	"	3	"	1
Samuel Canfield	4	1	5	"	"
Ebenezer Sage	2	1	5	"	1
Elijah Harrington	1	1	2	"	[illegible]
Jacob Sebor	1	2	4	"	[illegible]
William Richards	1	1	4	"	1
James Cornwell	2	1	2	"	"
Richard Alsop	2	1	4	"	"
Anna Hall	1	"	2	"	2
William W. Parsons Esqr.	1	"	3	"	"
Nathaniel Brown Junr.	1	2	2	"	"
Jane Brewster	1	1	3	"	"
Samuel Goodrich	1	3	3	"	"
Elizabeth Rawson			3		
	52	38	115	2	23

Names of Heads of Families	Free White Males of sixteen years and upwards, including Heads of Families	Free White Males under sixteen years	Free White Females, including Heads of Families
John Hall	1		
Mathew Talcott Esqr.	3	—	2
Timothy Starr	2		3
William Cleaver	1		
Elizabeth Bigelow	2	1	3
Timothy W. Bigelow	1		2
Bennet Eglistone	1		3
Joseph Sage	1		2
William Southmayd	2	1	1
Nehemiah Hubbard Junr.	4	1	3
Samuel Tuck	1	2	4
Joseph King	1		1
Samuel [illegible]	1		
William Cleaver Junr.	1		2
Andrew Campbell	2	3	[illegible]
William Nott	1	2	[illegible]
John Dickinson	1		
Mary Alsop		1	
Isaac Williams	1	[illegible]	
[illegible] Nott	1	3	
Hannah Banks			
Hez. Bailey	1	2	[illegible]
Samuel Cotton	1	2	[illegible]
Thomas Brigden	3	1	[illegible]
Jacob W[illegible]	[illegible]	[illegible]	[illegible]
John B[illegible]	1	1	[illegible]
Samuel [illegible]	[illegible]	1	3
Edward [illegible]	[illegible]	[illegible]	[illegible]
Jemima [illegible]	[illegible]	[illegible]	[illegible]
Sarah [illegible]	[illegible]	[illegible]	[illegible]

Source: National Archives Microfilm Publication M637, Roll 1 (Connecticut)

FIGURE 12 *1820 Census Return*

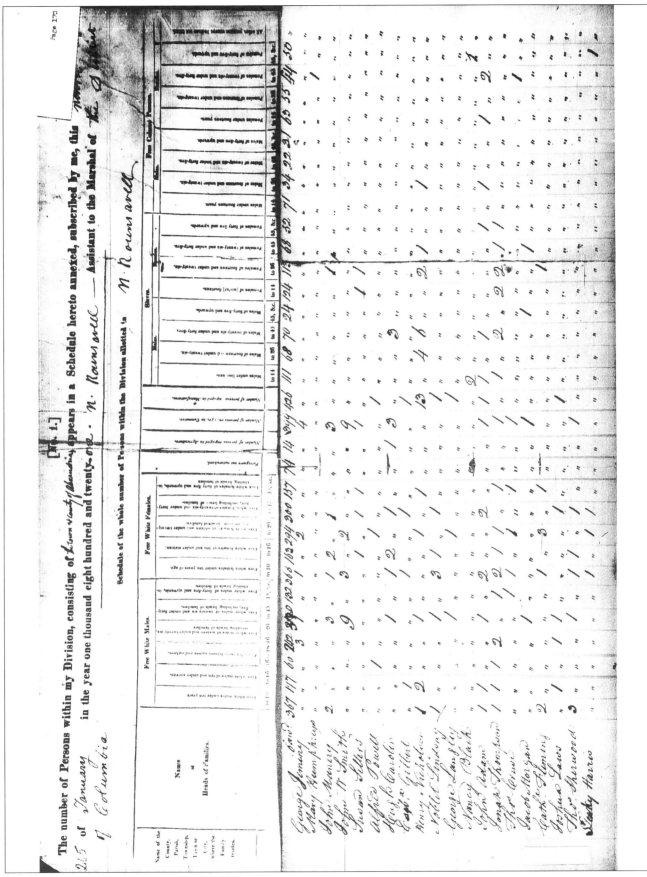

FIGURE 13 *1840 Census Return*

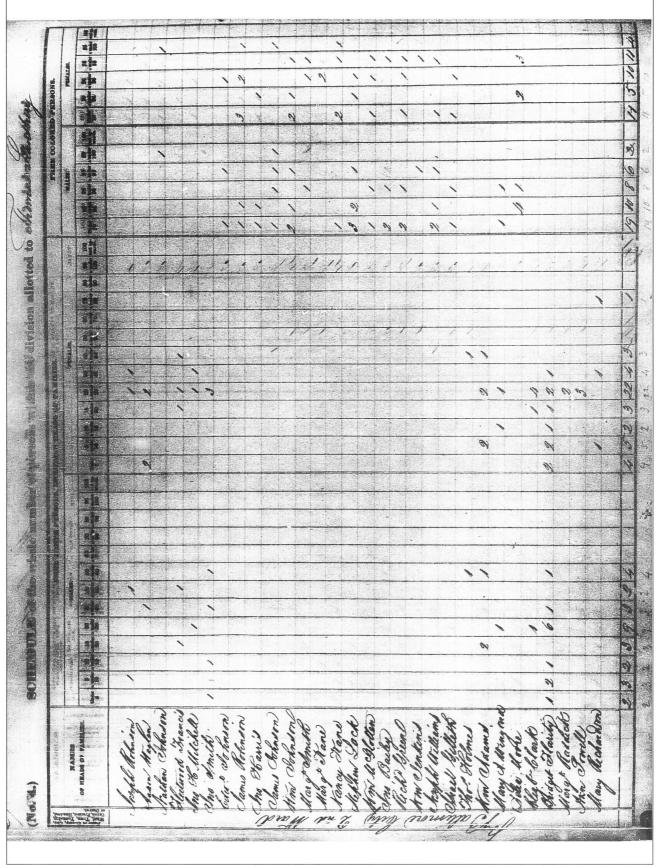

FIGURE 14 *1850 U.S. Census Return—Schedule 1*

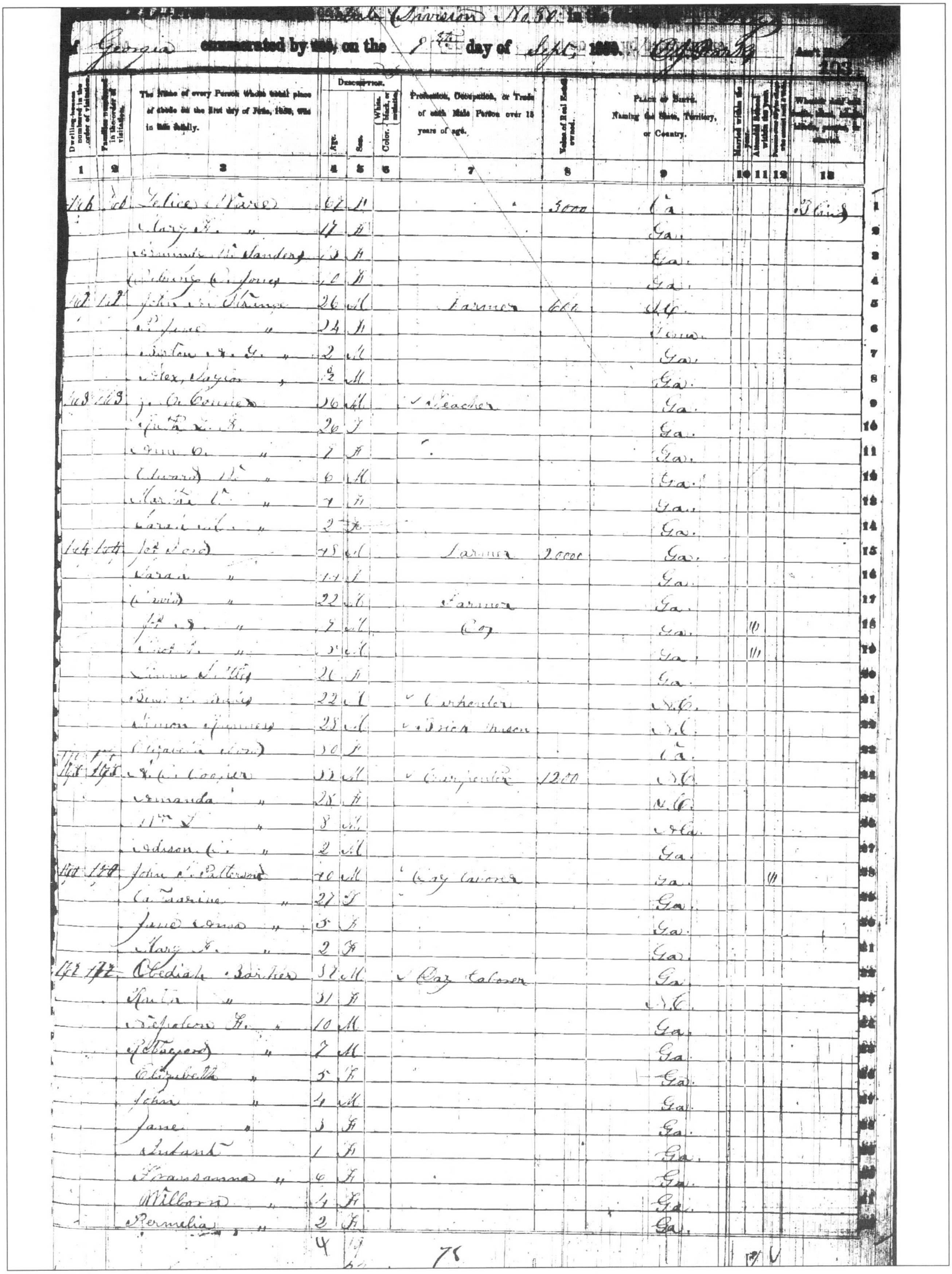

... Division No. 5[illegible] in the County of [illegible] State of Georgia enumerated by me, on the 8th day of Sept, 1850. [illegible] Ass't Marshal. 103

Dwelling-houses numbered in the order of visitation.	Families numbered in the order of visitation.	The Name of every Person whose usual place of abode on the first day of June, 1850, was in this family.	Age.	Sex.	Color. White, black, or mulatto.	Profession, Occupation, or Trade of each Male Person over 15 years of age.	Value of Real Estate owned.	Place of Birth. Naming the State, Territory, or Country.	Married within the year.	Attended School within the year.	Persons over 20 y'rs of age who cannot read & write.	Whether deaf and dumb, blind, insane, idiotic, pauper, or convict.	
1	2	3	4	5	6	7	8	9	10	11	12	13	
146	146	Felice [illegible] Ware	67	F			3000	Ga.				Blind	1
		Mary F. "	17	F				Ga.					2
		[illegible] Sanders	13	F				Ga.					3
		[illegible] Jones	10	F				Ga.					4
147	147	John [illegible]	26	M		Farmer	600	Ala.					5
		[illegible] Jane "	24	F				Tenn.					6
		[illegible] "	2	M				Ga.					7
		Alex. Taylor "	2/12	M				Ga.					8
148	148	J. O. Connor	36	M		Teacher		Ga.					9
		[illegible]	20	F				Ga.					10
		[illegible] "	7	F				Ga.					11
		Edward [illegible] "	6	M				Ga.					12
		Martha [illegible] "	4	F				Ga.					13
		[illegible] "	2	F				Ga.					14
149	149	Jos. Ford	48	M		Farmer	20000	Ga.					15
		Sarah "	44	F				Ga.					16
		David "	22	M		Farmer		Ga.					17
		[illegible] "	9	M		[illegible]		Ga.		1			18
		[illegible] "	5	M				Ga.		1			19
		[illegible]	20	F				Ga.					20
		[illegible]	22	M		Carpenter		N.C.					21
		[illegible]	28	M		Brick mason		N.C.					22
		[illegible]	30	F				Ga.					23
150	150	[illegible] Cooper	33	M		Carpenter	1200	N.C.					24
		Amanda "	28	F				N.C.					25
		[illegible] "	8	M				Ala.					26
		Addison [illegible] "	2	M				Ga.					27
151	151	John [illegible] Patterson	40	M		[illegible]		Ga.			1		28
		Catharine "	27	F				Ga.					29
		Jane Anna "	5	F				Ga.					30
		Mary F. "	2	F				Ga.					31
152	152	Obediah Barker	37	M		[illegible]		Ga.					32
		Ruth "	31	F				N.C.					33
		Napoleon B. "	10	M				Ga.					34
		[illegible] "	7	M				Ga.					35
		Elizabeth "	5	F				Ga.					36
		John	4	M				Ga.					37
		Jane	3	F				Ga.					38
		Infant	1	F				Ga.					39
		[illegible]sanna "	6	F				Ga.					40
		Milloom "	4	F				Ga.					41
		Permelia "	2	F				Ga.					42
			4	[illegible]		78							

Source: National Archives Microfilm Publication M432, Rolls 69, 90 (Floyd County, Georgia)

FIGURE 14 continued   *1850 U.S. Census Return—Schedule 2*

SCHEDULE 2.—Slave Inhabitants in _Sub Division No. 30_ in the County of _Hall_ State of _Georgia_, enumerated by me, on the _18_ day of _Septr_, 1850. _D. J. Parks_, Ass't Marshal.

NAMES OF SLAVE OWNERS.	Number of Slaves.	Age.	Sex.	Colour.	Fugitives from the State.	Number manumitted.	Deaf & dumb, blind, insane, or idiotic.	NAMES OF SLAVE OWNERS.	Number of Slaves.	Age.	Sex.	Colour.	Fugitives from the State.	Number manumitted.	Deaf & dumb, blind, insane, or idiotic.
1								1							
Daniel G. Mitchell	1	70	F	B				Q. E. Paine	1	6	F	M			
for Ford	1	51	M	B					1	5	F	B			
	1	50	M	B				Samuel T. Paine	1	1	F	M			
	1	46	M	B				John Trowbridge	1	24	M	B			
	1	46	M	B					1	8	F	B			
	1	32	M	B					1	17	F	B			
	1	28	M	B				James Brown	1	14	F	M			
	1	36	M	B				G. S. Coleman	1	28	F	B			
	1	22	M	B					1	18	F	B			
	1	20	M	B					1	23	M	B			
	1	20	M	B				Wm Gibbs	1	38	F	B			
	1	16	M	B					1	10	M	B			
	1	16	M	B				A. Washington	1	36	F	B			
	1	16	M	B					1	28	F	B			
	1	12	M	B					1	20	F	B			
	1	12	M	B				Wm R. Green	1	30	F	B			
	1	10	M	B					1	10	M	B			
	1	10	M	B					1	8	M	B			
	1	9	M	B					1	4	F	B			
A. D. Keefer	1	9	M	B					1	2	M	B			
Benj. Garrett	1	9	M	B					1	2	M	M			
	1	3	M	B					1	12	M	B			
	1	3	M	B					1	4	F	B			
	1	3	M	B				John Slade	1	14	F	B			
	1	2	M	B				L. Moore	1	50	M	B			
	1	2	M	B					1	45	F	B			
	1	38	F	B					1	42	F	B			
	1	34	F	B					1	23	M	B			
	1	38	F	B					1	22	M	B			
	1	30	F	B					1	26	F	B			
		18	F	M					1	8	F	B			
		16	F	B				John Reagan	1	5	F	B			
	1	18	F	B						3	M	B			
Samuel Hensley	1	15	F	B				G. C. Conner	1	62	F	B			
	1	12	F	B				Elizabeth Ford	1	45	M	B			
	1	11	F	B					1	35	M	B			
	1	9	F	B					1	13	F	B			
	1	8	F	B				George Wait	1	11	F	B			
James H. Davis	1	8	F	B					1	8	F	B			
	1	8	F	B					1	6	F	B			

(You will find more information about tracing Native American ancestors in chapter 7.)

Remember that microfilm copies of the 1790 to 1910 censuses and 1880 to 1920 census indexes can be rented through the National Archives microfilm rental program. These microfilms are also available through many of the research centers listed in Appendix A.

Most of the 1890 census was destroyed in 1921 by a fire in Washington, D.C. What is left, including an index, is on five rolls of film, National Archives microfilm publications M407 (three rolls) and M496 (two-roll index). Part of a special census of Union soldiers and veterans' widows taken in that year survived the fire and provides valuable information on a segment of the population that would otherwise be lost to researchers. Included are the states in alphabetical order from Kentucky to Wyoming and Washington, D.C. Only about half of the Kentucky returns survived. These schedules are on 118 rolls of microfilm, National Archives microfilm publication M123.

Other censuses may have been taken as part of the act establishing a territory or state. If such an enumeration were taken before or after an existing decennial census, you may find important information about ancestors who are less adequately described in the regular census.

Surname Indexes

Another reason censuses are so valuable is that the returns for many states have been indexed as to all heads of households appearing in a United States census for a specific state. This means you can find your ancestors' whereabouts knowing only their given names and surnames and the states in which they lived. If you are not sure of the state, you can search indexes for several likely states.

Surname indexes to United States censuses exist for many states and were produced by local societies or researchers trying to make census searching less time consuming. The censuses for the years 1830 to 1870 have been the most popular indexing projects. Most of these indexes were published as books until about five years ago. Now some of them are available on compact discs or on computer floppy disks. Local city and county libraries may have purchased census indexes for their state. Ask at the reference counter in your local library or the libraries in the area in which your ancestors lived. Many of the libraries identified in Appendix A have the published indexes for their state.

To use these indexes, first read the introduction to understand any abbreviations and how the index is organized. Next, turn to the part that contains the names from the census. You will note that all of the surnames of heads of families from the census are listed in alphabetical order: *Abbott* would be among the first entries and *Zundell* among the last. These names are further arranged in the alphabetical order of the first initial or first given name. Persons with a middle initial or a second surname are alphabetized after those with a single given name. Therefore, *Aaron Abbott* would be an early entry among the numerous *Abbotts* in an index. On the same line as each name in the index will be references to the community, county, and page number of the census in which that name appears. This information allows you to use a library catalog or a National Archives microfilm catalog to locate the film for the appropriate state and county. Once you have the needed microfilm, turn to the county and the page number shown in the index to find your family.

A unique census index that may help your research efforts is *Accelerated Indexing Systems, Inc. Microfiche Indexes of U.S. Census and Other Records.* Accelerated Indexing Systems is one of the many companies and public agencies publishing census indexes. After more than a decade of indexing, this publisher decided to create an index to all of the entries in its database of indexes. It amounts to a national index of censuses and other selected records. You search for your ancestor's name, and the index entry will tell you where the person lived and provide the page number of the census in which that person is recorded. The coverage is best for the period 1830 to 1880, although you will find entries from as early as 1607 and as late as 1906. This index is available at the Family History Library in Salt Lake City and at local LDS Family History Centers and at some of the research centers described in Appendix A.

Indexes are wonderful tools, but it is important that you understand their limitations. The production process that creates indexes requires high-speed data entry or extraction onto cards. As a result, your ancestors' names may be misspelled. Because the census pages are handwritten, an indexer may misread the name being entered. For example, an initial *F* may become an *E* and a *B* can be read as an *R, P,* or *K.* The only way to deal with this problem is to imagine as many variant spellings of your name as possible and check them out in the index. Persons with the surnames that match these spellings could be members of your family.

If you have difficulty reading census entries or handwritten census index entries, look at the way the enumerators or indexers formed letters and words. Make up an alphabet showing how each letter was written by these particular recorders at the time of the census.

Write the name you are seeking using letters from the alphabet you have constructed. Perhaps it is possible to see how the initial letter of the surname could have been read as something else. What about the given names? Are there combinations of letters within the surname or given names that could have caused them to be interpreted as something entirely different? If, for example, someone indexing a census entry looked at the name *Wright* and saw *Weight* or *Haight,* my ancestor would not be listed correctly.

The Soundex and Miracode Indexes

For the 1880, 1900, 1910, and 1920 censuses, special indexes were created by government-sponsored projects. These indexes are arranged according to the sound of a surname and are called *Soundexes.* Each index card contains an extract from a household's or individual's entry on the original census page. At the top of cards

from the 1900 census (see figure 15) is the name of an individual, usually the "head of family." Recorded on the card are the address of the family and the names, ages, birth month and year, and birthplace of each person in the family. In the upper right-hand corner of the card are spaces to specify the exact location of the family's census entry: volume, enumeration district (E.D.), sheet (page), and line. Be certain to copy all of the information from the cards that refer to your ancestors. The data will help you find the original census record.

The cards are organized by state, and under each state all of the cards are arranged by the first letter of a surname and then by code numbers assigned the remaining letters in the name.

Names are coded by writing the beginning letter of the surname—in my case W. Next, *a, e, i, o, u, y, w,* and *h* are crossed out of the name unless one of them is the initial letter in the surname. *Wright* thus becomes

FIGURE 15   *Soundex Card for Wilson G. Wright—1900 Census*

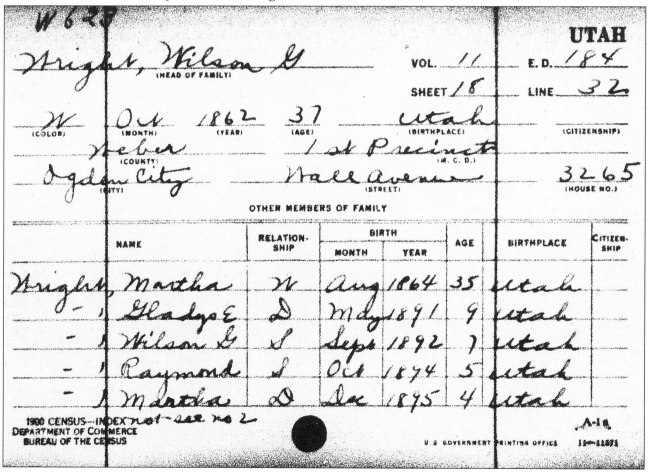

Source: National Archives Microfilm Publication T1074, Roll 29 (Utah)

WRGT. Only the first three of the remaining letters after the first letter are given a numeric value from the following table.

1 = b, p, f, v
2 = c, s, k, g, j, q, x, z
3 = d, t
4 = l
5 = m, n
6 = r

Thus, the index code number for *Wright* is *W–623*. Double consonants that fall together in a name are given one number. The name *Lassen*, for example, would receive the code number *L–250*. Notice that a zero is added to make the third digit of the code because after eliminating *a, e,* and one *s* for Lassen, *LSN* is left. The code must always have three digits, but no more than three, after the initial letter of the name. If your name is *Shakespeare,* the code would be *S–221,* using the first three allowable letters after *S* (S-ksp) even though there were four letters left in the name after crossing out the other six letters. You will notice that both *k* and *s* have the same value (2).

Bradley Steuart has compiled an index of codes for a large number of surnames, *The Soundex Reference Guide.* For more details on the Soundex, read Charles Stephenson's 1980 *Prologue* article, "The Methodology of Historical Census Record Linkage: A User's Guide to the Soundex."

Within each section devoted to a Soundex code, the cards are arranged alphabetically by the given names of the heads of household. Abel W–623 (Wright and similar names) will be at the beginning of the W–623 index film and Zebidee W–623 will be near the end.

The Soundex for the 1880 census included only those families with one or more children under the age of ten years. The 1900 Soundex covered all household heads and included separate cards for those individuals in the household with a surname different from the head of the family.

Only seven states are covered in the Soundex head-of-household indexes to the 1910 census: Alabama, Georgia, Louisiana, Mississippi, South Carolina, Tennessee, and Texas. A similar type of index, Miracode, was used in preparing the 1910 census indexes for fourteen additional states: Arkansas, California, Florida, Illinois, Kansas, Kentucky, Michigan, Missouri, North Carolina, Ohio, Oklahoma, Pennsylvania, Virginia, and West Virginia. The Miracode system uses a different format for the index card, but the arrangement of the index is basically the same as with the Soundex system.

The Soundex for the 1920 census covers all states and territories and includes separate cards for nonrelatives enumerated in a household.

To find where your ancestor appears in the 1900 census, for example, you need only determine the code for your name and look in the microfilmed index for the name of the person who was the head of the household at the time of the census. Remember that each state has its own index on several rolls of microfilm. With the information gleaned from the Soundex, you can obtain a microfilm of the census sheets for the county in which your ancestors lived and find the census entry that describes your family.

Maps, Directories, and Guides

Sometimes the census for the area you want is not indexed, or your ancestor was not captured in the index—even though you are confident that the person lived there. Resources are available to help you overcome these obstacles.

One of the most important aids in using census population schedules or enumerations was described in chapter 4—local directories. From the latter part of the eighteenth century until the present, local directories have been published as a register of the people, businesses, government offices, churches, and other community organizations in cities and counties across America. Directories generally serve as a credible substitute for an enumeration of the local population. Since directories will list your family and its address, this information may help you find ancestors in unindexed census returns.

With a local map and a directory in hand, you can try to figure out how enumerators conducted the census in an area. Street names or other addresses are listed at the top of the census pages after 1880. In earlier censuses you may find a post office address. Sometimes the enumerator also wrote street names or other identifying information in the margin of the census page. Even without any information about where the census enumerator found each family, you can check your directory and determine where each family lived. By looking for each family's location on a contemporary map, you can retrace the steps of the enumerators who carried out the census in that area. Once you feel you have established the arrangement of census entries for the place in which your family lived, it is easier to estimate where you might expect to find them on the microfilms of the census schedules. Such searches take a lot of time—especially in large cities—but are worth it if you find your family.

NARA has microfilmed the existing descriptions of census enumeration districts and some street indexes for selected cities. It also has filmed maps of the enumeration districts for 1910. These tools show you which microfilms contain enumeration districts or streets you are seeking. You can find these at your regional National Archives branch under the titles *Descriptions of Census Enumeration Districts, 1830–1890 and 1910–1950* (microfilm publication T1224), and *Descriptions of Census Enumeration District Descriptions, 1900* (microfilm publication T1210).

Several publications will help you identify and interpret census records. The U.S. Bureau of the Census's *200 Years of U.S. Census Taking: Population and Housing Questions, 1790–1990* and its reprint describe the instructions given to enumerators. This information will help you understand what the entries about your family mean. In addition, four catalogs from the National Archives in Washington, D.C., list the microfilms available from NARA that will help you when ordering films for rental or purchase: *Federal Population Censuses 1790–1890: A Catalog of Microfilm Copies of the Schedules, The 1900 Federal Population Census: A Catalog of Microfilm Copies of the Schedules, The 1910 Federal Population Census: A Catalog of Microfilm Copies of the Schedules,* and *The 1920 Federal Population Census: Catalog of National Archives Microfilm.*

Errors and Omissions in Census Records

You must be cautious in using census data. The most common errors involve ages, birthplaces, and spellings of names for each person enumerated. An example will illustrate what I mean.

Hetty Petersen died in 1909. Her death certificate gave a birth date of February 19, 1837. From the compilers David N. McBride and Jan N. McBride's *Cemetery Inscriptions of Highland County, Ohio,* I found that the birth date on her headstone was April 30, 1834. I have not located an obituary, which might help. In the meantime, I decided to trace her in censuses. In each census she is shown as the wife of Adam Cunningham Post. The following chart shows the discrepancies across censuses. Question marks precede information that would be deduced from that provided in the census. Two birth years are listed because the correct year would depend on whether her birthday came before or after the census day.

Census	Age	Birth Date
1900		June 1841
1880	44	?1836/1837
1870	30	?1840/1841
1860	24	?1836/1837

When you find ancestors in a census, it may add more confusion to the search or shed more light. That is the way it is with censuses: They are essential in our research, but we must recognize some of the information may be incorrect.

Why are some ancestors missing from censuses? Often, we do not know the death date of an ancestor and, thus, assume that the person will be listed in a census. If the census was taken after the person's death, he or she will not be listed there. Another reason an ancestor may not be found in a census is that the person was not home and the enumerator did not call again. In fact, some ancestors deliberately may have avoided the census taker, perhaps because they were suspicious of what the government might do to them or because they may have had reason to fear being discovered if they had broken the law or were avoiding creditors. Others were boarders or hired hands who were simply overlooked. Furthermore, ancestors often moved from where they were in the last census or where we think they were. Sometimes we think they are not there because we cannot find them in an index to the census. The omission of their names in an index may have had nothing to do with the census enumerator—perhaps an indexer overlooked them or misspelled their names. Check under several spellings of your family's name before you conclude it is not in an index. If all else fails and you know the county where your family was supposed to have lived, search through all of the entries for the county on the microfilm of the original census sheets.

As described in chapter 4, you can also check local records such as tax lists, draft registration records, printed directories, school records, and land records to see if they document your ancestors in the area. Contact the local county clerk, historical society, or school board to determine if such records are available. As mentioned earlier, directories also are a great substitute for census records.

Using Census Records

To help you apply what you have learned about censuses in your research, let me share some additional examples from my family's history.

My grandfather was born in 1894. The first time he was recorded by a census taker was in 1900. I asked him where he and his parents were living in 1900 and learned that they were in Utah. Checking at some local libraries, I found that the university where I teach had a set of microfilmed census returns for 1900 as well as the microfilms containing the Soundex to the returns from each state. Another library in the community had a second set.

You may have to travel to one of the regional National Archives for 1900 census returns or borrow microfilms through the nearest LDS Family History Center, a branch of the Family History Library in Salt Lake City, Utah. Many of the libraries listed in Appendix A also have complete sets of censuses and census index microfilms. In addition, other libraries in your state may collect census microfilms. Your local interlibrary loan librarian may be able to give you some guidance in finding them or arrange for you to borrow copies from another library.

When I arrived at the library to use the 1900 census, I first had to code my grandfather's surname—Wright—so that I could search for his name in the Soundex to the 1900 census. Next, I had to find the microfilm with the portion of the index cards that includes W–623.

If the index microfilms and the films of the original census schedules are available at one of your local libraries, it should also have the National Archives catalog that describes this collection: *1900 Federal Population Census: A Catalog of Microfilm Copies of the Schedules.* Beginning on page 32 of this publication are the numbers of the 1900 census index microfilms arranged by state. On page 76 are microfilm roll numbers for Utah (see figure 16). There are twenty-nine rolls listed under T–1074, the microfilm publication number for Utah. Film number 29 contains the index cards coded W–600 through Z–565. In other words, the census returns are indexed for each state, not the returns for the country as a whole.

After finding the film, I placed it on a microfilm reader and soon found a Soundex card for a family head named Wilson G. Wright (see figure 15). His wife was named Martha, and among their six children I found my grandfather, Raymond. In the upper-right corner of the card I found the census enumeration district number (184), the sheet/page number (18), and the line number (32) on the census page listing this family. At the top of the card was also a description of where they lived: 3265 Wall Avenue, Ogden City, Weber County, Utah.

The next step took me back to the catalog of National Archives census microfilms where, on page 27, I found the microfilm containing Weber County, Utah, census schedules: microfilm 1688. On page 18 and line 32 in Weber County's enumeration district 184, I found Wilson G. Wright and, on the lines below his name, his wife Martha and their children (figure 17, see pages 82–83).

From the 1900 census entry for my grandfather's family, I learned the month and year of each family member's birth and the state in which each was born. Another column of the census schedule contains the state or country of birth for each person's parents. My great-grandparents, Wilson G. and Martha Agnes, were born in Utah in 1862 and 1864. Wilson's father and mother were born in Connecticut. Martha's father was born in Vermont and her mother in Scotland.

The 1900 census also has a column for the number of children born to the wife and the number still living. My great-grandmother had given birth to seven children and six were living. Another column contains the number of years my great-grandparents had been married: twelve years. Other columns—blank for my family—provide space for the year of immigration to the United States, the number of years in the United States, and whether or not a person was a naturalized citizen. In the column headed "Occupation, Trade, or Profession," my great-grandfather listed himself as a teamster. Under the same heading is a column for the number of months unemployed. A zero in that space showed that Wilson G. Wright had not been out of work during the previous year.

The "Education" section of the 1900 census asks for information about who attended school within the previous year and for how many months, along with whether or not each person could read, speak, and write English.

FIGURE 16 *1900 Census Soundex Microfilms by State*

#	From	Thru
198.	P-362	thru P-400 Elisha
199.	P-400 Eliza	thru P-412 Trawick
200.	P-412 Uleses	thru P-455
201.	P-456	thru P-525 Geo.
202.	P-525 H. C.	thru P-600 Rimona
203.	P-600 Robt.	thru P-620 Justo
204.	P-620 K. B.	thru P-623 Wilhelmina
205.	P-623 Will	thru P-626 John**
206.	P-626 John**	thru P-635
207.	P-636	thru Q-351
208.	Q-400	thru R-100 Preather L.
209.	R-100 R.	thru R-152 Joel W.
210.	R-152 John	thru R-163 Alice P.
211.	R-163 Allen	thru R-200 Alejandro
212.	R-200 Alex	thru R-200 John G.
213.	R-200 Jospeh	thru R-223
214.	R-225	thru R-245
215.	R-246	thru R-262 Ozie G.
216.	R-262 P. R.	thru R-300 Dave S.
217.	R-300 David	thru R-320 Samson M.
218.	R-320 Samuel	thru R-352
219.	R-355	thru R-400 Polley
220.	R-400 R. H.	thru R-500 Ruth
221.	R-500 S.	thru R-534 Gus B.
222.	R-534 H. A.	thru R-560 Eugene
223.	R-560 Fabis	thru S-100 Josef**
224.	S-100 Joseph**	thru S-145
225.	S-146	thru S-162 Penix
226.	S-162 Peter	thru S-200 Lou M.
227.	S-200 Louis	thru S-300 Ann
228.	S-300 Anna	thru S-310 Lea G.
229.	S-310 Lee	thru S-316 Eugene N.
230.	S-316 F. H.	thru S-330 Uno H.
231.	S-330 V. H.	thru S-350 Joel L.
232.	S-350 John	thru S-356
233.	S-360	thru S-363 James A.**
234.	S-363 James B.**	thru S-365 Martin R.
235.	S-365 Mary	thru S-420 Emeline
236.	S-420 Emil	thru S-432 Martin
237.	S-432 Mary	thru S-462 Isaac G.
238.	S-462 J. H.	thru S-514 Richard M.
239.	S-514 Robt.	thru S-524 Emily
240.	S-524 Emma	thru S-530 Charlie W.
241.	S-530 Charlotte	thru S-530 James**
242.	S-530 James A.**	thru S-530 Mary**
243.	S-530 Mary**	thru S-530 William**
244.	S-530 William**	thru S-536 Gertrude
245.	S-536 George	thru S-550 Juan
246.	S-550 Julia	thru S-563 Joe
247.	S-563 John	thru S-626
248.	S-630	thru S-665
249.	T-000	thru T-260 Eliza M.
250.	T-260 Elizabeth	thru T-360
251.	T-362	thru T-460 Charles G.**
252.	T-460 Charles H.**	thru T-460 Sylvester
253.	T-460 T. A.	thru T-512/513* Louie
254.	T-512/513* Louis	thru T-520 Guy
255.	T-520 H.	thru T-525 Homer
256.	T-525 Horace	thru T-600 Rutha
257.	T-600 S. L.	thru T-630 David H.
258.	T-630 Earl H.	thru T-653
259.	T-654	thru U-300/326* H.
260.	U-300/326* J.	thru V-250 Cora
261.	V-250 D. H.	thru V-464/465* Evarista
262.	V-464/465* F.	thru V-660
263.	W-000	thru W-162/163* LizzieL.
264.	W-162/163* M. C.	thru W-240 Julia
265.	W-240 Leain	thru W-256 Charles**
266.	W-256 Charles**	thru W-300 J. Z.
267.	W-300 Jack	thru W-300 Tommie
268.	W-300 Tony	thru W-325 Alberta
269.	W-325 Alex	thru W-330 Rufus
270.	W-330 S. C.	thru W-362 Joel
271.	W-362 John	thru W-410 Lusee
272.	W-410 M. A.	thru W-420 John E.**
273.	W-420 John F.**	thru W-425 Cardon
274.	W-425 Carl	thru W-425 Santa Anna
275.	W-425 Sarah	thru W-426 Larry
276.	W-426 Laura	thru W-436 Myrtle
277.	W-436 N. N.	thru W-452 Ed E.**
278.	W-452 Ed. F.**	thru W-452 John
279.	W-452 Jno.	thru W-452 Robert E.**
280.	W-452 Robert F.**	thru W-463 Hugh
281.	W-463 Gordon	thru W-535 Mott
282.	W-535 Nannie R.	thru W-623 Myrtle C.
283.	W-623 N. J.	thru W-635 Vester J.
284.	W-635 W.	thru Y-320 Fred
285.	Y-320 G. M.	thru Y-326 Lou
286.	Y-526 Major	thru Z-660

UTAH. T-1074

#	From	Thru
1.	A-000	thru B-120/164* Iver
2.	B-120/164* J. Henry	thru B-460/463* Jennie
3.	B-460/463* John	thru B-650
4.	B-652	thru C-450/452* George**
5.	C-450/452* George**	thru C-642/645* Isaac V.
6.	C-642/645* Isabelle	thru D-555
7.	D-560	thru F-453
8.	F-455	thru F-666
9.	G-000	thru G-663
10.	H-000	thru H-500
11.	H-510	thru H-663
12.	I-100	thru I-520/523* Sylvester F.
13.	J-520/523* T. H.	thru K-513
14.	K-514	thru K-656
15.	L-000	thru L-563
16.	L-600	thru M-320
17.	M-321	thru M-620
18.	M-621	thru M-660
19.	N-000	thru O-420/425* Cristine
20.	O-420/425* Dagney	thru P-400
21.	P-410	thru R-165
22.	R-200	thru S-116
23.	S-120	thru S-400 Justie W.
24.	S-400 Less	thru S-566
25.	S-600	thru S-666
26.	T-000	thru V-655
27.	W-000	thru W-420
28.	W-421	thru W-563
29.	W-600	thru Z-565

VERMONT. T-1075

#	From	Thru
1.	A-100	thru A-625/646* Maude
2.	A-625/646* Milton A.	thru B-240/246* Everett N.
3.	B-240/246* F. Rush	thru B-420 Grace E.
4.	B-420 H. C.	thru B-540/553* Frederick
5.	B-540/553* George	thru B-636
6.	B-640	thru B-666
7.	C-155	thru C-420
8.	C-421	thru C-535
9.	C-536	thru C-650 Irene
10.	C-650 James	thru D-250/251* Earl J.
11.	D-250/251* Edgar E.	thru D-565
12.	D-600	thru E-463
13.	E-500	thru F-460/463* Oscar W.
14.	F-460/463* Parker A.	thru G-166
15.	G-200	thru G-600
16.	G-610	thru H-156
17.	H-160	thru H-400/416* Ezra R.
18.	H-400/416* F. Burton	thru H-552
19.	H-553	thru J-300/360* Justin W.
20.	J-300/360* L. Belle	thru K-420/426* Ivan U.
21.	K-420/426* James	thru L-150/156* Joel G.
22.	L-150/156* John	thru L-500 Lucy
23.	L-500 M. Antionnette	thru M-200 Katherine
24.	M-200 Laura	thru M-260 Issac H.
25.	M-260 James	thru M-550
26.	M-552	thru M-634
27.	M-635	thru O-165 Julia
28.	O-165 Kate	thru P-320 Joseph**
29.	P-320 Joseph**	thru P-620 Nurtha
30.	P-620 Olin	thru R-000
31.	R-100	thru R-300/316* Jonas G.
32.	R-300/316* Joseph	thru S-143 Elisha S.
33.	S-143 Eliza	thru S-350 Lynn
34.	S-350 M. H.	thru S-510/515* Leon
35.	L-510/515* Leonard H.	thru S-620/623* Irving
36.	S-620/623* James	thru T-500 James O.
37.	T-500 Jane	thru V-523

* Indicates mixed codes continued on next roll.   ** Indicates same given name continued on next roll.

Source: National Archives and Records Administration, *1900 Federal Population Census: A Catalog of Microfilm Copies of the Schedules* (page 76)

The whole family answered yes to the language questions, and the two oldest children had attended school for nine months. The other children, ages 5, 4, 3, and 1, had not been in school during the previous year.

The 1900 census lists whether a family owned or rented their home. My great-grandfather rented the house in which he lived with his family.

From the 1900 census information I now knew to search through the marriage records for Weber County, Utah, because Martha and Wilson Wright had been married for twelve years in 1900. Although I did not find their marriage records in Weber County, I did find them in the records of Cache County, the neighboring county north of Weber.

Next, I checked to see if I could find the same family in the 1910 census. It is indexed for twenty-one states, and Utah is not one of them. Yet, my curiosity had been piqued, so I decided to see if I could find the Wilson Wright family by looking through the microfilmed census schedules for Ogden, Utah. When I found the family, my great-grandmother, listed as Martha in the 1900 census, was not recorded. Research in local obituaries—on film at the Harold B. Lee Library, Brigham Young University—produced the following from the September 3, 1900, issue of the *Ogden Standard Examiner:*

> Died. Wright-Agnes Bingham, wife of Wilson G. Wright, of pneumonia at her home 3271 Wall Avenue, Sunday, Sept. 2nd, at 10:45 a.m.

Church records showed that Martha Agnes died six days after the birth of her seventh child, a daughter. Wilson had not remarried by the time of the 1910 census. He is listed as the head of household in a family that showed no mother and the same six children listed in the 1900 census. The child born in 1900 is not shown for some unknown reason. As a widower father working to support and raise six children, it is possible that my great-grandfather had arranged to have someone else care for her.

The 1900 and 1910 censuses taught me a lot about my grandfather and his father's family. But I wondered if earlier censuses could help me find my second great-grandparents. I know from the 1900 census that Wilson G. Wright—my great-grandfather—was born in October

1862 and his wife, Martha, in August 1864, both in Utah. Since censuses seldom give a wife's maiden name, I used Martha's marriage record and obituary to learn she was a Bingham. From the marriage record I determined her parents were Sanford and Agnes Bingham. Since I know her month and year of birth, I can search civil and religious birth records in Weber County to see how many Martha Binghams were born to a Sanford and Agnes in the appropriate month and year (1864). To verify her family data I could also look for her as a 6-year-old in the 1880 census with Sanford Bingham as the head of household and Agnes listed as the wife. For now, however, I will try to find out more about Wilson G. Wright's father.

Wilson would have been about 18 years old when the 1880 census was recorded. There is a Soundex for 1880, so I could have used the same code—W–623—to find all of the Wrights in Utah with children aged 10 and under for that census year. Instead, I chose a surname index published in book form that was easier to use: Ronald V. Jackson, and others, editors, *Utah 1880 Federal Census Index.* It lists all household heads in the 1880 Utah census including more than 100 Wright households. To narrow the search I needed to review what I already knew about Wilson and his parents: According to the 1900 and 1910 censuses, both Wilson's mom and dad were born in Connecticut, and he was born in Utah. In 1900 and 1910 the family lived in Ogden, Utah. A search of the indexes turned up eleven Wright families in Ogden. Now I needed to look at these entries to learn how many of them listed parents born in Connecticut with an 18-year-old son named Wilson who was born in Utah.

The 1880 census lists names of enumerated persons; their race, sex, age, relationship to the head of the household, citizenship status, profession, number of months unemployed, health (sick, handicapped), and education (attended school, able to read and write); the places of birth of each person enumerated; and their parents' birthplace (the state or country). This last column of the 1880 census will help because I know that Wilson's father was born in Connecticut. Using the information found in the index, I turned to page 15 of enumeration district 97 (line 1) where I found a family of eight children with their mother, Aurelia Wright, age 37, as the head of the household.

FIGURE 17 *1900 Census Return*

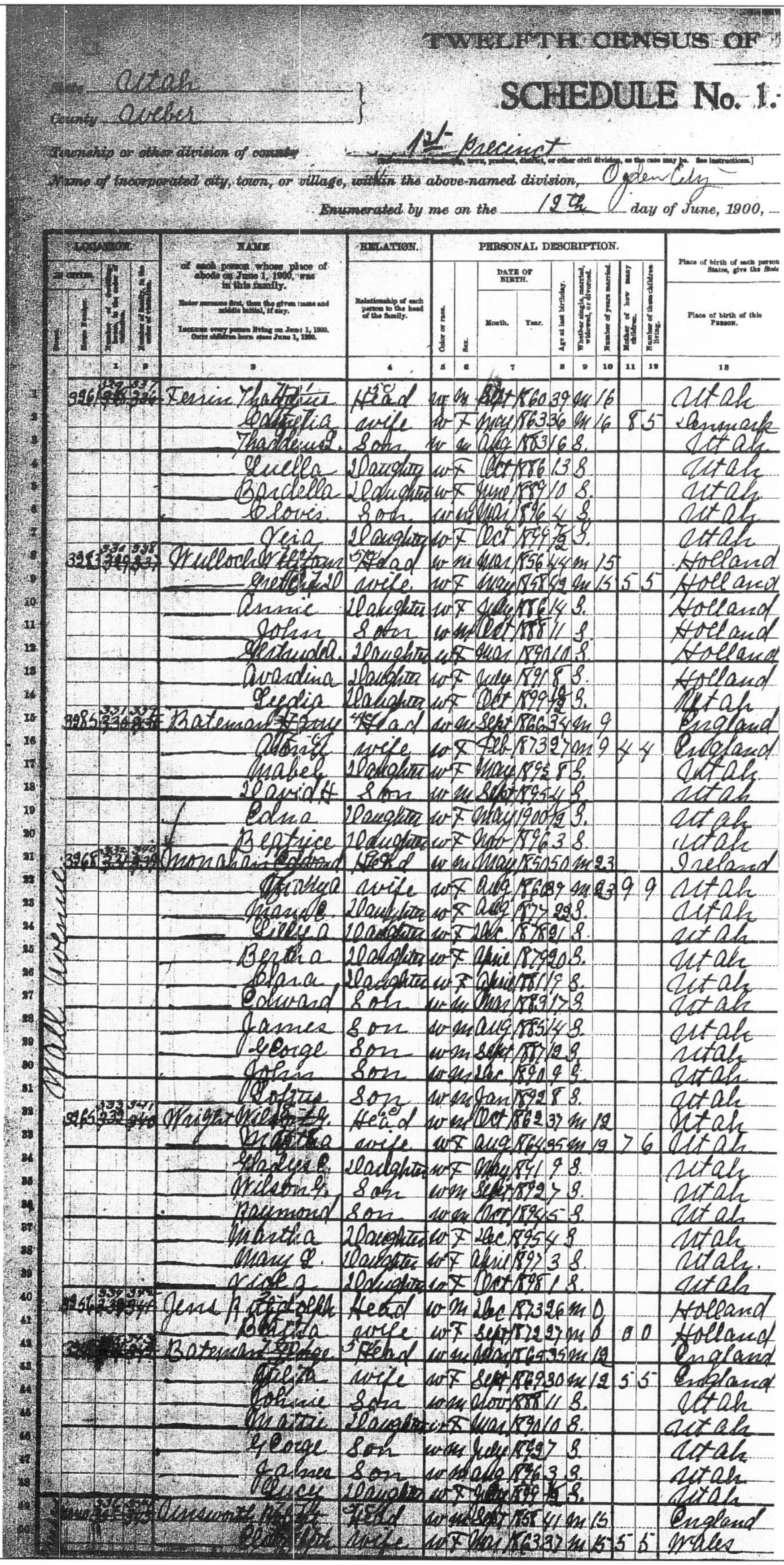

TWELFTH CENSUS OF

SCHEDULE No. 1.

State: Utah
County: Weber
Township or other division of county: 1st Precinct
Name of incorporated city, town, or village, within the above-named division: Ogden City
Enumerated by me on the 12th day of June, 1900

Line	Name	Relation	Color	Sex	Month	Year	Age	Marital	Yrs married	Mother of how many	Living	Place of birth
1	Ferrin, Thaddeus	Head	W	M	Sept	1860	39	M	16			Utah
2	[illegible]	Wife	W	F	May	1863	36	M	16	8	5	Denmark
3	Thaddeus L.	Son	W	M	Aug	1883	16	S				Utah
4	Luella	Daughter	W	F	Oct	1886	13	S				Utah
5	Bardella	Daughter	W	F	June	1889	10	S				Utah
6	Clovis	Son	W	M	Mar	1896	4	S				Utah
7	Veia	Daughter	W	F	Oct	1899	7/12	S				Utah
8	Wullock, William	Head	W	M	Mar	1856	44	M	15			Holland
9	[illegible]	Wife	W	F	May	1858	[illegible]	M	15	5	5	Holland
10	Annie	Daughter	W	F	July	1886	14	S				Holland
11	John	Son	W	M	Oct	1888	11	S				Holland
12	[illegible]	Daughter	W	F	Mar	1890	10	S				Holland
13	Avardina	Daughter	W	F	July	1891	8	S				Holland
14	Lydia	Daughter	W	F	Oct	1899	7/12	S				Utah
15	Bateman, Henry	Head	W	M	Sept	1866	33	M	9			England
16	[illegible]	Wife	W	F	Feb	1873	27	M	9	4	4	England
17	Mabel	Daughter	W	F	May	1892	8	S				Utah
18	David H	Son	W	M	Sept	1895	4	S				Utah
19	Edna	Daughter	W	F	May	1900	[illegible]	S				Utah
20	Beatrice	Daughter	W	F	Nov	1896	3	S				Utah
21	Monahan, Edward	Head	W	M	May	1850	50	M	23			Ireland
22	[illegible]	Wife	W	F	Aug	1860	39	M	23	9	9	Utah
23	Maude	Daughter	W	F	Aug	1877	22	S				Utah
24	Lilly A	Daughter	W	F	Dec	1878	21	S				Utah
25	Bertha	Daughter	W	F	April	1879	20	S				Utah
26	Clara	Daughter	W	F	April	1881	19	S				Utah
27	Edward	Son	W	M	Mar	1883	17	S				Utah
28	James	Son	W	M	Aug	1885	14	S				Utah
29	George	Son	W	M	Sept	1887	12	S				Utah
30	John	Son	W	M	Dec	1890	9	S				Utah
31	[illegible]	Son	W	M	Jan	1892	8	S				Utah
32	Wright, [illegible]	Head	W	M	Oct	1862	37	M	12			Utah
33	[illegible]	Wife	W	F	Aug	1864	35	M	12	7	6	Utah
34	[illegible]	Daughter	W	F	May	1891	9	S				Utah
35	Wilson L.	Son	W	M	Sept	1892	7	S				Utah
36	Raymond	Son	W	M	Nov	1894	5	S				Utah
37	Martha	Daughter	W	F	Dec	1895	4	S				Utah
38	Mary L.	Daughter	W	F	April	1897	3	S				Utah
39	[illegible]	Daughter	W	F	Oct	1898	1	S				Utah
40	Jens, [illegible]	Head	W	M	Dec	1873	26	M	0			Holland
41	[illegible]	Wife	W	F	Sept	1872	27	M	0	0	0	Holland
42	Bateman, [illegible]	Head	W	M	Mar	1865	35	M	12			England
43	[illegible]	Wife	W	F	Sept	1869	30	M	12	5	5	England
44	Johnie	Son	W	M	Nov	1888	11	S				Utah
45	Mattie	Daughter	W	F	Mar	1890	10	S				Utah
46	George	Son	W	M	July	1892	7	S				Utah
47	James	Son	W	M	Aug	1896	3	S				Utah
48	Lucy	Daughter	W	F	July	1899	[illegible]	S				Utah
49	Ainsworth, [illegible]	Head	W	M	Sept	1858	41	M	15			England
50	[illegible]	Wife	W	F	Mar	1863	37	M	15	5	5	Wales

Source: National Archives Microfilm Publication T623, Roll 1688 (Weber County, Utah)

FIGURE 17 continued

THE UNITED STATES. 102 A

—POPULATION. { Supervisor's District No. _273_ } Sheet No.
{ Enumeration District No. _184_ } 18

Name of Institution, X

Ward of city, _1st_

Josie F. Kimball , Enumerator. 3460

Place of birth of Father of this person.	Place of birth of Mother of this person.	Year of Immigration to the United States.	Number of years in the United States.	Naturalization.	Occupation	Months not employed.	Attended school (in months).	Can read.	Can write.	Can speak English.	Owned or rented.	Owned free or mortgaged.	Farm or house.	Number of farm schedule.	
14	15	16	17	18	19	20	21	22	23	24	25	26	27	28	
England	England				R.R. Contractor	0		yes	yes	yes	O	F	H		1
Denmark	Denmark	1874	26					yes	yes						2
Utah	Denmark				At School		9	yes	yes	yes					3
Utah	Denmark				At School		9	yes	yes	yes					4
Utah	Denmark				At School		9	yes	yes	yes					5
Utah	Denmark														6
Utah	Denmark														7
Holland	Holland	1895	5	Al	Farmer	0		yes	yes	yes	R		H		8
Holland	Holland	1897	3					yes	yes	yes					9
Holland	Holland	1897	3		At School		9	yes	yes	yes					10
Holland	Holland	1897	3		At School		9	yes	yes	yes					11
Holland	Holland	1897	3		At School		9	yes	yes	yes					12
Holland	Holland	1897	8		At School		9	yes	yes	yes					13
Holland	Holland														14
England	England	1889	18	Na	Rock Mason	0		yes	yes	yes	R		H		15
England	England	1874	26					yes	yes	yes					16
England	England				At School		9	yes	yes	yes					17
England	England														18
England	England														19
England	England														20
Ireland	Ireland	1870	30	Na	Miner	0		yes	yes	yes	O	F	H		21
England	England							yes	yes	yes					22
Ireland	Utah				Laundress	0		yes	yes	yes					23
Ireland	Utah				Laundress	0		yes	yes	yes					24
Ireland	Utah				Laundress	0		yes	yes	yes					25
Ireland	Utah				Servant	0		yes	yes	yes					26
Ireland	Utah				At School		9	yes	yes	yes					27
Ireland	Utah				At School		9	yes	yes	yes					28
Ireland	Utah				At School		9	yes	yes	yes					29
Ireland	Utah				At School		9	yes	yes	yes					30
Ireland	Utah				At School		9	yes	yes	yes					31
Connecticut	Connecticut				Teamster	0		yes	yes	yes	R		H		32
Vermont	Scotland							yes	yes	yes					33
Utah	Utah				At School		9	yes	yes	yes					34
Utah	Utah				At School		9	yes	yes	yes					35
Utah	Utah														36
Utah	Utah														37
Utah	Utah														38
Utah	Utah														39
Holland	Holland	1879	1	Al	Clerk in Dry Store	0		yes	yes	yes	R		H		40
Holland	Holland	1888	2												41
England	England	1889	18	Na	Stone Mason	0		yes	yes	yes	O	F	H		42
England	England	1880	20					yes	yes	yes					43
England	England				At School		9	yes	yes	yes					44
England	England				At School		9	yes	yes	yes					45
England	England				At School		9	yes	yes	yes					46
England	England														47
England	England														48
England	England	1886	14	Al	Janitor	0		yes	yes	yes	R		H		49
Wales	Wales	1886	14					yes	yes	yes					50

The census taker listed her occupation as "keeps house" and her birthplace as Illinois. Her parents' birthplace was recorded as Canada. The second child in the family was an 18-year-old son named Wilson who gave his profession as "butcher." His birthplace was Utah, and his father's birthplace was Connecticut.

I had found an 18-year-old Utah native named Wilson in a household with a father born in Connecticut, but the birthplace of the mother did not match information in the 1900 census. Since enumerators often made mistakes, I thought that this could be the Wilson Wright I was looking for.

To verify the birthplace of Aurelia Wright and prove that she was my great-grandfather's mother, I decided to look for her family in the 1870 census. However, before putting away the microfilms of the 1880 census, I copied two entries that had caught my eye. On page 20 of the enumeration district in which Aurelia and her family lived, I found a person who could have been her father-in-law: Josiah Wright, age 65, a farmer. Both he and his wife, Susan, were born in Connecticut. On page 23 of this district I found a Gilbert Wright age 41 with his wife, Annie, and their six children. Gilbert was born in Connecticut and Annie in England. Could Gilbert be a brother to Wilson's father? Maybe these people will also show up in the 1870 census of Utah.

Before finding the 1870 census film for Weber County, I checked to see if our library had any published indexes to this census. What luck! In the library catalog under *Utah—Census—Indexes* I found Ronald Vern Jackson's *Utah 1870,* containing an index to the 1870 census of Utah. In the index I found a reference to a Wilson Wright on page 492 of the Weber County returns for the 1870 census of Utah. Next, I found the microfilm copy of the census schedules and there, among entries for Ogden City, I found Wilson Wright, age 37, a farmer, born in Connecticut. His wife is listed as Orillia (note spelling change from 1880 census), age 28, from Illinois. Six children are recorded, including a 7-year-old son named Wilson born in Utah. Now I know the names of my second great-grandfather and grandmother.

Why was father Wilson not in the 1880 census? He could have been away at the time, he and his wife may have been separated or divorced,

or he might have died between 1870 and 1880. From local church records, obituaries, and death records I learned that he died in 1876 and that his middle name was Andrew. Since he and his son have the same first name, knowing their middle names is important for future research. The fact that he was alive in the 1870 census and not enumerated in 1880 helped me narrow my search in local records for his death.

On page 476 of the 1870 Weber County census returns I also found a Josiah Wright, age 60, born in Connecticut and his wife, Susan, age 60, also from Connecticut. In the 1880 census I had found a Josiah, age 65, and his wife, Susan, age 60, both from Connecticut. Again, the ages do not seem correct, but Josiah is a candidate for being the father of Wilson Andrew Wright. Perhaps looking at some earlier census returns will help determine Josiah's relationship to Wilson Andrew.

The 1850 census was the first to list all household members, and it may be a good place to look. I need to find a Josiah with a wife named Susan, both about 30 or 35 years old, and a son named Wilson, who is about 17. The question is, where was Josiah in 1850? He does not show up in the 1850 census for Utah. Was he in Connecticut?

As for many states, there is an index published for the 1850 United States census of Connecticut: *Connecticut 1850 Census Index* edited by Ronald Vern Jackson and G. Ronald Teeples. Your local public or college library or historical society will probably have census indexes for many of the censuses for your state. The same will be true of such agencies in the state where your ancestors lived.

In the index I found a Josiah Wright, a Josiah Wright Jr., and a Benjamin Wright all on the same page of the census schedules for Middlesex County, Connecticut. All three were in the town of Westbrook. There were several other Wright families in Westbrook, as well as some in neighboring Hartford County. The Wrights from Westbrook did not match the information I had gotten from later censuses: Josiah Wright Jr. was 26 years old and married to Phoebe. Josiah Wright was 65 years old and married to Fanny. If the Josiah I was looking for was not in Connecticut or Utah in 1850, where was he?

Before looking further, I need to see what I can find out about the early settlers of Utah. Perhaps there was some kind of emigration pattern they followed that would let me know where Wilson A. Wright's father was in 1850.

If you cannot find a previous residence for an ancestor or locate that person in censuses, turn to local histories. Often, local histories explain population growth by discussing where groups of new residents came from. This is especially true of those immigrating to the United States and of pioneers founding new communities. For example, most of the early settlers in Utah were Mormons—members of the Church of Jesus Christ of Latter-day Saints. They left the center they had established in Nauvoo, Illinois, during the winter of 1846–1847. Their destination was to be the Great Salt Lake Valley. With a little searching I came across a survey of the history of the Latter-day Saints by William Edwin Berrett, *The Restored Church: A Brief History of the Growth and Doctrines of the Church of Jesus Christ of Latter-day Saints.*

Since Wilson and his family could have been among the Mormon immigrants, I was anxious to learn about their activities. The first group of these pioneers arrived in the Great Salt Lake Valley in July 1847. Others followed throughout the summer and fall. Since my family was not there by the 1850 census, they must have stopped somewhere along the way. On page 278 of Berrett's book, I found an important clue: "In 1850 there were 7,828 Saints on the Indian lands of Iowa." Maybe I could find Wilson A. and his father Josiah in the 1850 census for Iowa.

Using census surname indexes first for Iowa in 1850 and then Connecticut for 1840 and earlier, I was able to identify Wilson Andrew Wright's father and mother (Josiah and Susan), brothers, and sisters. I learned that the family had indeed originated in Connecticut.

United States censuses before 1850 list only the head of household by name; therefore, some researchers do not use these earlier records because they think the identities of ancestors cannot be confirmed unless all

the names of family members are known. However, it *is* possible to identify persons in the pre-1850 censuses that could be your forebears. I will continue to use the example of Wilson Andrew Wright's ancestors from Connecticut to illustrate this point.

From the 1850 Iowa census I knew the names and ages of Josiah Wright's wife and children. This information helped me find him in the 1840 Connecticut census. Using published indexes, I first isolated all Josiah Wrights in Connecticut in 1840. Next, I checked the census schedules for Josiah Wrights with a wife and children who would match the ages I found in the Iowa 1850 census—minus ten years. The 1840 census had the following age categories for each sex—males and females were enumerated separately: "under 5," "5 and under 10," "10 and under 15," "15 and under 20," "20 and under 30," "30 and under 40," "40 and under 50," "50 and under 60," and so on to "100 and older." In an area in which both the surname Wright and the given names in Josiah's family were common (Westbrook), I found a Josiah A. Wright with the correct number of children in each age category and an adult female in the appropriate age category—if Susan's age was correct on the 1850 Iowa census.

Josiah first appears in the 1830 census, and his father and other ancestors can be traced in every federal census for Connecticut back to the first, taken in 1790. I will use local vital records, church records, cemetery records, obituaries, probate records, and other resources in Connecticut to verify names, birth dates, birthplaces, and ancestors for the persons I have discovered in my census survey. For example, I can search through the birth records for Westbrook, Connecticut, to see if I can find the births of Wilson and his brothers and sisters. There or in a nearby town I may also find birth records for Wilson's father and mother. I will want to find the marriage record for Josiah and Susan to learn her maiden name and verify her age. With that data I can search through local birth records to find her birth and the names of her parents.

Research in United States censuses enabled me to follow my ancestors from their home in Connecticut to Iowa and finally to Utah. Censuses are important records in helping us draw a broad picture of families and their movements. They are especially helpful in learning where ancestors lived. For families that moved often, tracking the state of birth of children in post-1850 censuses may lead to local records such as births, marriages, cemetery records, land records, employment, and school records among many others. Remember to start with the most-modern census and move backward in time. The 1920 census available at regional National Archives branches and public libraries is indexed for every state and territory so that you will need only to know which state your kin lived in to find them (first in the index and then on the census page that describes them).

Military Records

Is there anyone in your family who served in the military? Perhaps a brother, sister, son or daughter, parent, or spouse who served in Vietnam, Korea, or World War II? Our grandfathers and great-grandfathers may have served in World War I. Most families can name a living family member who served in the military. That service may have been in a state National Guard unit, a federal reserve unit, or in the regular Army, Air Force, Coast Guard, Marines, or Navy.

Military Records and Family History

The military service of family members and ancestors has resulted in the creation of records that are important links between the present and the past. Beginning with the Civil War, draft records have identified persons eligible to serve in the military. When a person enters the service, induction or enlistment records are created. Thereafter, each person's career in the military is recorded in individual service records. Veterans have always been eligible for a number of benefits designed to repay them for their service. We are familiar with the education benefit available to former service men and women today. In the past they were rewarded with land grants and pensions. Again, records detail the benefits your ancestors received, and in the process these records tell us a great deal about ancestors' lives. On the following pages we will learn what such records contain, how they can be used to help you better understand your family's past, and where you can find these records. It is not just the soldiers, sailors, marines, and airforce we learn about in records created by the military: wives—or widows—and soldiers' children are also described.

Why would you want to find ancestors' military records? It may verify some things you have already found elsewhere: age, birthplace, and dependents. What you cannot find elsewhere is the information pertaining to their military service: unit; rank; place of enlistment/discharge; physical description; occupation; military assignment; and, if prisoners of war, where they were imprisoned. If your veteran ancestors or dependents had a claim on bounty land, you will learn where that land was and be able to track what happened to it. You may not be able to find all of these facts for each ancestor, but you will never know until you search.

Although post-World War I military records may contain information about a person's birthplace and age, earlier records often give only the place of enlistment and information about the unit in which the person served. Many of the service and pension records for volunteers are indexed; however, you must have an idea of when and where the ancestors served if you want to find their records.

Draft Registration Documents

The draft was first used during the Civil War. It was enacted through the Conscription Act of March 3, 1863. These draft records are available at the National Archives in Washington, D.C. They have not been microfilmed and are arranged by the United States congressional districts of the time. Knowing the state and county in which your ancestor lived in 1863, you can look up the congressional district in the *Congressional Directory for the Second Session of the Thirty-Eighth Congress of the United States of America* published by the U. S. House of Representatives. Your librarian may need to borrow it from another library. Once you know the congressional district, request that the staff at the National Archives search for the registration file for your ancestor.

Two records were created by the 1863 conscription process: consolidated lists and descriptive rolls. Consolidated lists provide the ancestor's birth date, state or country of birth, place of residence, occupation, and marital status as of July 1, 1863. The descriptive lists add a physical description and place of birth to the information in the consolidated lists. A book on the subject of conscription in the North provides further details on this source: James W. Geary's *We Need Men: The Union Draft in the Civil War.* The author's appendix on how to use Record Group 110 (records of the Provost Marshal General's Bureau), which contains the consolidated lists and descriptive rolls compiled by bureau officials, is especially helpful.

For men born between 1872 and 1900, World War I draft registration cards are available and have been microfilmed by the National Archives (microfilm publication M1509). The entire collection of some twenty-four million cards (one card for each person registered) is organized into state sections that are further subdivided into separate sections for each county or large city in the state and filed in alphabetical order by the surname of the enrolled person. Cards provide a registrant's name, age, birth date, address, nearest relative, occupation, employer, and, in most cases, birthplace. On some cards a father's birthplace is also listed. The Family History Library has acquired this huge collection of microfilm. Visit a nearby LDS Family History Center and ask one of the volunteer librarians to help you consult the *Family History Library Catalog.* You will find that the catalog is available in two formats, microfiche and compact disc; you may use either one to find the microfilm you need. Check the microfiche version of the Family History Library catalog's author/title section for the author entry "United States—Selective Service System" or under the title "World War I Selective Service System Draft Registration Cards 1917–1918." On the compact disc version of the Family History Library catalog select the menu option: "locality search." Check under the locality heading *United States* and the topic *Military Records—World War, 1914–1918.* There you will find an entry with the same author and title as shown in the microfiche. Both versions of the catalog will provide the latest information on this valuable collection, including the microfilm numbers for the rolls containing your ancestors.

If you do not live near an LDS Family History Center, contact the nearest regional National Archives office to inquire about the availability of these microfilms in your area. (See Appendix A for the address.) You can also access your ancestor's World War I draft card from the National Archives Southeast Regional Office.

For information about the men registered for the draft during World War II and later, contact the Records Division of the Selective Service System (see Appendix A). In addition, the staff at the nearest regional National Archives or your state archives or historical society may have information about the post-World War I draft records from your state.

Military Service Records

Personnel files for the military are called *service records.* They allow you to learn about where your ancestor served, what their assignments were, who their officers and fellow service men/women were, and even how much they earned. Where ages are given, you can compare your ancestors' ages and income to those of their fellow soldiers and their officers.

In military record keeping, there is a distinction between regular and volunteer/conscripted soldiers. Regular soldiers enlisted for a longer period—say, five years—and made the military a career, a way of earning a living; their time is not usually affected by the length of a war. Volunteers or persons who are drafted become part of a military unit to serve in a specific war or campaign. Their service usually ends when the conflict is over or their period of enlistment is up. These are the so-called citizen soldiers who leave family and employment to defend their country.

For the regular Army, Navy, and Marines there are no centralized records until the first part of this century. You must consult several record groups to uncover your ancestor's military history, pension rolls, service records, correspondence registers, muster rolls, and the like. Records for volunteers, on the other hand, can be found in several series of compiled service records now housed at the National Archives, many of which are available on microfilm at local archives and libraries. The military service records of volunteers have been abstracted onto cards and placed in "jackets" at the National Archives, each one bearing the soldier's name, rank, and military unit. Name indexes are arranged by period: Revolutionary, post-Revolutionary, 1812, etc. Check first the microfilmed state index for information about when ancestors served and in which units. Consult the National Archives *Military Service Records: A Select Catalog of National Archive Microfilm Publications* for the microfilms of indexes and service records that relate to your volunteer soldier ancestor. A section in this catalog also describes filmed records and indexes for those in the regular armed forces.

For descendants of Civil War soldiers and sailors, a massive indexing project to create an index to all of the soldiers who served in the Civil War has begun. It is sponsored by the National Park Service, the Federation of Genealogical Societies, and the Genealogical Society of Utah. You can track its progress in the Federation of Genealogical Societies *Forum,* published quarterly. For more information write to the Federation of Genealogical Societies in Salt Lake City.

Military Benefit Records

The most-valuable military records for vital data are the pension applications. These often give information about the birth of the person as well as facts about family beneficiaries. Pension records will also tell you where and when an ancestor served because the applicant or heirs had to prove service before a pension would be issued. Knowing how much a person received in pension payments may help you determine what a soldier relative's standard of living was while on pension.

From the Revolution until 1855, soldiers could also receive land in return for their service. Bounty land warrants were issued to veterans entitling them or their heirs or agents to take possession of a specified amount of federal land. The records generated in support of these claims—applications and warrants—are indexed and available for research on microfilm. They include documentation of a person's military service and may name family members and their relationship to the veteran. An age and residence for the veteran or an heir may be given. For those who would like to learn more about the practice of providing land to veterans, see James W. Oberly's *Sixty Million Acres: American Veterans and the Public Lands before the Civil War.*

Those with Revolutionary War interests will want to know of the National Genealogical Society's *Index of Revolutionary War Pension Applications in the National Archives.* The introductions to the index and to the microfilmed pension and bounty land warrant files provide a good summary of how these records came to be and what they contain. The index provides the name of the applicant (the soldier, his widow, or a child) and the number of the pension file or bounty land warrant file. Other family members may be mentioned in the application or in the papers filed to prove that the applicant was eligible to apply for the benefits. The typical file contains about thirty pages of records, including evidence of identity or service and papers showing any action regarding the claim for benefits. File numbers in the index with an *S* prefix were for surviving veterans, and those with a *W* prefix were for applications from veterans' widows. Those index numbers with the symbol *BLWT* refer to bounty land applications.

If you find the name of an ancestor in the *Index,* you can go to your nearest regional National Archive, LDS Family History Center, or another library and use one of the 2,670 rolls of microfilm for the 80,000 pension and bounty land warrant files in National Archives microfilm publication M804. From the National Archives catalog, *Military Service Records in the National Archives of the United States* or the LDS Family History Library catalog you can identify which of the rolls has your ancestor's file on it. Films can be rented from the National Archives Microfilm Rental Program, purchased from the Fulfillment Center of the National Archives, or viewed in person at a nearby research center (see Appendix A for addresses).

A book that will help you find Revolutionary War veterans who applied for bounty land is Clifford Neal Smith's *Federal Land Series: A Calendar of Archival Materials on the Land Patents Issued by the United States Government, with Subject, Tract, and Name Indexes.*

Locating Military Records

In chapter 4 you learned that the records of state and local militia and National Guard units are normally found at the state archives or historical society. It is the National Archives and Records Administration's responsibility to care for the records created by units of the United States Army, Air Force, Coast Guard, Marines, and Navy. This includes records for local units placed under federal command, which accounted for a large number of soldiers and sailors in the era prior to World War I: career military persons, volunteers, and inductees.

Requests for information about ancestors from military records created prior to World War I, including pension and bounty land claims, should be sent to the General Reference Branch (NNRG) of the National Archives and Records Administration (see Appendix A for address). Your local library, historical society, or regional national archives may have copies of NATF Form 80, which you must use to request information from veterans' records. For information about records documenting military service from World War I to the present, you may write to the National Personnel Records Center (Military Records) (see Appendix A). The National Personnel Records Center requires Standard Form 180, "Request Pertaining to Military Records," for nonfamily history information and NARA Form 13043 for genealogical requests.

Be aware that in 1973 a fire at the National Personnel Center destroyed some of the records for persons who were on active duty prior to 1960. The surviving records are now in a computer database accessible by a person's military service number—not the social security number. To find ancestors' service numbers, check to see if there is a copy of their discharge papers or any other pages from their time of service. At the state archives or state historical society in the state where they lived, see if there is a veterans' index with information about their military service. If not, contact the local Department of Veterans Affairs to determine if it has records that might reveal ancestors' service numbers.

Guides to Military Records

Your local public or college library will have books about military records. Following are some key titles that you can use to learn about military records, where to find them, and how to use them in your research. The subject headings you find in your local library catalog for these books should be used to perform subject searches in your library's catalog to discover other books about these topics.

James Neagles's *U.S. Military Records: A Guide to Federal and State Sources* covers the period from the Revolution to the present. It serves as a guide to sources and to research centers with materials of value to those seeking military ancestors. The overview of military records and their history provided in *U.S. Military Records* makes it a good starting point in your search for information about your military ancestors.

NARA in Washington, D.C., has published several important reference books that will help you. *Guide to Genealogical Research in the National Archives,* section B, chapters 4 through 9, describes the military records preserved by the National Archives that apply to questions genealogists often ask. Included are several good bibliographies of important publications, including indexes, that provide help for the researcher with a soldier ancestor. A more-detailed description is found in *Guide to the National Archives of the United States,* with chapters on the records of the Departments of the Army, Navy, Air Force, and, under the Department of Transportation, the records of the Coast Guard. Your local library will likely have a copy of these books. It may also have the pamphlet *Military Service Records in the National Archives of the United States* that describes many of the U.S. military records available on microfilm. If not, you can buy copies of all three publications from the National Archives Fulfillment Center or the National Archives Trust Fund (see Appendix A).

These books will provide you with background about the creation of military records and also provide the National Archives microfilm numbers. The bibliographies in *Guide to Genealogical Research in the National Archives* list books that will help you reconstruct the lives of ancestors who served in the military from the Revolutionary War to the present.

Equal in value to the foregoing titles is *Register of Federal United States Military Records: A Guide to Manuscript Sources Available at the Genealogical Library in Salt Lake City and the National Archives in Washington, D.C.,* by Marilyn Deputy and others. These volumes were prepared by the reference staff of the LDS Family History Library and published by the library for its own patrons and the patrons of LDS Family History Centers. Heritage Book's publication of these volumes made this important information available to researchers and librarians in general. A fourth volume was published by the library in 1987 and revised in 1989 under the same title as the original three volumes. This last volume is available only through the Family History Library. The volumes of this series cover the major military records available to researchers dating from the Revolution to World War II and include a brief description of the records and a list of the numbers of the Family History Library microfilms containing the records. The primary value of this set is to indicate which records you can order for use at a local LDS Family History Center or regional National Archives.

Your local library may also have a copy of *The Archives: A Guide to the National Archives Field Branches* by Szucs and Luebking. This book provides the addresses of the regional archives and descriptions of military records available there. Along with these descriptions the authors indicate which of the National Archives microfilms of military records are available at each regional archives.

A brief introduction to the use of military records is also found in the National Archives pamphlet *Using Records in the National Archives for Genealogical Research.* Another publication that you will want to have when searching for military ancestors is the Family History Library's *Research Outline: U.S. Military Records,* published by the Church of Jesus Christ of Latter-day Saints.

Tracking down Revolutionary War ancestors will be aided by James C. and Lila L. Neagles's *Locating Your Revolutionary War Ancestor: A Guide to the Military Records.* For ancestors serving in the military before 1900 refer to *A Bibliography of Military Name Lists from Pre-1675 to 1900* by Lois Horowitz. If you are interested in Civil War soldiers or history, consult Charles Dornbusch's *Military Bibliography of the Civil War* and Kenneth Nelson's *Genealogical Journal* article "Civil War Sources for Genealogical Research."

Land Records

The seventeenth- and eighteenth-century colonists of North America came to settle on land granted them by the monarchs of England, France, and Spain or by their deputies, the colonial governors. Title to a specific plot of land was conveyed in a patent, similar to the deeds we use today. The patent specified where the land was, the size of the parcel being purchased, the amount of payment, and the new owner and certified that the applicant would receive title to the land. These patents were issued by local land offices, town clerks, and colonial governors' offices.

To make it easier to identify each parcel of land that had been surveyed prior to the granting of a patent, local government offices developed plat books containing maps that showed where each piece of land was located and who owned it. Today your county clerk has plats of your community. Often the names of the lot owners are written inside the outlines of the parcels of land or lots. Since elevations, landmarks, streams, streets, and other features are shown, these plat books can help you discover what the area was like when your family lived there.

Whether land was obtained from the state or national government or from a private citizen, records were created to track ownership. From chapter 4 you learned that land transfers between private citizens were recorded at local county or town clerk's offices. These records are found in state archives or historical societies as well as local clerk's offices. Land sold by state governments to private citizens was documented in state land records, which are also available at state archives and historical societies. The focus here will be upon records that documented the transfer of land from the federal government to private citizens.

Some ancestors bought land from the United States government as an investment, selling it without ever living on it or even seeing it. Perhaps your ancestor bought the land from a land investor or speculator. The deeds recording the sale of former federal land to your relative are found in local county land records under the name of your ancestor as the buyer or the name of the seller. The federal government also gave large blocks of land to state governments that, in turn, were sold to generate revenue on the local level. These records are found today in state archives or historical societies.

The records spawned by federal land sales or land grants help you learn about the role your ancestors played in settling this country. The records created by this process help you catch a glimpse of your ancestors' world in terms of their physical environment. Knowing how much land was worth at the time it was sold also helps you understand the economic climate of your family's hometown, township, or county.

The Creation of the Public Domain

The original thirteen states plus Hawaii, Kentucky, Maine, Tennessee, Texas, Vermont, and West Virginia have controlled the lands within their boundaries since statehood. All other states were created from the public domain—land administered by the national government. Among the public land states were those formed from land purchased or taken after the Revolution from other nations—France, England, Spain, Russia, and Mexico. The following list shows states that were created from public domain land.

Public Domain States

Alabama	Illinois	Missouri	Oregon
Alaska	Indiana	Montana	South Dakota
Arizona	Iowa	Nebraska	Utah
Arkansas	Kansas	Nevada	Washington
California	Louisiana	New Mexico	Wisconsin
Colorado	Michigan	North Dakota	Wyoming
Florida	Minnesota	Ohio	
Idaho	Mississippi	Oklahoma	

The original settlers in areas that belonged to other nations had claims to land granted them by those governments before the land became part of the United States. As the United States expanded its boundaries, these claims were investigated by land commissions appointed by Congress. Applicants were required to produce documents and witnesses proving their right to the land in question. If the proof was convincing, the claim would be approved. The claims presented from 1789 to 1837 are covered in *American State Papers: Public Lands* from the United States Congress, for which a consolidated index has been prepared under the title *Grassroots of America* by Phillip W. McMullin. Claims from 1789 to 1891 were compiled alphabetically by the name of the claimer and published in the *Congressional Serial Set* (First to Fifty-first Congresses) from the U.S. House of Representatives. Talk to the government documents librarian at your local college or university to learn if this series is available there. These government publications are arranged by session of Congress. You can learn more about private land claims in *Guide to Genealogical Research in the National Archives*, chapters 15 and 16.

Types of Land Records

Earlier in this chapter you learned that between 1776 and 1855 Congress passed numerous acts giving land to military veterans in return for their service. The government also gave other citizens opportunities to get some of the public domain land. Land sales began early in our nation's history and were based on government surveys conducted as early as 1785. If your ancestor was the original owner of public domain land, he or she may appear in several types of records, as explained in the following paragraphs.

Plat maps were made from original surveys of the public domain. They were used at the local land offices to pinpoint land parcels prospective owners wished to acquire. Along with these maps, local land offices often had access to surveyors' field notes, which provided written descriptions of the area and its terrain. The plat maps show the exact location of every section of land within a township. Each township is six miles square and divided into 36 sections of 640 acres each.

Townships are identified by a number that describes their position relative to a surveyor's line running east and west (appearing as a horizontal line on a map) through the area called a *base line* and a second line running north and south (vertical line) called a *meridian*. Figure 18 shows the base lines and meridians used to survey all public domain land. At specified distances on either side of the meridian and the base line, surveyors project parallel lines, each with a consecutive number east or west of the meridian and north or south of the base line. The area of land between the meridian and the first parallel line to the west (left on a map) has a range number of 1 west. The land between the base line and the first parallel line to the south (below on a map) has a township number of 1 south. Notice at the top of the map in figure 19 that the township is described as "No. 72 N. (north), Range No. 35 W. (west), 5th Mer. (meridian)." This particular township lies 72 lines north of the base line and 35 lines west of the fifth principal meridian.

If you look closely at figure 19 you will see that each 640-acre section is assigned a consecutive number from 1 through 36. The numbering begins in the upper right-hand corner and ends with section 36 in the lower right-hand corner. Sections could be divided in many ways if someone did not want to buy the whole 640 acres. Many plat maps show the names of those who acquired land written on the section where their property was located.

Tract books are probably the first record of a person's application for public domain land. Staff at local land offices would record the name of the applicant, the legal description of the land, and the amount of money paid (shown in figure 20). The payment could have been an installment or full payment—unless the land was being given to the applicant in exchange for residence upon or improvements to the land. A column for the receipt number or the certificate number and another for the price per acre of the land were provided. When you multiply the number of acres purchased by the price per acre, you can quickly determine whether your ancestor paid for the land in several payments or one. Receipts are issued for payments made.

When all of the requirements were met for receiving the land, a final certificate/certificate of purchase was issued by the local land office that was sent to the General Land Office (today the Bureau of Land Management) so that a patent for the land could be given to the applicant. A final certificate normally identified the new landowner by name and residence and described the land the owner was receiving. It also listed the payment history and where the government's copy of the patent was filed. The number of the final certificate was also recorded in the local tract book. A second set of tract books was kept by the General Land Office in Washington, D.C.

Land entry files are the files containing applications from persons who wanted to own public domain land. Each applicant's file was first set up at the local land office when the person filed a request (entry) for land. The General Land Office would also have a land entry file for the applicant because that office would keep track of any documents or certificates sent from the local land office as proof the applicant had qualified for a land patent.

There were several programs under which a person could obtain title to public domain land. Separate land entry files exist at the National Archives for each program.

During most of this nation's history, public domain land was sold to citizens for full payment in cash. The land entry files for these transactions are referred to at the National Archives as *cash entry files*. From 1800 to 1820, public land could be bought using installment payments. A buyer made a down payment and then paid for the land in several subsequent partial payments. The files for these sales are referred to as *credit entry files*. Sometimes applicants preempted the land they wanted to buy. A *preemption claim* is one in which the prospective buyer has already occupied or begun to use the land before purchasing it. Land entry files for applicants preempting land are filed with the cash entry files at the National Archives.

In 1842 in Florida and in 1851 in the Oregon Territory, the government decided to give away land in the hope that it would encourage settlement in these areas. The objective was to fortify the government's claims in these areas by moving settlers onto the lands. Property acquired under these circumstances is known as *donation land*. The donation land entry files have their own separate files at the National Archives.

The Homestead Act of 1862 encouraged persons to obtain land by living on it and making improvements. This program provided an unheard-of opportunity for scores of immigrants looking for a place to settle. The land entry files for homestead applications are more likely than cash land entry files to contain naturalization

FIGURE 18 *Public Domain Land Principal Meridians and Base Lines*

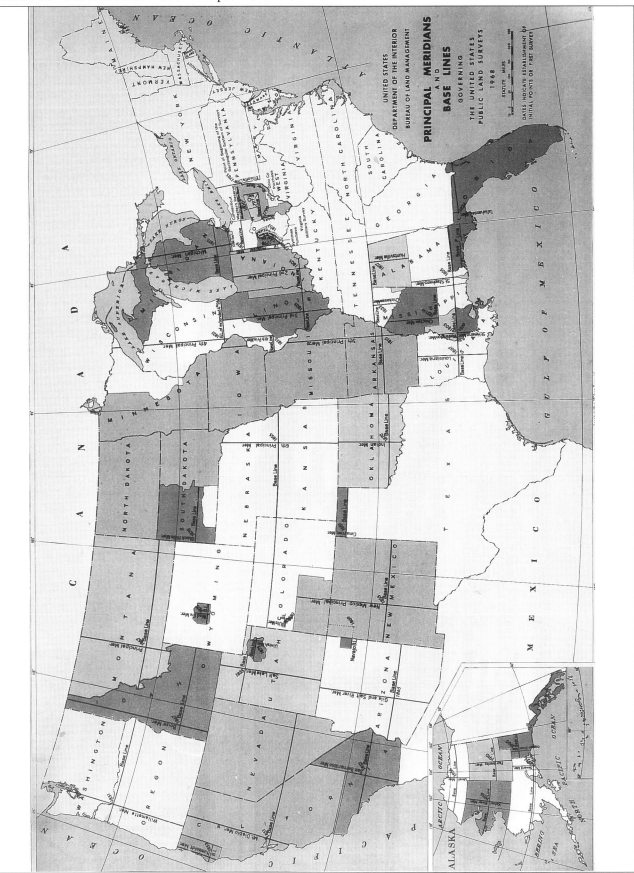

Source: United States Bureau of Land Management, Washington, D.C., 1968

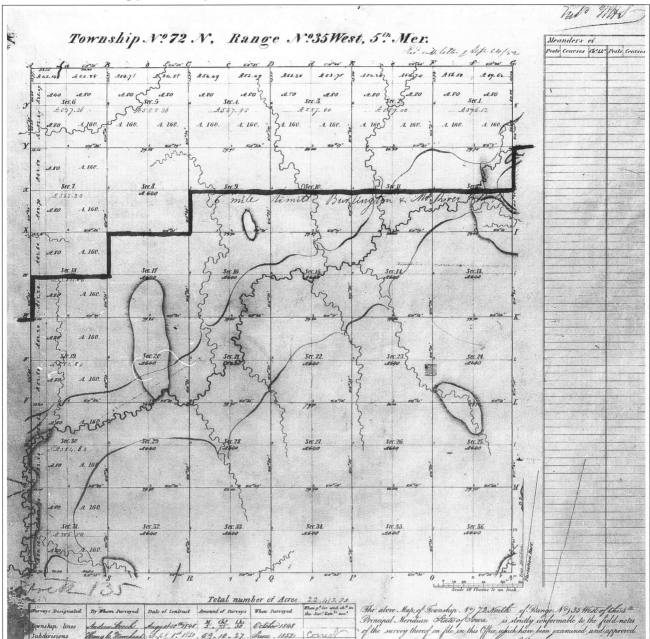

Source: National Archives Microfilm Publication T1234, *Township Plats of Selected States* (Family History Library Film 1578356)

FIGURE 20 *Land Office Tract Book for Kanesville, Iowa, 1853–1854*

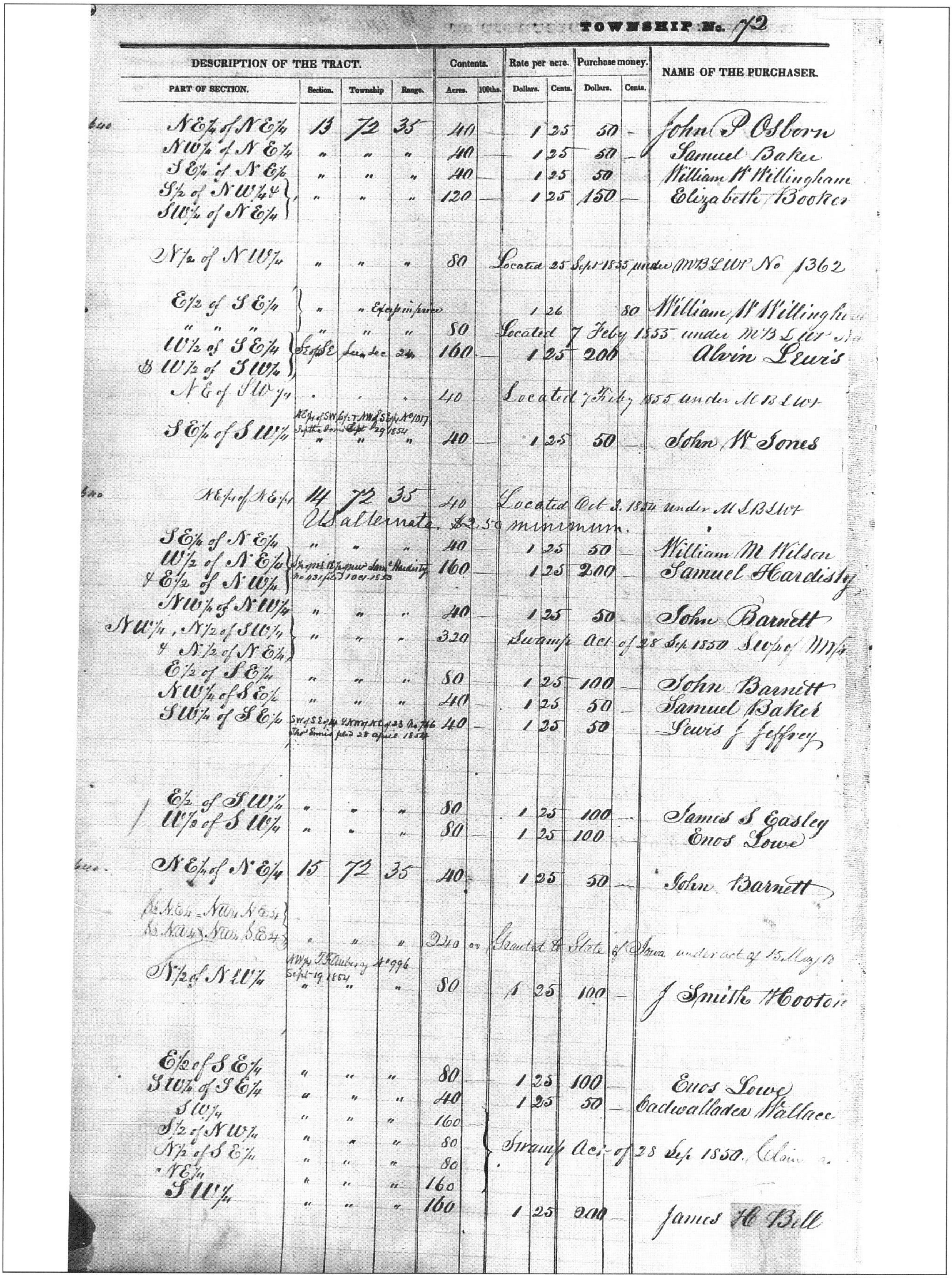

DESCRIPTION OF THE TRACT.				Contents		Rate per acre		Purchase money		NAME OF THE PURCHASER.
PART OF SECTION.	Section.	Township	Range.	Acres.	100ths.	Dollars.	Cents.	Dollars.	Cents.	
N E¼ of N E¼	13	72	35	40		1	25	50	—	John P. Osborn
N W¼ of N E¼	"	"	"	40		1	25	50		Samuel Baker
S E¼ of N E¼	"	"	"	40		1	25	50		William W. Willingham
S½ of N W¼ &	"	"	"	120		1	25	150	—	Elizabeth Booker
S W¼ of N E¼										
N½ of N W¼	"	"	"	80		Located 25 Sept 1855 under M B L W No 1362					
E½ of S E¼	"	" Except in price				1	26		80	William W. Willingham
W½ of S E¼	S E of S E	Sec Dec 24.		80		Located 7 Feby 1855 under M B L W No				
S W¼ of S W¼				160	—	1	25	200	—	Alvin Lewis
N E of S W¼				40		Located 7 Feby 1855 under M B L W				
S E¼ of S W¼	N E¼ of S W 6¼ T A W (S E¼ No 1017) Sept 29 1854			40		1	25	50	—	John W. Jones
N E¼ of N E¼	14	72	35	40		Located Oct 3 1854 under M S B L W				
	U S alternate $2.50 minimum.									
S E¼ of N E¼	"	"	"	40		1	25	50	—	William M. Wilson
W½ of N E¼				160		1	25	200	—	Samuel Hardisty
& E½ of N W¼										
N W¼ of N W¼	"	"	"	40		1	25	50	—	John Barnett
N W¼, N½ of S W¼	"	"	"	320		Swamp Act of 28 Sep 1850 S W¼ of N W¼				
& N½ of N E¼										
E½ of S E¼	"	"	"	80		1	25	100	—	John Barnett
N W¼ of S E¼	"	"	"	40		1	25	50	—	Samuel Baker
S W¼ of S E¼	S W¼ S E¼ & N W¼ No 746 That Smith Sept 28 April 1854			40	—	1	25	50	—	Lewis J. Jeffrey
E½ of S W¼	"	"	"	80		1	25	100	—	James S. Easley
W½ of S W¼	"	"	"	80		1	25	100	—	Enos Lowe
N E¼ of N E¼	15	72	35	40		1	25	50	—	John Barnett
S N E¼ N W¼ N E¼, S N E¼ N W¼ S E¼	"	"	"	240 or		Granted to State of Iowa under act of 15 May 18				
N½ of N W¼	A W¼ T Kaulway No 996 Sept 19 1854			80		1	25	100	—	J. Smith Hooton
E½ of S E¼	"	"	"	80		1	25	100	—	Enos Lowe
S W¼ of S E¼	"	"	"	40		1	25	50	—	Cadwallader Wallace
S W¼	"	"	"	160						
S½ of N W¼	"	"	"	80		Swamp Act of 28 Sep 1850, Alvin				
N½ of S E¼	"	"	"	80						
N E¼	"	"	"	160						
S W¼	"	"	"	160		1	25	200	—	James H. Bell

Source: United States Bureau of Land Management, *Tract Books* (Family History Library Microfilm 1445563)

DATE OF SALE.	Number of receipt and certificate of purchase.	TO WHOM PATENTED.	DATE OF PATENT.	Where recorded.	
				Volume.	Page.
Sept 13 1853	880				
Oct 1 1853	921				
Feby 7 1855	5032				
Aprul 28 1854	1926				
Act of 3 March 1855					
Feby 7 1855	5041				
3636 Act 28 Sept 1850					
June 28 1855	7403				
No 8081 act March 22 1852					
Oct 3 1854	3542				
No 96942 act Sept 28 1850					
April 28 1854	1927				
Oct 3 1854	3537	Indemnity granted March 9/65 Reft No 15727.			
Oct 3 1854	3540	Indemnity granted March 9/65 Reft No 15727.			
Approved 354 February 1857					
Nov 6 1854	4323				
Jany 10 1854	1316				
Feby 7 1855	5038				
Oct 18 1854	4047	Paid in MtBL Scrip Indemnity granted March 9/65 Reft 15727			
July 22 1854	3131	Indemnity granted March 9/65 Reft No 15727.			
Oct 3 1854	3539	Indemnity granted March 9/65 Reft 15727.			
Le Burlington & Missouri River Rail Road. Approved 3d March 1862.					
Aug 9 1855	8196	John L Aubrey assignee			
July 22 1854	3132	Indemnity granted March 9/65 Reft 15727.			
May 18 1855	6399				
Except for Mr. Jno. 35 Aca. Survey Co. Reg. Reject Oct 25 1861					
July 5 1854	2918	Indemnity granted March 9/65 Reft 15727.			

certificates and personal information about the claimant and any dependents. Ages, names, places of residence, and descriptions of the property and improvements made upon it are some of the facts family historians can find in homestead entry files. Knowing what an ancestor did to make the required improvements to a homestead can tell a lot about the effort and energy such enterprises required.

If your ancestors were the original owners of public domain land, you will want to find their land entry file, a copy of their land patent, a copy of the plat map showing their land, and a copy of their entry in the tract book for their land. Each of these sources will provide something to help you understand your forebears, the community in which they lived, and the lives they led there.

Two agencies have the responsibility to preserve federal land records or microfilm copies of them: the National Archives and the Bureau of Land Management (check Appendix A for addresses). If you have trouble finding your ancestors' land records, call, write, or visit the nearest regional National Archives or Bureau of Land Management office. In the following pages you will learn which records are within each agency. Some of the land records have been microfilmed and are available at genealogical research centers also listed in Appendix A. Remember, however, that for most records kept at the national level, duplicate sets created by officials at local land offices may be at the nearest regional National Archives; Bureau of Land Management office; library, county, or state archives; or historical society. The following section describes how you can find and use records available at the National Archives and Bureau of Land Management.

Using Land Entry Files and Tract Books

Land entry files for buyers, homesteaders, and recipients of donation or preemption land are available through the National Archives in Washington, D.C. Some of the land entry files at the National Archives are indexed, but many of them are not. First check to see if your ancestor's claim appears in an index of applicants for public domain land. The following chart will help you determine if your ancestors can be found in one of these indexes.

Pre-1908 Land Entry Files Indexed at the National Archives and Records Administration

State	Record Type
Alabama	Cash entry
Alaska	Cash entry
Arizona	Cash entry
Florida	Cash entry
Louisiana	Cash entry
Nevada	Cash entry
Oregon	Donation entry
Utah	Cash entry
Washington	Donation entry

For all public domain land states, the land entry files (cash sales and homestead files) created from 1908 to 1973 are indexed and at the National Archives, arranged numerically by patent number. Two card indexes at the National Archives help researchers find the patent number issued to a forebear and, ultimately, the land entry file of the ancestor. The first index is arranged alphabetically by applicants' names. On the card for each person you will find the name of the land office where the application or claim was registered and the serial number of the person's application. With this information you can use the second index to find the number of the patent issued to each successful applicant. This patent number index is arranged first by land office, then by application serial number. Searching among the cards for the land office where your ancestor applied should produce a card with the application serial number and the number of the patent. You will find the land entry file under this patent number.

To find the unindexed records for your ancestor's land you must have a description of the land that includes the state, name of the land office, range and township numbers, description of the property, receipt or final certificate numbers, date of purchase, and the name of the buyer. You can find all of this information in the tract book in which your ancestor's land transaction is recorded. The original set of General Land Office tract books is divided between the National Archives and the Bureau of Land Management Eastern States Office. The Bureau of Land Management has the tract books for the states east of the Mississippi as well as for Arkansas, Iowa, Louisiana, Minnesota, and Missouri. The same office has an index of applicants recorded in the tract books for parts of Ohio in the period 1800 to 1820. The public domain land lying in other states is covered by tract books at the National Archives in Washington, D.C.

Once you have the description of your ancestor's property, you can find the land entry file, land patent, and even the plat map and surveyors' notes for the area. Following are the steps you take to find the description of their land claim in a tract book.

1. Find your ancestor on a U.S. census near the time the person settled in an area in which he or she purchased federal land. Ask your local librarian to help you find and use the indexes to censuses

that are available for many of the public domain land states. In the index you should find your ancestor's name, the county of residence, and the page number of the census that lists that person.

2. Obtain a copy of the census page listing your ancestor and note the town, county, township, etc., in which your family lived at the time of the census.

3. Most libraries will have the *Rand McNally Commercial Atlas & Marketing Guide.* Use the latest edition to find the locality in which your ancestors were living. Note the range numbers and township numbers shown on the atlas page for this area. (Refer to figure 18 to help orient yourself. You may want to look at figure 19 again to see what a township looks like on a plat map and how it is described in terms of its township and range numbers.) It is unlikely that the atlas will show the exact section where your family lived, but you can determine the approximate range and township numbers that encompass the area. Since the tract books you are seeking are arranged by township and range numbers, the data you glean from the atlas will help you find the microfilm containing the tract book for the general area in which your family lived. (You will see how this works in the example that follows.)

4. Obtain a copy of the microfilmed tract books for the range and township numbers that include the land your ancestors purchased. Microfilms are available at LDS Family History Centers, at several of the genealogical research centers in Appendix A, and for purchase from the Bureau of Land Management. You may also write to the National Archives or the Bureau of Land Management Eastern States Office for copies.

5. Search the tract books looking for your ancestor in the column titled "Name of Purchaser."

6. Once you find the entry in a tract book, note the part of the section the person purchased and the section number, township, range, and the land district. Now you have the legal description of the land your ancestor bought. This information will help you find other federal land records relating to your ancestor's property.

Let's use an example from Iowa to show how these steps lead to the tract book describing your ancestor's property.

✺ ————————————————

Suppose that steps 1 and 2 led you to your ancestor, Samuel Baker, living in western Ad-

ams County, Iowa, according to the 1860 U.S. census. At a local library, find a recent edition of the *Rand McNally Commercial Atlas & Marketing Guide,* turn to the pages that show the state of Iowa and locate Adams County (southwestern Iowa). You notice numbered scales running from east to west across the state about an inch from the northern border of the state, through the middle of the state, and again about an inch from the southern border. You also find a dark line running north and south along the western borders of Jackson and Clinton counties near the eastern border of the state. In fine print this line is identified as the fifth principal meridian. The numbers on the east-west scales start at this line. The first number to the west is 1 west and the first number east of the meridian is 1 east. These are range numbers, east or west of the meridian.

With some more-careful looking, you find other scales on the eastern and western sides of the state running from north to south—with the lower numbers at the south end of the scale. The same scale runs through the middle of the state. These are township numbers. They have their starting point farther south at what surveyors call a "base line" that runs through the middle of Arkansas. The fifth principal meridian and the base line in Arkansas provided the starting points for the Federal Land Office surveys of Iowa. Using the range and township numbers from the atlas page you can see that Adams County lies between ranges 31 and 36 west and townships 70 and 74 north. Your next step is to learn if a local library has the Bureau of Land Management microfilms of the tract books for this area.

A local librarian refers you to a nearby LDS Family History Center where you can rent microfilms from the Family History Library in Salt Lake City, Utah. At the Family History Center you search the LDS Family History Library catalog and find three microfilms for Iowa showing tract books including townships from 68 to 77 north and ranges 28 to 45 west. (Family History Library Microfilms 1445561, 1445562, and 1445563, *Tract Books,* 1265 microfilm reels, Washington, D.C: U.S. Bureau of Land Management, 1957).

A search of the *Tract Books* reveals the name of your ancestor on the pages for township 72 north, range 35 west (figure 20). His name is the second entry on the page and shows that his land is in section 13 of the township. You can see at the top of the page that his forty acres of land are in the Kanesville, Iowa, land office district (today, Council Bluffs, Iowa). The parcel of land he bought is the "NW 1/4 of NE 1/4" in section 13 of the township. He paid $1.25 per acre in cash ($50) on October 1, 1853, and was issued receipt/certificate of purchase number 921. (You also notice that he bought another 40 acres as reflected in receipt 1316.) Knowing the date of the transaction, the description of the tract, and the receipt/certificate number will help you write to the National Archives or Bureau of Land Management for Samuel Baker's land entry file and patent. You could also request copies of the township plat for this area and the surveyor's field notes. In your request you will specify that the land is the northwest 1/4 of northeast 1/4 of section 13 in township 72 north, range 35 west in the Kanesville district of Iowa.

_____ ☯

Using Plat Maps and Field Notes

As each township was surveyed, the local land office and the General Land Office each received copies of plat maps for the area. You may find the local copy at a library, historical society, or archive near the land office. The National Archives has filmed about 20,000 General Land Office plat maps and more than 22,000 such maps from local land offices (*Township Plats of Selected States*, microfilm publication T1234, 69 rolls). The states covered are Alabama, Illinois, Indiana, Iowa, Kansas, Mississippi, Missouri, Wisconsin, portions of Ohio, Oklahoma, Oregon, and Washington. These maps are arranged on the microfilms by state, principal meridian, and then by the range and township number of the township. For example, if you are looking in a local library catalog for the microfilm with your ancestor Samuel Baker's township plat, look for the film containing plat maps for Iowa, the fifth principal meridian, and the township and range numbers that include his property (township 72 north, range 35 west). This is the same information you would use if you were writing to the National Archives or Bureau of Land Management for help with your search.

To find the surveyor's field notes from the area where your forebear obtained land, contact the Bureau of Land Management Eastern States Office for the states under its jurisdiction. For other states, contact the local office of the Bureau of Land Management. Remember

to include the description of your ancestor's property in the request for information.

Using Patent Copies

Because patents were given to successful applicants for public domain land, the Bureau of Land Management has copies of these records only. If the original patent is not among your family's papers, try to find the pre-1908 patent copy stored in volumes arranged by state and then by local land offices. In each land office volume, patents are arranged by township and range numbers. The patents for Alabama, Arkansas, Florida, Illinois, Indiana, Iowa, Louisiana, Michigan, Minnesota, Mississippi, Missouri, Ohio, and Wisconsin are at the Bureau of Land Management Eastern States Office. The Bureau of Land Management is creating a computer index of the land patents at this office; to date, the records for Arkansas, Louisiana, Florida, Michigan, and Minnesota are available. The rest are scheduled for inclusion by the end of 1996. The pre-1908 land patents for the other public domain land states are at the National Archives in Washington, D.C. This and other information is available in a brochure from the Bureau of Land Management Eastern States Office entitled *Land Records, Where They Came from, How We Got Them.*

To request a patent copy, you will need information from the appropriate tract book. In your request to the National Archives or Bureau of Land Management Eastern States Office, include the state where the land was purchased, name of the land office, certificate/receipt number, and the description of the tract purchased.

Patents issued from 1908 to 1973 are easy to find. The record copies of the patents are actually at the Bureau of Land Management, but the indexes that lead to them are at the National Archives. You were introduced to these indexes earlier as we discussed land entry files for this period. The indexes will help you find the number of the patent your relative received. Using the patent number, you can order a duplicate of the patent copy from the Bureau of Land Management. To track patent copies of ancestors who acquired public domain land after 1973, contact the nearest Bureau of Land Management office for help.

Social Security and Railroad Retirement Board Records

The Social Security Act of August 1934 not only paved the way to ease the suffering of the aged and unemployed but it also provided a record-keeping system that may help you in your family history research. Remember that railroad workers, government employees, and some of the self-employed did not participate in social security. However, self-employed persons could elect to participate under special social security guidelines.

Agencies responsible for ancestors' retirement payments maintained files on them that contain valuable information. From enrollment applications we learn birth dates and places, occupations, and residences at the time the form was filled out. When a person became eligible for retirement benefits or the person's death made family members eligible, more forms had to be filled out with updated information on family members, current addresses, and employment history. By obtaining copies of ancestors' files, you discover facts that will provide important data for your family's history.

You can write to the Social Security Administration to request copies of family members' files. The Railroad Retirement Board, Office of Personnel Management (for federal employees), or state-sponsored retirement agencies (for state and local employees) also have records about relatives whose pensions they administer. The state, county, or city personnel department can provide information about former government employees in their jurisdictions. In many states public employee associations can provide information about where to look for records of ancestors who were public employees. (The term *public employees* includes ancestors who worked for state and local government as well as for local school boards.)

The government offices section of your telephone book is the place to start your search for the nearest office of one of these agencies. If your town does not have many federal offices, check the telephone directory for the state capital or another large city to find the number of the Social Security Administration or other United States government offices. For example, in the United States government section of the Salt Lake City telephone directory I found a listing for the Social Security Administration, the Railroad Retirement Board, and the telephone numbers of my federal representative and senator. These elected officials maintain local offices that provide addresses or telephone numbers to contact for information about any federal agency. Local libraries often have *The United States Government Manual 1993–1994* from the Office of the Federal Register, which lists addresses and telephone numbers of office holders and United States agencies.

To find information about ancestors in social security records or the records of other government retirement agencies, you must be able to furnish data about when and where your ancestor registered for benefits or where they were employed. Knowing a person's social security number will always expedite the search. For example, assume that you are trying to find the birthplace or deathplace of a great-grandparent who died in the 1960s. Knowing where the person applied for a social security number would give you a place to start looking for records that might list a birthplace and date. The same is true if you could learn where the person died. You can also request copies of a relative's social security number application or application for benefits and other information in the file. Call your local Social Security Administration office for instructions or write to the Social Security Administration (see Appendix A). Request a copy of the SS-5 form, "Application for a Social Security Number Card."

There is also an index to deceased persons with social security numbers. You have access to this information from the LDS Family History Library in Salt Lake City or one of its Family History Centers (see Appendix A). The FamilySearch Social Security Death Index (see chapter 3) provides the social security number of the deceased, where the person applied for it, and the place, month, and year of death. It includes only persons who died before 1989.

The government created a special retirement fund administered by the Railroad Retirement Board for those involved in the nation's railroads. For those with railroader ancestors, see Wendy L. Elliott's article "Railroad Records for Genealogical Research" in the *National Genealogical Society Quarterly*. The local Railroad Retirement Board office telephone number is listed under United States government in the telephone directory; however, it may deal only with living retirees in the area. Files for all railroad employees are found only at the headquarters office of the Railroad Retirement Board (see Appendix A). In pursuing information about my father, I wrote a letter to the Railroad Retirement Board that produced some valuable information.

⸎ ————————————

The letter I received explained that since my father died before reaching retirement, his records were less complete than if he had retired. Nonetheless, this agency provided me with quite a bit of new data about my father. The answer I received included copies of five documents. The first was an "Employee's Statement of Compensated Service Rendered Prior to January 1, 1937, to Employers under the Railroad Retirement Act of 1937," dated October 24, 1940, and signed by my father. It was a record of his employment with the Southern Pacific Company from June 1936—just prior to his sixteenth birthday—to October 1940. He had worked as a section laborer and as a rodman on a survey crew. From 1936 to the end of 1938, he began work each year in June and quit in the late fall or early winter—probably to continue schooling. Since his father and uncle were both employed by the railroad, it is likely they helped him find these jobs during the time he was not in school. The next document was a "Certification of Service and Compensation." It detailed my father's pay from 1937 to September 1972.

The third document was a copy of his honorable discharge as a private first class in the 361st Infantry Regiment. It was dated October 24, 1945, at Fort Douglas, Utah. I was four years old at the time and can still remember my dad coming through the gate of the home where I lived with my mom in Farmington, Utah. The exact date had always eluded me, but according to this evidence it was late in October 1945.

Attached next to his discharge was another service-related document: "Enlistment Record and Report of Separation." It was signed by my father and dated October 25, 1945. It contained his birth date, a physical description, and his service record. He began active duty at Fort Douglas February 2, 1944. He was wounded April 27, 1945, just eleven days before V-E Day (May 8, 1945) and was shipped home August 14, 1945.

The "Notice of Death and Statement of Compensation" was the last document in the packet. This listed his death, the last day he worked, and the pay he had received in the months preceding his death.

I had learned more about my dad from the documents ferreted out from his employer, the government, and his union than I had learned from him while he was alive. The examples given here show that you can learn a lot about ancestors if you will contact employers and others who had responsibility for them—that is, if you go beyond census records, vital records, wills, and cemetery records.

Notes

1. National Archives and Records Administration, *Guide to Genealogical Research in the National Archives* (Washington, D.C.: The Administration, 1985), 199.

2. Ibid., 201–202.

3. National Archives and Records Administration, *Guide to Records in the National Archives: Rocky Mountain Region* (Washington, D.C.: The Administration, 1989), 15.

4. ———, *Guide to Records in the National Archives: Mid-Atlantic Region* (Washington, D.C.: The Administration, 1989), 18.

5. ———. *Guide to Records in the National Archives: Southeast Region* (Washington, D.C.: The Administration, 1989), 19.

6. Val D. Greenwood. *The Researcher's Guide to American Genealogy,* 2d ed. (Baltimore: Genealogical Publishing Co., 1990), 226–235. Greenwood also provides a list of locations where mortality schedules are found. Some of the other schedules may well be at the same institutions.

7. An update on these records appeared in the National Society of the Daughters of the American Revolution Library's "Continental Columns," *Newsletter of the NSDAR Library* 1, no 1 (winter 1993): 3–4.

8. National Archives and Records Administration, *Guide to Genealogical Research in the National Archives,* rev. ed. (Washington, D.C.: The Administration, 1985), 19–21.

CHAPTER 7

⪦⪧

Learning about Your Ethnic Origins

People who live in the United States trace their origins to many different cultures. Only the Native Americans trace their roots back to the aboriginal inhabitants of the United States; the rest came here from other nations. Most came voluntarily, but African American slaves, English convicts, and indentured servants had little choice. As you move back in time learning about ancestors, you will encounter difficulties identifying progenitors who lived in cultures with record-keeping practices and customs that are foreign to you. The information you seek may be in another country or at Bureau of Indian Affairs offices on a Native American reservation. Stories about your family's early history may be in the memories of older relatives or neighbors or carved on a totem.

This chapter will introduce you to steps you can follow to discover your ethnic heritage. It is not a complete guide to researching the origins of families from all of the ethnic groups living in the United States. Its primary focus is on immigrant ethnic groups with the exception of sections about Native American ethnic groups. This chapter is a primer, a basic guide to resources and methods that will help most Americans discover their ethnic immigrant ancestors' hometown so they can continue their research in other countries. The model used is immigration from Europe to the United States because, at present, there are more resources available to trace European immigrant origins than other immigrant ethnic groups. Regardless of your heritage, however, the instructions presented here are based on methods and resources that are common to many immigrant ethnic groups in the United States. Once you have exhausted the possibilities for information about your family presented in this chapter, it is time to consult with the staff at one of the research centers listed in Appendix A or B or contact one of the ethnic organizations referred to in this chapter for help specific to your ethnic heritage.

ETHNIC RESOURCES FOR FAMILY HISTORY RESEARCHERS

For much of its history, America was viewed as a melting pot. National and local government leaders as well as immigrants themselves wanted to overcome cultural and language differences by making everyone an American—compliant with majority attitudes and customs. Many persons wanted to believe that there was an American culture that all members of all ethnic groups joined or became assimilated into. However, the fact is that America is made up of many groups with cultural heritages or identities that are still an inseparable part of each person's identity.

The census enumerators in 1980 and again in 1990 asked us about our ancestry. The statistical reports for these censuses testify vividly about the ethnic diversity that is the United States today. One reason genealogy and family history research is so popular is because Americans identify with their ancestral origins in other countries. Part of being Americans has become identifying ourselves with one or more of the many ethnic, national, or racial groups that make up this patchwork we call American society. Some of us like to think it is our diversity that provides hope for this nation's future.

This great interest in maintaining contact with our racial origins lies at the core of the many fraternal groups, societies, institutions, and publications that will help you learn more about your family and your heritage. Such sources are particularly important for learning about immigrants to this country after the middle of the nineteenth century and about Native Americans and African Americans.

It may seem obvious, but one of the most important records any fraternal organization or society has is a membership file. If you think an ancestor may have joined an ethnic organization, ask a member if the organization has a membership record for your ancestor. The record may provide additional information about an ancestor's life and interests, perhaps including your ancestor's birthplace and family members' names.

Sometimes you know that your relatives were active in a local or national ethnic organization because among their papers you found membership cards, award certificates, or copies of newsletters or magazines published by the society or fraternity to which they belonged. If you have no clues that they were involved in such activities, it still pays to check with organizations in the community that may have interested them. Even if membership records have not been indexed, they are usually in alphabetical or chronological order. Knowing when your ancestor lived in the community helps you narrow your search to a range of years. Overlooking this source may rob you of important facts about your family.

Universities in the state in which your ancestor settled may have organizations or programs to educate the public about the state's ethnic groups. They may also have programs in the language or history of these groups. For example, in 1968 the University of Texas at San Antonio established the Institute of Texan Cultures as part of the University of Texas system of higher education. It supports research about the many cultures brought to Texas by immigrants from many parts of the world and by Native Americans and African Americans. Another of the Institute's goals is to provide materials to teachers and the general public that will educate Texans and others about the state's rich cultural heritage. The Institute's many books, pamphlets, videos, exhibits, filmstrips, and other types of presentations provide invaluable insight into the origins, history, and culture of such diverse groups as Lebanese and Syrian Texans, African American Texans, Czech Texans, Chinese Texans, German Texans, Native American Texans, Jewish Texans, and Swedish Texans.

The Balch Institute of Philadelphia is another agency that has contributed a great deal to preserving the ethnic heritage of this nation. Its library contains a rich collection of materials about American ethnic groups. In 1984 the Institute joined with Temple University to found the Temple University–Balch Institute Center for Immigration Research. Scholars at this center have used data taken from United States ship's passenger mani-

fests to produce several indexes to these lists, including Ira Glazier and Michael Tepper's *The Famine Immigrants* and Ira Glazier and P. William Filby's *Germans to America* and *Italians to America,* which will be discussed later in the chapter. Like the Institute of Texan Cultures, Balch Institute also publishes books and pamphlets that will help you learn about ethnic immigrant ancestors.

The Immigration History Research Center at the University of Minnesota also collects materials about ethnic groups. It publishes books, pamphlets, and periodicals of great value to those of us learning about our ethnic origins.

The American Historical Society of Germans from Russia in Lincoln, Nebraska, and the Germans from Russia Heritage Society in Bismarck, North Dakota, were formed to preserve the heritage of those hardy immigrants to the plains of the United States and Canada who near the beginning of this century came from Russia but spoke German. Their ancestors were immigrants to Russia after 1763 when the Russian Empress Catherine and her successors provided land and privileges to entice German farmers and artisans to come to Russia to increase the empire's productivity.

You can readily locate organizations with a focus on a specific cultural or national group. Again, your local public or college library is the place to start. The reference librarian can help you find a few of the many ethnic directories in print. In them you will find hundreds of organizations dedicated to preserving the culture, traditions, and history of the many ethnic groups in the United States.

These organizations publish newsletters and magazines that contain articles about current activities among their members and, occasionally, articles on genealogy and family history along with articles that teach you about the history and culture of your family's original homelands. You can place ads in these publications to help you find your cousins so that you can exchange information about your common ancestors. Ethnic societies support a number of other activities that can help you, such as producing language guides, histories, and other titles that will help you discover information about your ethnic roots.

Finding Ethnic Organizations

As you compile your family's history, it may help to join organizations in the United States founded to promote or commemorate ethnic identity. In addition to the institutions listed in Appendix B, many others are listed in guides to ethnic organizations that you will find at local public or college libraries. Start with Deborah M. Burek, Karen E. Koek, and Annette Novallo's *Encyclopedia of Associations*. Look first in the name and keyword index under the name of the ethnic group of interest. Under *Korea, Korean,* the twenty-fifth edition shows seventy entries. Under *Italia, Italian, Italiana, Italiano, Italo,* and *Italy* are 177 entries. The entries in this encyclopedia will describe the organization including when it was founded, the number of members, its purposes and activities, publications, and address and telephone number. Most of the organizations listed are national or international in scope. For local ethnic associations check the *Encyclopedia of Associations: Regional, State, and Local Organizations* edited by Grant J. Eldridge.

With the help of your local reference librarian, you will find that libraries generally have several books about ethnic organizations in the United States. Search in the library's catalog under the subject *Minorities—United States—Societies—Directories.* In addition check the following subject headings—remembering that not all library catalogers place the same books under the same subject headings: *Minorities—United States—Information Sources, Ethnic Press—United States, Ethnicity—United States—Bibliography/Directories, Immigrants—United States—Bibliography,* and the many subheadings under the subjects *Emigration* and *Immigration.* Under these subject headings you will probably encounter books compiled by Lubomyr R. Wynar nearly twenty years ago that still have value today: *Encyclopedic Directory of Ethnic Organizations in the United States* and, with Anna T. Wynar, *Encyclopedic Directory of Ethnic Newspapers and Periodicals.*

If you would like to add some details from ethnic periodicals to your family history, refer to *Ethnic Press in the United States* edited by Sally M. Miller. This book contains articles about the history, content, and impact of periodical publishing by members of twenty-seven American ethnic groups. The bibliographies following each article are a great place to find additional information about publications by each of these groups.

Books about Our Ethnic Origins

For short but accurate histories of American ethnic groups, refer to the *Harvard Encyclopedia of American Ethnic Groups* edited by Stephan Thernstrom. Although the bibliographies for articles are now a bit dated, the titles listed are valuable aids to understanding the many groups that make up American society. In searching for books listed in the *Harvard Encyclopedia,* you will encounter newer titles on the shelves next to these older

books and find that they will draw you into subject headings in the library catalog that will further your research. In other words, check the subject headings assigned to the books you find in Thernstrom's *Harvard Encyclopedia* for more-recent books about the ethnic groups of interest.

A good introduction to non-European family history research is *Ethnic Genealogy: A Research Guide* edited by Jessie Carney Smith. The authors of the book's various chapters are experts in researching family histories and genealogies through libraries and archives. Most of the book deals with methods and resources for ethnic genealogical research.

Family history and genealogy research manuals exist for many ethnic groups. A new title that will help those of Polish origin is Rosemary A. Chorzempa's *Korzenie Polskie: Polish Roots.* The author covers the history, geography, ethnic groups, and records of Poland. The book includes lists of addresses that researchers may write to for information about their families.

To find research handbooks for your ethnic group, check the catalog at your local public or college library under the subject heading for the country from which your family originated. Search under the subheading *Genealogy* to see if there are books in the library about research method. If not, ask for help in checking the catalogs of other libraries in your state and region.

Be sure to read some of the books that family historians and genealogists have written about their ethnic heritage. *The Kidwells: A Family Odyssey* by Dwayne E. Walls and Dorothy S. Redford's *Somerset Homecoming: Recovering a Lost Heritage* are well-written African American family histories. In both cases, the search for family origins began on the front porch or in the living room of family members. Parents, siblings, grandparents, aunts, uncles, and cousins all had to be contacted. The amount of information relatives have is not important, only their willingness to share it. A single letter, photograph, or certificate may be the missing piece of the puzzle. Talk with your local librarian about histories written by other persons with your same ethnic background. See what you can learn from these authors about tracking family origins.

Biographies will give you some good ideas about how to pursue information about ancestors. Again, let your local librarian help you search for biographies about persons with your same ethnic origins. Often you can find biographies from the area in which your family lived in this country by performing a subject search in the computer catalog or card catalog under the county as a subject. Subheadings for the county will include *Biography, Genealogy,* and *History,* among others.

DOCUMENTING ETHNIC ORIGINS IN THE FAMILY ARCHIVES

Immigrant ancestors did not always pass on information about their origins to descendants. They may have been hesitant to discuss their former homeland because they wanted their families to fit in as Americans; thus, they downplayed their origins and traditions. Often the second or third generation of descendants were the first to become curious about their heritage. They collected mementos, artifacts, stories, and documents that could become the foundation for your research. Therefore, the first step in your research is to find the relatives who have these materials today. In chapter 4 you were introduced to interviewing techniques that will help you gather the stories and oral traditions that abound in every family. Often they tell of the village in a far-off land in which your family lived before immigrating to the United States.

You can refer to chapter 4 for more help in finding and interpreting family records. To see more clearly how family records aid your search for immigrant origins, consider the following scenario.

Pretend that your second great-grandfather (great-great-grandfather) came to America about 1850 from Ireland. He married in the United States to another Irish immigrant. Your great-grandfather was the second son of this Irish immigrant couple and the third child in a family of four girls and two boys. You do not know your second great-grandfather and grandmother's hometowns in Ireland and are stymied in efforts to trace your Irish heritage. Any government records you find in America simply list Ireland as their place of birth or prior residence. How are you going to find their birthplaces so you can trace their families in the local records of Ireland? The facts you need may be among the family papers of one of your cousins.

Perhaps in the years after their arrival in America, your Irish ancestors received letters from family and friends living in their old hometowns. They had kept as souvenirs their tickets from the ship that brought them here and papers from home that had been required by various officials as they made their way from Ireland to the United States. A family Bible, first owned by the grandfather of your immigrant ancestor, listed the birthplaces of

each family member and whom they married. As your second great-grandparents aged, they passed these family treasures to their youngest child, a daughter, who showed real interest in them. None of the other children—among them your great-grandfather—received any of their parents' records. This great-grandaunt, who never married, passed the family papers to her nephew, your first cousin, twice removed (the son of her oldest brother). Your cousin found that each of his children had an interest in these items, so he divided them among his four children—your second cousins, once removed. Each of these cousins married and passed that share of the family archives to his or her children—your third cousins—in photocopy form, leaving the original with their oldest child. Your job is to find one of these third cousins—who are actually about your same age. (For help with these relationships refer to figure 2 in chapter 2.)

You may have several hundred third cousins, all descended from the same Irish immigrants you are seeking. They probably inherited stories, documents, and artifacts that may have come from your second great-grandparents. The question is, how do you find these cousins?

Following is an example of how a researcher used telephone directories to find relatives who held material in their family archives about an immigrant ancestor.

One of my students at Brigham Young University knew that her immigrant ancestor from Germany settled with several brothers in a large eastern seaboard city in the latter half of the nineteenth century. With the help of the reference librarian she found the telephone listings for her surname in that town. To her surprise, there were several people with the same given names and surname as her immigrant ancestor and his brothers. The student called one of them and discovered that the man was the direct descendant of her immigrant ancestor's brother. This cousin not only had information about the ancestor's birthplace but had facts about the immigrant ancestor's parents as well.

Placing ads in newspapers for the area in which your immigrant ancestor settled or queries in the newsletters of genealogical societies are other means of finding relatives who may hold documents or other information in their family archives.

The National Genealogical Society (*NGS Newsletter*) and New England Historic Genealogical Society (*NEXUS*) are examples of national organizations that publish such queries. The same is true of Everton Publishers' *The Genealogical Helper*, American Genealogical Lending Library's and Historical Resources' *Heritage Quest*, and the Connecticut Society of Genealogists' *The Connecticut Nutmegger*, all of which have nationwide circulation. Look in Elizabeth Bentley's *Genealogists' Address Book* and Mary K. Meyer's *Directory of Genealogical Societies in the United States and Canada* to find the addresses of genealogical societies, family organizations, and genealogical periodicals that apply to surnames or localities of interest to you.

Native American Family Archives

The most important source for finding out about Native American ancestors is through the family archives. Oral traditions will help you begin the search for Native American ancestors. From older members of the family and tribe you can learn about naming practices and marriage and inheritance customs that are an essential part of your heritage. In Native American tribes where totems are a part of history, these emblems will help you learn about family origins. Talk to members of your tribe who are familiar with the meaning of totems and their role in tribal and personal life.

Follow the guidelines given in chapter 4 to help you prepare for interviews you will conduct in search of your family history. Researchers from the University of Utah have been conducting oral history interviews with Native Americans for many years. Check with the history departments or reference librarians at universities or colleges in the areas in which your family lived and ask if they know of any projects involving your tribe. Unknown to you, some of your ancestors may have been interviewed during one of these oral history projects.

Chinese Family Archives

Frank Ching's book *Ancestors: 900 Years in the Life of a Chinese Family* demonstrates the critical roles of family records and oral evidence in compiling Chinese family histories and genealogies. This book also shows how a genealogy can be turned into an interesting family history.

From 1977 until 1988 Ching sought his ancestors. His search started with an uncle he had never known—the brother of his mother. It included visits to half-brothers and sisters as well as cousins. From his half-sister Margaret he received a plastic bag containing a bundle of old books, among them the *Ancestral Genealogy of the Qin Clan of Wuxi*. Many Chinese families have kept such clan genealogies. This particular genealogy traced the author's ancestry back thirty-three generations to the eleventh century and a prominent poet of the Song Dynasty of emperors, Qin Guan.

With the aid of cousins he did not know before his search began, Ching uncovered ancestral shrines and graveyards. From talks with librarians and archivists he discovered seventeen additional volumes of his clan's genealogy. Several volumes turned up in the rare books collection of Columbia University's East Asian Library.

The author learned that during China's Cultural Revolution many clan genealogies in private hands were destroyed or hidden to protect individuals from persecution. A considerable number are still in existence today, however, as witnesses of Chinese dedication to preserving family history.

In the 1930s and 1940s many clan genealogies were acquired by American universities as part of a growing interest in Asian studies. You should contact your local university to speak with Asian specialists there in the hope of locating some of these clan genealogy collections. The LDS Family History Library has been acquiring microfilm copies of clan genealogies from American universities as well as archives and libraries in Asia. The catalog to this collection is not automated and, thus, must be searched in Salt Lake City. A knowledge of Chinese characters is essential in using this card catalog.

Dr. Basil Yang, a Chinese specialist and genealogist at the Harold B. Lee Library of Brigham Young University, cautions that the biggest stumbling block for Asian-American genealogists is correctly interpreting the Chinese characters that stand for the family's name. You will not be able to pursue your research for Chinese ancestors unless you can accurately reconstruct the American name in Chinese characters. Here again, older family members and documents from the family archives will be the biggest helps. You may also want to seek help at nearby universities with Chinese language programs.

African American Family Archives

There are few records in Africa that tell the stories of the families that were raided to provide slaves for the Western Hemisphere. After arriving in South America, the Caribbean, or North America, slaves were seldom mentioned in records by name until they were freed. If you have African American ancestors who came to America as slaves, you must begin your search by interviewing parents, grandparents, aunts, uncles, cousins, and older brothers and sisters. They will provide clues to help you find your ancestors in government, religious, and other records. You must rely heavily on oral information passed from one generation to the next since your family left Africa. It is difficult for African Americans to identify the African families from which they are descended. Unless ancestors immigrated to the United States after the middle of the nineteenth century, most families' oral traditions do not include descriptions of the locality in Africa where the family originated. If you do succeed in tracing your family to its home in Africa, it will be on the basis of evidence passed by word of mouth from one generation to the next.

Even before the Civil War there were numerous free African Americans. If this is the case with your family, oral traditions and family records will still be the starting point to lead you to local and national records documenting your family's history. If your family came here as immigrants from Africa after the middle of the nineteenth century, the oral and written sources in the family archives will likewise guide you to passenger lists, naturalization records, censuses, and other records discussed in chapters 5 and 6 that will detail your ancestors' lives.

IMMIGRANTS IN PUBLISHED RESOURCES

Chapter 4 taught you to look for the research others have completed before you start your own search in original records. The same principle applies in your efforts to find information about an immigrant ancestor. If you ignore this step, you could waste time duplicating research efforts of other persons interested in your

family. Numerous indexes and other published materials can make finding ancestors' origins easier. They are based on research in the censuses, passenger lists, naturalization records, passport records, and religious records you will learn about later in the chapter.

If your immigrant ancestors came to the United States many years ago, you should seek published resources as well as manuscript or typescript genealogies, biographies, and family histories created nearer the time when these progenitors lived. Researchers and family members who lived one hundred years ago, for example, may have had access to information that is now lost. Finding these materials is easy if you know where your family settled after they arrived. Follow the approach outlined in chapter 5, contacting libraries, historical societies, and other record-collecting agencies in the area in which your immigrant ancestors settled, to learn about resources held in repositories there.

The New England Historic Genealogical Society Library in Boston is an example of a library that has one of the nation's largest book and manuscript collections about early New England and the other areas in the United States where New Englanders settled. The New Haven (Connecticut) Colony Historical Society is another repository possessing a unique collection of resources including local histories, biographies, and genealogies that describe the seventeenth-, eighteenth-, and nineteenth-century immigrants to New England. Appendixes A and B will help you find other research centers for areas in which your immigrant ancestors lived. Many libraries with large collections of books about early American immigrants make their holdings known through computer catalog hookups and published catalogs of their holdings. The interlibrary loan librarian at one of your local libraries can help you search such catalogs for books about your immigrant family or for histories of the communities in which they settled.

Indexes to Ships' Passenger Lists and Immigration Records

One of the earliest compilations of eighteenth- and early nineteenth-century German immigrants is I. Daniel Rupp's *A Collection of Upwards of 30,000 Names of German, Swiss, Dutch, French and Other Immigrants in Pennsylvania from 1726–1776.* It was based on passenger lists turned in at North American ports before the Revolution. The same sources were used for Strassburger and Hinke's *Pennsylvania German Pioneers: A Publication of Original Lists of Arrivals in the Port of*

Philadelphia from 1727 to 1808, with separate volumes for a transcription of the passenger lists and facsimiles of the original lists. The facsimiles were included to help researchers who wanted to see the original lists rather than accept the spelling of personal names presented by the indexers.

The most exhaustive guide to published lists of passengers and immigrants is P. William Filby's *Passenger and Immigration Lists Bibliography: 1538–1900*. The entries in the *Bibliography* identify ships by name, ports of embarkation and arrival, and dates of arrival in the United States. Of equal importance is the massive index Filby compiled with the aid of Mary K. Meyer and, later, Dorothy M. Lower under the title *Passenger and Immigration Lists Index*. This index contains the names of passengers and immigrants found in published lists included in Filby's *Bibliography* as well as newly discovered lists. Because this is an ongoing project, new volumes include previously undiscovered passengers, so it pays to check each new volume. Each *Index* entry identifies a passenger in terms of when and where the person arrived and upon which ship. Any other data given in the ship's list, such as age, is also included. Excluded from consideration in these titles are the United States customs and immigration passenger lists discussed later in this chapter; thus, Filby's works are of particular importance if you think your ancestor came before federal passenger lists were created (1820).

Trudy Schenk, Ruth Froelke, and Inge Bork have used microfilms of emigration papers from the Duchy of Württemberg to compile a multivolume index with the title *The Württemberg Emigration Index*. Thousands of German emigrants are identified in this index by name, birthplace, birth date, and date of departure. Most of the entries are from the last quarter of the eighteenth century to about 1900. Gary Zimmerman and Marian Wolferts's *German Immigrants: Lists of Passengers Bound from Bremen to New York, 1847–1871, with Places of Origin* is another important index covering ships arriving at New York.

The National Archives no longer owns the original federal passenger arrival records dating from 1820, but it has microfilm copies. Many of the originals were given to the Center for Immigration Research at the Balch Institute in Philadelphia. To date, three series of indexes to the federal passenger lists have been published as a result of research at the Center. *The Famine Immigrants*, edited by Glazier and Tepper, lists Irish immigrants arriving at the Port of New York from 1846 to 1851; *Germans to America*, edited by Glazier and Filby, indexes German immigrants in U.S. passenger lists beginning in 1850. Several new volumes of Glazier

and Filby's work appear each year, and the latest volume lists German immigrants arriving through 1879. Be aware that the volumes from 1850 to 1855 of *Germans to America* include only passenger lists in which 80 percent of the passengers were from Germany. Germans arriving on ships carrying large numbers of passengers from other countries were not included in these early volumes. The newest series, *Italians to America 1880–1899*, edited by Glazier and Filby, indexes Italian immigrants in U.S. passenger lists.

Robert P. Swierenga is an author/editor familiar to Americans with Dutch origins. Using U.S. passenger lists, emigration records from the Netherlands, and U.S. census data, he has identified thousands of Dutch immigrants who came to America between 1820 and 1880. See his *Dutch Emigrants to the United States, South Africa, South America, and Southeast Asia, 1835–1880* and *Dutch Immigrants in U.S. Ship Passenger Manifests, 1820–1880* if you have Dutch ancestry.

Aside from passenger lists and immigration records, other resources such as court records, newspapers, religious records, etc., describe immigrants and their origins. A number of books have been written using these other sources to identify immigrants to the United States from several different countries. Ask your local librarian to help you find similar books about immigrants from your ancestors' countries. Check library catalogs using the country name as the subject. Look under the subheadings *Immigration, Emigration*. Following are some examples of books on immigrants from the British Isles and from Germany.

Books about Immigrants from the British Isles

One of the most important titles about English emigrants to the United States before the American Revolution is Peter Wilson Coldham's *Complete Book of Emigrants 1607–1776*. Its four volumes covering the period from 1607 to 1776 are unique for their use of English court and port records to trace emigrants from England to its colonies in the Western Hemisphere. Another Coldham book, *Emigrants in Chains*, will help you understand the social history behind forced emigration to the Americas from England during this period.

Michael Tepper's *Immigrants to the Middle Colonies* is based upon passenger lists and related data published in the *New York Genealogical and Biographical Record*. Some of the articles provide facts about immigrant places of origin in England. Tepper's *New World Immigrants* covers primarily English immigrants and is based on passenger lists and related information found in a broad assortment of genealogical and historical periodicals. Many of Tepper's sources would be accessible only to knowledgeable researchers.

For those whose immigrant ancestors came to New England, compiler Gary B. Roberts's three-volume *English Origins of New England Families: From the New England Historical and Genealogical Register* will prove essential. It is valuable because few libraries have a complete set of *The New England Historical and Genealogical Register* published by the New England Historic Genealogical Society since 1847. Over the years researchers here and abroad have contributed numerous articles to the *Register* on the English, Irish, Welsh, and Scottish origins of New England families. *English Origins* contains a large number of *Register* articles and makes the information in the articles more accessible by providing a name index.

If your Irish ancestors immigrated before 1900, you probably do not know an exact town of origin—unless the family archives has produced one—because no passenger lists provide this information until nearly the end of the nineteenth century. For those whose ancestors' Irish hometown is unknown, the New England Historic Genealogical Society recently began a series called *The Search for Missing Friends: Irish Immigrant Advertisements in the Boston* Pilot, Ruth-Ann Harris, Donald M. Jacobs, and B. Emer O'Keeffe, editors. Volume 1 covers the years from 1831 to 1850; volume 2 covers 1850 to 1853. During and after the potato famine, thousands of Irish fleeing starvation and poverty sought to find relatives who were already in the United States. The *Pilot* was Boston's leading Catholic newspaper and an ideal place to publish advertisements in search of lost kin. Ads included places of origin for about 85 percent of the persons being sought as well as other information such as arrival date and last known residence. Anyone with Irish roots should check these volumes.

Books about Immigrants from Germany

The first German colony in America was founded at Germantown, Pennsylvania, in 1683. From that time until about 1915, Germans made up a substantial proportion of the total number of persons immigrating to the United States. In the 1990 census 57 million persons reported German ancestry, more than any other ancestry group. Don Yoder has published several books that identify many of the early German settlers in Pennsylvania, including *Pennsylvania German Immigrants,*

1709–1786. Based on a series of articles he wrote for the *Yearbook* of the Pennsylvania German Folklore Society, the book translates eighteenth-century immigrant lists and puts the people on them in the context of the German immigration to America during that time. Entries provide information about an immigrant's origins in Germany, list members of his or her family, and indicate where the family settled. Checking your local library catalog or the catalogs of your interlibrary loan librarian for Don Yoder as an author will produce several books to help you find German settlers in Pennsylvania.

Annette Kunselman Burgert is another researcher who has uncovered the origins and histories of many early German settlers. Her series *Eighteenth-Century Emigrants from German-Speaking Lands to North America* is another important resource for tracing immigrants back to their German hometowns. The three volumes published to date detail origins of German-speaking immigrants from southwestern Germany and western France (Alsace).

Descendants of seventeenth-century New York German families will recognize the name of Henry Z. Jones. His research and writing has identified many early German settlers that you would not otherwise find. In his *The Palatine Families of New York, 1710* and *More Palatine Families,* hundreds of entries identify immigrants, their German hometowns, and where they settled in the United States. He also provides valuable background about the history of the period and how it affected these immigrants.

American Local Histories and Immigrants

Perhaps your ancestors are not to be found in passenger list indexes or books about immigrants to the United States. If so, local histories may help you learn the names of towns in which immigrant ancestors lived before coming to the United States, especially if they immigrated to America in the seventeenth, eighteenth, and early nineteenth centuries. Although you may think that your ancestors came here alone, many people came in groups in which members were bound to each other by blood, friendship, or religion and settled in the same area.

Sometimes local histories will mention your family by name; more often, they focus on the leaders of the community who may have led a group to the United States that included your ancestors. If your ancestor did not come with them, perhaps they settled in this particular town because many in the community came from their home region or town. Letters from successful immigrants or their visits to European hometowns may have provided motivation to your family to immigrate. If your ancestors did come from the same area as the immigrants mentioned in local histories, this information may lead you to the records that chronicle their lives before immigration.

Local histories are more likely to be found at libraries or historical societies near where your ancestors settled. Most of the libraries listed in Appendix A have large collections of local histories from many localities. In chapter 4 are more suggestions about how to find local histories.

The Immigrant Experience

Immigrants to America seldom came here on an impulse. Their decision was carefully made with much planning and forethought. Many of them had become migrants in Europe, traveling from one locality to another seeking employment to sustain them and provide savings toward passage to America. They traveled in family groups as well as alone; however, the solitary immigrant seems to be an exception. A careful look at passenger lists and United States censuses will show you that many of these newcomers traveled to their new homes with friends and family, and many of your ancestors' fellow passengers were from the same hometown areas as they. Compare the people you find recorded with your ancestors on the passenger list against those listed on the census as their neighbors. It may surprise you that some of the same people who came here with them continued to live near them. See if you can find records about these other persons or their descendants in local historical societies or record offices. Their obituaries, christenings, or marriages could mention a place of origin. Their employment records could also contain clues. When you fail to find information about your own family in existing records, you can find facts about those who traveled with them or settled near them to help you overcome research obstacles.

Many books have been written about immigrants. Your ancestor may not be named in these books, but you could enrich any family history or genealogy you may write with information from other researchers and authors. The readers of your family history will be curious about how your immigrant ancestors fit into the larger picture of millions of immigrants coming to the United States at various times in its history. Following are some examples of books you might find in the catalogs of local public or college libraries under *United*

States—Emigration and Immigration and its many subheadings such as *Social Aspects* and *Biography*.

American Mosaic: The Immigrant Experience in the Words of Those Who Lived It by Joan Morrison and Charlotte Fox Zabusky is filled with personal remembrances of immigrants whose experiences may have been similar to those of your ancestors. If your ancestors left no narratives about their experiences, a book such as this will help you understand what it meant to be an immigrant.

Women Who Dared: The History of Finnish American Women, edited by Carl Ross and Marianne Wargelin Brown, is another book that will help you understand immigrant ancestors' lives even if they did not leave any evidence of their own activities. Francesco Cordasco's *The Immigrant Woman in North America: An Annotated Bibliography of Selected References* includes many experiences that will help you discover more about what immigration meant to the women in your family. These two titles were found under the Library of Congress subject headings *Women Immigrants—United States—History* and *Women Immigrants—United States—Bibliography.*

It is also important that you understand the history of immigration to this country. A good introduction to the nineteenth- and twentieth-century European immigration to the United States is *A Century of European Migrations, 1830–1930* edited by Rudolph J. Vecoli and Suzanne M. Sinke. Marcus Lee Hansen's classic treatment *The Atlantic Migration, 1607–1860* is another good book to read if you would like to place the immigration of earlier European ancestors in perspective. To find additional books, check the catalog at your local public or college library to see what it has under the subject *United States—Emigration and Immigration* and the subheading *History*.

You will need the background that books about immigration provide if your family history or genealogy is to have the interpretive quality that so many lack. Readers deserve a family story that has been placed in the context of history—international, national, and local.

TRACING ETHNIC ORIGINS THROUGH LOCAL, STATE, AND NATIONAL RECORDS

If all of your efforts to find the name of your ancestor's birthplace among family records and published resources fail, look at some of the local, state, and national sources generated in this country. A number of records were created to identify people coming into the United States: passenger lists, naturalization records, and passport and visa applications. These documents may provide information that will lead to an immigrant ancestor's origin. Other records that may contain facts about a person's birthplace, including draft registration records, social security records, and censuses, were explained in chapter 6. As outlined in chapter 5, local religious records, histories, and obituaries may provide clues about ancestors' birthplaces, and, as mentioned earlier in this chapter, ethnic, social, or fraternal groups may also have records about an immigrant ancestor that disclose a birthplace in the home country. Any record that lists a registrant's birthplace is of interest. The following sections look at a few of these records to demonstrate how you can use them to discover an immigrant ancestor's place of origin.

The Census

If your family came to this country during the nineteenth or twentieth centuries, censuses may help pinpoint a date of arrival and at least a country of origin. A few census takers even wrote down the names of immigrants' hometowns. It is likely that these cases occurred when the persons being questioned supplied that information rather than just the name of the country, kingdom, or principality in which they lived prior to their arrival in the United States. Both state and federal censuses should be searched. In some cases state census takers were required to ask immigrants to name their hometown.

Censuses also reveal the composition of your immigrant ancestor's American neighborhood. Often you will find that many of his or her neighbors were also immigrants from the same country as your family. When you cannot find local or federal records about your ancestor, try to find records for other family members or neighbors that are shown in the censuses. The dates and places on the records of these neighbors and relatives may well be similar to those for your progenitor, if they had been recorded, because most of our ancestors came here with other family members or friends. Once in the United States, they often settled in areas with others who spoke their native language and shared their traditions.

If your ancestors came to America before 1900, the federal decennial censuses can help you learn when your ancestors arrived in America. If they are in the 1860 census, for example, but do not appear in the 1850 enumeration, they may have arrived after 1850 but before 1860. Again, noting the ages and birthplaces of the children may narrow the span of years in which

they might have arrived. If the 1860 census shows the ancestors with a five-year-old son born in the United States and a seven-year-old daughter born in France, you can assume the family arrived between 1853 and 1855—between the birth of the daughter and the son.

After tracking down records or memories from or about twentieth-century immigrant progenitors, look them up in the 1900, 1910, and 1920 censuses if they arrived early enough to be included. These records will tell you the year ancestors immigrated and their citizenship status: naturalized or alien. The 1920 census also provided a space for the year of naturalization. The instructions provided in chapters 5 and 6 will help you gather state and federal census data about your immigrant ancestors.

After analyzing the facts garnered from censuses, you probably have an idea about the date immigrant ancestors arrived in this country and perhaps even the name of the port. The following section will help you to begin reconstructing ancestors' lives as newly arrived immigrants by starting at their port of entry to the United States.

Ships' Passenger Lists

Why would you want to find your ancestors on a customs or immigration passenger list? Depending on the time of arrival, the entry may tell you where your immigrant ancestor last lived or his or her birthplace. Before U.S. immigration passenger lists required a last place of residence or birthplace, some captains complied with American regulations by turning in passenger lists compiled in the home port. They often had to file a complete list of passengers—noting birthplaces or last residence—with local port authorities before leaving for their American destination. The port of Bremen, Germany, is an example. In their multivolume work *German Immigrants: Lists of Passengers Bound from Bremen to New York*, Zimmerman and Wolfert compiled towns of origin for about 20 percent of the passengers they identified coming from Bremen to New York from 1847 to 1871. The majority of ships' masters did not follow this example but made up new lists upon arrival in the United States, providing only the minimum data required by U.S. officials for each passenger.

Another value of passenger lists is that they name other family members and former neighbors of your ancestor. You can also learn which port they left from so that if passenger lists exist at the port of departure, you can try to gain access to them. Finding ancestors on passenger lists also isolates the dates of their arrivals.

This knowledge will save time as you search for ancestors in other records that are chronologically arranged. For example, if they arrived in 1875, you would not expect to find them in the 1870 census.

Congress enacted laws in 1819 requiring that ships' masters file a list of passengers and crew at the port of arrival. A minimum of information for each passenger—name, age, sex, occupation, country of origin, and the country where he or she intended to settle is generally all you will find in passenger lists from 1819 through 1892. Persons who died during the crossing were also to be listed by name, and each list provided the name of the ship, master (captain), ports of embarkation and arrival, and the date of arrival. Figure 21 shows an example of this type of passenger list. These records were collected by officers of the United States Customs Service at more than one hundred ports—including inland ports on the Great Lakes and navigable rivers. The National Archives microfilmed these original passenger lists as well as copies and abstracts of original passenger lists made at local customs offices and sent each quarter to the Secretary of State. The abstracts contain the same information as found on the original passenger lists, although some of the names and terms may be abbreviated. These copies and abstracts generally include the period from 1820 to about 1900, but coverage varies for each port. Microfilm copies are available at some of the centers listed in Appendixes A and B, at the National Archives in Washington, D.C., and at its regional archives.

Federal legislation in 1882 required the registration of immigrants on separate passenger lists. An act of March 3, 1891, created the forerunner of the present-day Immigration and Naturalization Service: The Office of Superintendent of Immigration. By 1893 standardized federal forms provided spaces for the marital status, last residence, destination, and previous travel in the United States of each immigrant, and the names, addresses, and relationships of relatives each was planning to meet (see figure 22). These forms became known as "immigration passenger lists/manifests" and were required of each ship's captain as the ship docked at a United States port.

In 1903 a column for race was added, and in 1906 a description of the immigrant and his or her place of birth. In 1907 the forms were expanded to include the name and address of the person's nearest relative in the country of origin (see figure 23). Passenger lists also named American citizens on board. The National Archives received microfilm copies of these records from the Immigration and Naturalization Service; the original records were destroyed. Again, copies of these records are available through the National Archives and at many of the research centers listed in the appendixes.

Crew lists were also turned in. Your ancestors may have worked their ways across the ocean, or they may have been stowaways who were discovered and required to work in exchange for passage to America. Crew lists name crew members and list their ages, nationalities, where and when they joined the crew, and other information about their service aboard ship.

By traveling to the town a passenger list reveals as your ancestor's place of origin or by writing to religious or government offices in that community, you may be able to obtain copies of christening, birth, marriage, or death records that will identify the parents and siblings of your forebear. These local records, in turn, will help you trace your ancestors back to earlier generations.

Locating Passenger Lists

Now that you know how to use passenger lists, you probably want to know where you can go to search them. Many researchers cannot find ancestors in passenger records because they do not know when immigrant ancestors arrived in the United States or the names of the ports at which they arrived. This problem can be overcome because the ships' passenger lists turned in at many ports of entry were indexed by the federal government. These indexes have been microfilmed by the National Archives and Records Administration and are available at its offices and at many of the research centers in Appendix A.

Microfilmed indexes to federal passenger lists exist for Atlantic and Gulf Coast ports dating from 1820. New York passenger arrivals are indexed for 1820 to 1846 and for 1897 to 1948. The previously cited works of Glazier, Filby, Tepper, Zimmerman, and Wohlfert were designed to cover the period when passenger records of the busiest immigration port—New York—were not indexed.

You can buy a complete catalog of the National Archives passenger arrival microfilms from National Archives Trust Fund Board (see Appendix A for address). Ask for *Immigrant & Passenger Arrivals: A Select Catalog of National Archives Microfilm Publications.* Using this catalog you can find the microfilms that contain the passenger lists or indexes listing your ancestors. If you wish to buy a copy of the microfilm, the catalog provides instructions on current prices and where to write. If you are planning to rent copies, obtain them through interlibrary loan, or travel to a research center to use them, this catalog will help you identify exactly which microfilms you should search. A National Archives facility or a research center with

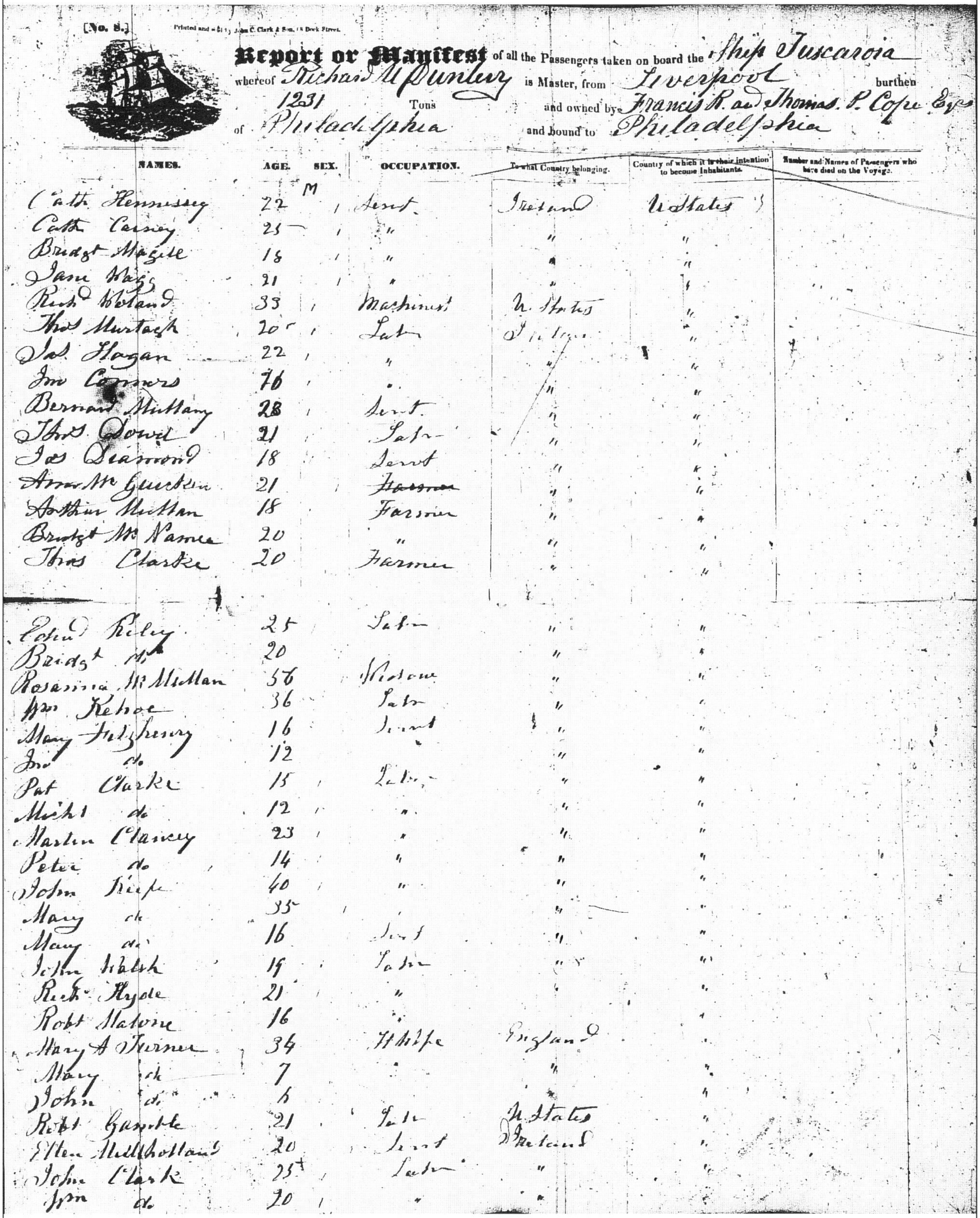

[No. 8.] Printed and sold by John C. Clark & Son, 60 Dock Street.

Report or Manifest of all the Passengers taken on board the Ship Tuscarora whereof Richard M Dunlevy is Master, from Liverpool burthen 1231 Tons and owned by Francis R. and Thomas P. Cope Esqs of Philadelphia and bound to Philadelphia

NAMES.	AGE.	SEX.	OCCUPATION.	To what Country belonging.	Country of which it is their intention to become Inhabitants.	Number and Names of Passengers who have died on the Voyage.
Cath. Hennessy	22	M /	Servt	Ireland	U States	
Cath Carney	23	/	"	"	"	
Bridgt Magille	18	/	"	"	"	
Jane Mag	21	/	"	"	"	
Richd Weland	33	/	Machinist	U. States	"	
Thos Murtagh	20	/	Labr	Ireland	"	
Jas. Hagan	22	/	"	"	"	
Jno Connors	76	/	"	"	"	
Bernard Mullany	28	/	Servt.	"	"	
Thos. Dowd	21		Labr	"	"	
Jas Diamond	18		Servt	"	"	
~~Anne McGuicken~~	21		~~Farmer~~	"	"	
Arthur Mullan	18		Farmer	"	"	
Bridgt McNamee	20		"	"	"	
Thos Clarke	20		Farmer	"	"	
Edwd Riley	25		Labr	"	"	
Bridgt do	20			"	"	
Rosanna McMullan	56		Widow	"	"	
Wm Kehoe	36		Labr	"	"	
Mary Fitzhenry	16		Servt	"	"	
Jno do	12			"	"	
Pat Clarke	15	/	Labr	"	"	
Michl do	12	/	"	"	"	
Martin Clancy	23	/	"	"	"	
Peter do	14	/	"	"	"	
John Keefe	40	/	"	"	"	
Mary do	35	/	"	"	"	
Mary do	16		Servt	"	"	
John Walsh	19		Labr	"	"	
Richd Hyde	21		"	"	"	
Robt Malone	16		"	"	"	
Mary A Turner	34		Wife	England	"	
Mary do	7		"	"	"	
John do	6			"	"	
Robt Gamble	21		Labr	U. States	"	
Ellen Mullholland	20		Servt	Ireland	"	
John Clark	25	/	Labr	"	"	
Wm do	20	/	"	"	"	

Source: National Archives Microfilm Publication M425, Roll 83 (Philadelphia, Jan. 12–Dec. 10, 1860)

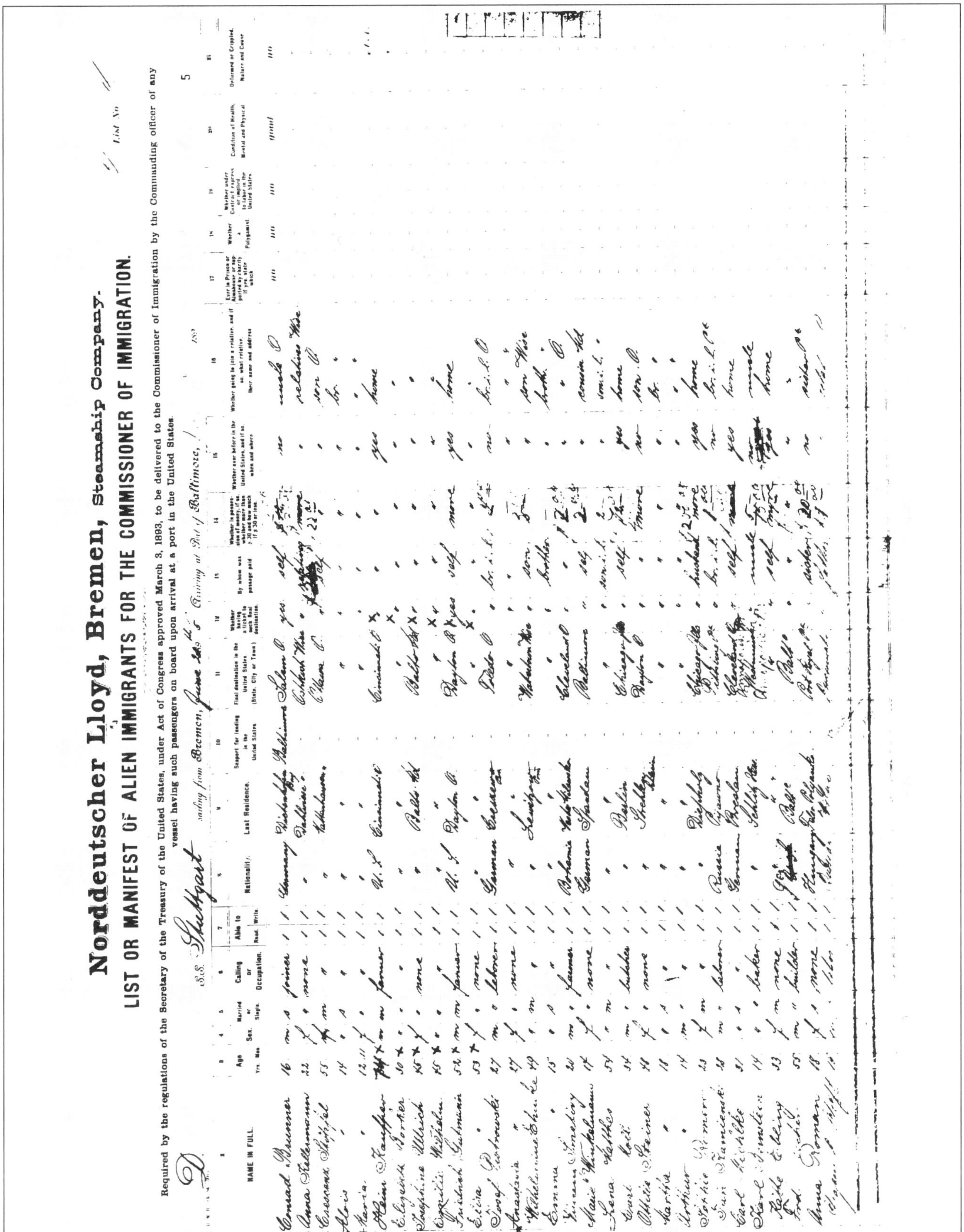

FIGURE 22   *Passenger List, 1895*

Source: National Archives Microfilm Publication T844, Roll 6 (Baltimore, Sept. 5, 1894–Dec. 28, 1895)

FIGURE 23 *Passenger List, 1910*

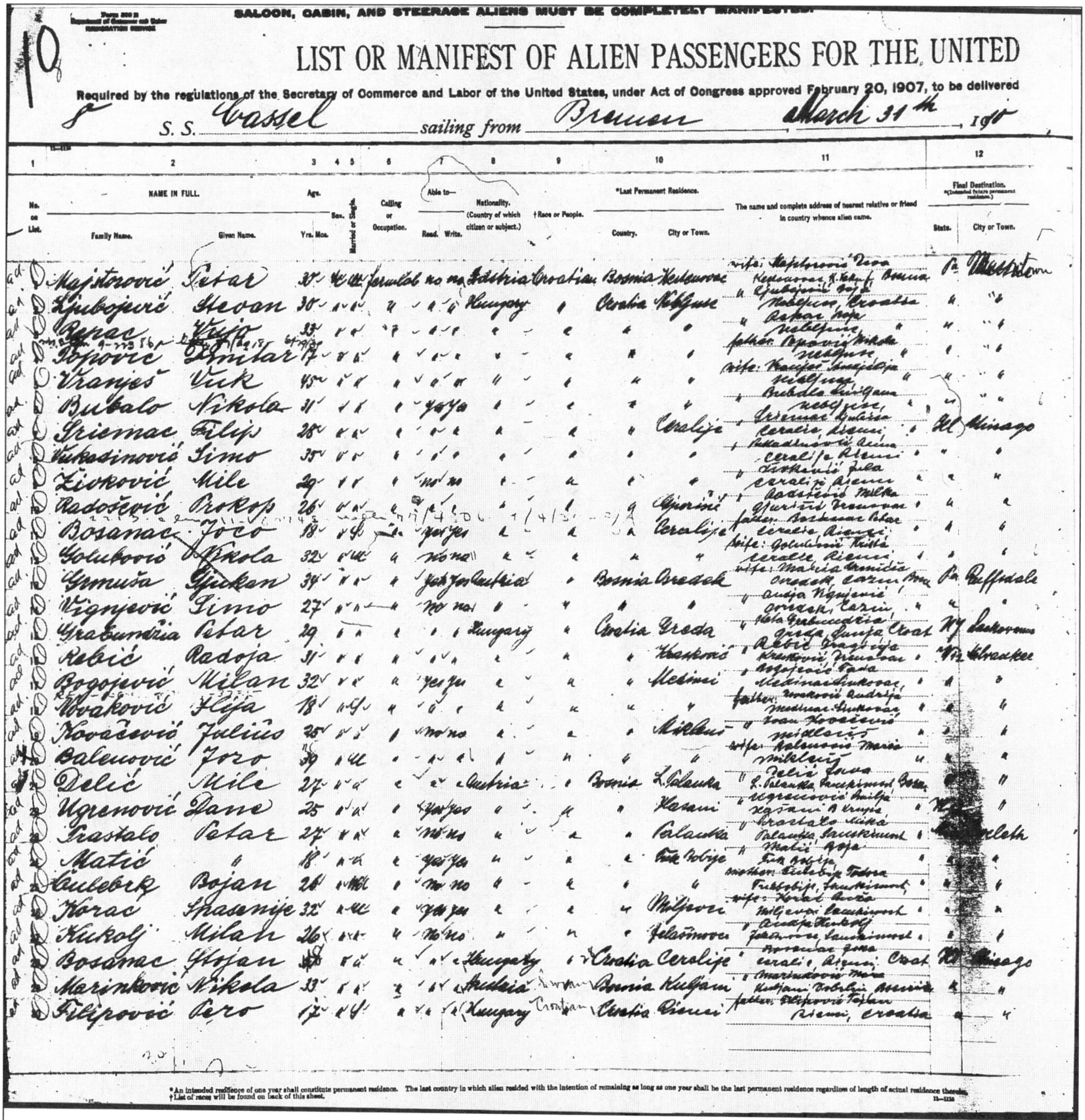

Source: National Archives Microfilm Publication T844, Roll 80 (Baltimore, Apr. 13, 1910–May 15, 1910)

FIGURE 23   continued

THIS SHEET IS FOR STEERAGE PASSENGERS.

STATES IMMIGRATION OFFICER AT PORT OF ARRIVAL.

to the United States Immigration Officer by the Commanding Officer of any vessel having such passengers on board upon arrival at a port in the United States.

Arriving at Port of *Baltimore* , APR 13 1910 , 19

REVIEWED WL.   List 8

microfilm copies available for research will have catalogs there for your use. In chapter 6 you were shown the steps to follow for buying or renting microfilms from the National Archives.

The National Archives provides microfilm copies of Records Group 36: Records of the U.S. Customs Service 1820–1891 and Records Group 85: Records of the Immigration and Naturalization Service, 1891–1957. In addition to the original passenger lists and registers of vessels arriving at many ports, microfilmed indexes to many of these records are available. You will find a list of the microfilms available for each port in the catalog *Immigrant & Passenger Arrivals* noted earlier. Chapter 2 of the National Archives and Records Administration's *Guide to Genealogical Research in the National Archives* provides a good description of these records, including the dates of microfilmed indexes and passenger lists for each port and the National Archives microfilm publication numbers for these records to be used when buying or renting the microfilm you need for your research.

If your previous research has revealed the date of your ancestor's arrival, the port, and the name of the ship he or she came on, use the microfilm of the passenger lists for that port. On each microfilm, the passenger lists are arranged in chronological order. You would look on the microfilm showing the records for ships docking at the port on the day your ancestor arrived. Look for the ship's name on the first page of each set of passenger lists. Once you have discovered the list for your ancestor's ship, you should be able to find his or her name on the passenger list.

If you do not know the entry port for your ancestors but have an approximate arrival date, use the National Archives catalog of microfilmed passenger list indexes that exist for all of the larger ports (except the New York index, in which there is a gap from 1847 to 1896). These indexes will reveal the date your ancestors arrived and the name of their ship. Find the microfilmed passenger list for their ship, and there you will discover your ancestors' notation.

Perhaps you know the port of entry but not the date of arrival or the name of your ancestor's ship. The passenger list indexes are again the resource to use. Search the index for your ancestor's port of entry until you find his or her name, then go to the microfilm showing the arrivals for the day indicated in the index.

If you know the name of the port and the year of arrival, but no indexes exist for your ancestor's port of entry or the indexes do not cover the year in which he or she arrived, use the microfilmed registers of ships arriving at U.S. ports to find the name of the ship. In the catalog *Immigrant & Passenger Arrivals* you will note that most ports kept a register of arriving ships arranged by date. Search the microfilmed register for your ancestor's port of entry and make a list of ships arriving during the time you feel he or she came to the United States. If you have an idea about the port or ports of embarkation your ancestor may have used, list only ships arriving from those ports. Next, find the microfilmed passenger lists for these ships and search the lists for your ancestor.

If your ancestor arrived at New York, Baltimore, Boston, or Philadelphia, there is another means of finding the ship: the Immigration Information Bureau's *Morton Allan Directory of European Passenger Steamship Arrivals* lists the names of all ships arriving at New York from 1890 to 1930 and those arriving at Baltimore, Boston, and Philadelphia from 1904 to 1926. It provides the date of arrival and the port each ship came from and lists the ships under the company that owned them. This directory can narrow your search for ancestors in passenger arrival lists. If you know when an ancestor arrived, this directory will name the ships that arrived in the United States at that time. If you have any clues about the port your ancestor's ship left from, you can narrow your list of ships to include only those ships that arrived at the appropriate time from the appropriate embarkation port. For example, if your ancestor came to one of these ports from Italy and arrived in May or June 1905, make a list of ships arriving here during those two months that came from Italian or French ports along the Mediterranean or Adriatic shore: Trieste, Venice, Genoa, Nice, and Marseille are examples.

What if you have no access to passenger list microfilms? If you know the name of the ship your ancestor arrived on and its date and port of arrival, the National Archives General Reference Branch in Washington, D.C., will provide a copy of the passenger list page on which your ancestor's name appears. If you do not have this information, staff at the Reference Services Branch will search for a person's records if the records for the port are indexed. To perform this search you must furnish the name of the passenger, the port of arrival, and an approximate date of arrival. There is a fee for these searches, and requests must be made on NATF form 81 "Order for Copies of Passenger Arrival Records." If a nearby research library or National Archives office cannot provide the forms, write to the Reference Service Branch (see Appendix A).

Ellis Island Arrivals

Although other immigrant receiving stations have older traditions, Ellis Island in New York Harbor has become a national shrine to the American immigrant. It opened its doors on January 1, 1892, and was closed November 3, 1954. A destructive fire temporarily closed it from June 14, 1897, to December 17, 1900, and immigrants were received at the New York Barge Office—which had served as the processing center before Ellis Island. Because of its role as the entry point to America's busiest port, and because its years of service encompass the high-water mark of immigration to this country, millions of Americans revere myths about the role of Ellis Island in their family history.

The New York passenger arrival records document the arrival of persons who entered the United States through Ellis Island. Other records were created as immigrants passed by the customs, immigration, and health officials at the facility. If you are interested in learning more about Ellis Island and information you can find there, write to the Ellis Island address listed in Appendix B.

Although efforts are under way to collect oral histories from employees who worked at Ellis Island as well as immigrants who arrived there, little is available for research at this time. In the future, officials hope to have a computer database containing all of the passenger arrival lists for Ellis Island indexed in such a way that visitors to the island can track down their ancestor's entry on the arrival lists. At the present time, exhibits that depict activities on Ellis Island during the height of its use as an immigrant receiving station are open to the public.[1]

The Ships That Brought Immigrants

Among the agencies you will find in Appendix B are museums at various ports that have collections of photographs as well as other artifacts from ships such as the one your ancestors boarded to come to America. A useful guide to these repositories is Hartley Edward Howe's *North America's Maritime Museums: An Annotated Guide*. Several other books provide you with the histories, descriptions, and photographs of sailing ships and steamships used in the immigrant trade: Eugene W. Smith's *Passenger Ships of the World Past and Present*, Michael J. Anuta's *Ships of our Ancestors*, Arnold Kludas's *Great Passenger Ships of the World*, and Carl C. Cutler's *Queens of the Western Ocean: The Story of America's Mail and Passenger Sailing Lines*. Books such as these will help you enrich your family's history by adding information about the ship in which immigrant ancestors traveled to the United States.

If you would like to learn more details about the process your ancestors followed to get here, refer to Michael Tepper's *American Passenger Arrival Records: A Guide to the Records of Immigrants Arriving at American Ports by Sail and Steam* and to John P. Colletta's *They Came in Ships*.

Passport Records

If your immigrant ancestor decided to visit the place of his or her birth, there would be records about that trip. The National Archives has in its collections a large number of passport applications dating from the late eighteenth century. Prior to about 1850 relatively few people applied for passports, and the information applications contain is meager. Applications generally provide travelers' current residences and, after 1869, their towns of birth and citizenship status. By 1889 applicants had to give their father's nationality. Most applications contain a physical description and by about 1910 a photograph, which may be of interest if you have no photographs of these ancestors or are trying to identify photos you have in your files.

Passport applications and several indexes to them (National Archives Record Groups 59 and 84) are available on microfilm from the National Archives. Record Group 84 also contains records of the Department of State from 1791 to 1925. You can request National Archives' staff to search the indexes for you or you can purchase films of interest from that office (see Appendix A). Your ancestors who lived abroad for extended periods often filed for passports or identity certificates at United States embassies and consulates abroad. Check with the research centers listed in Appendix A to see if they have the microfilms of Record Groups 59 and 84. The LDS Family History Library has a set available in Salt Lake City or through its branch Family History Centers.

Citizenship Records

Censuses and passenger arrival records are important, but so are local records that might contain information about a newcomer's former residence. Among the most valuable are naturalization records. During the colonial era, immigrants were expected to take an oath of allegiance to the monarch under whose authority the colonial government operated. After the founding of the United States, laws were eventually adopted that standardized the process a person followed to become a citizen. Although citizenship was a matter regulated by federal law, the provisions of these laws were administered by local and federal officials. Immigrants to the United States from other countries who wished to apply for citizenship did so at federal courts or any common law court of record, that is, a court with a clerk.

The first step in the naturalization process was to file a "declaration of intention" to naturalize at a local court. From 1798 to 1828 this could have been preceded by filing for a "certificate of report and registry" at a local court of record when the immigrant first arrived. In creating this report and registry, the clerk of the court was supposed to learn the alien's name, age, birthplace, nation of origin and allegiance, place of embarkation, and place of intended settlement. Not all clerks complied with the regulation; many recorded only an immigrant's name, age, and country of origin. Although the enforcement of the federal law requiring the report and registration was not uniform, you might find quite a bit of information about an immigrant ancestor who appeared before the local court clerk to file the required report. In some areas the declaration of intention to naturalize was combined with the registry and report. Not all immigrants filed their declaration of intention as soon as they arrived; the law prescribed that it had to be filed three years before they took the oath of citizenship. Since immigrants generally had to have five years' residence at the time of becoming a citizen, an alien could have lived in the United States for two years or longer before filing his or her declaration of intention. After 1911 most immigrants entering the country were registered by immigration authorities at the port of entry and given a certificate of arrival. This certificate replaced the declaration of intention to naturalize and had to be produced when a person filed a petition for naturalization.

The next step in becoming a citizen was to fulfill the residency requirement and file a petition at a nearby court to become naturalized. For most of our history, an alien had to live in the United States for a total of five years and in the state in which he or she applied for one year. If all requirements were met, a naturalization certificate would be issued after the applicant had taken an oath of allegiance to the Constitution and government of the United States.

Courts near where your ancestor lived should have at least a declaration of intention, petition for naturalization, and a record that a certificate of naturalization was issued. Normally, your ancestor was given a record of each action and the court also made an official record in its proceedings. Many courts kept separate records for actions involving naturalization, so you may be able to find copies of naturalization records among your ancestor's papers or court documents.

If you would like to know more about the history of naturalization in the United States, refer to John Newman's *Naturalization Processes and Procedures, 1790–1985*, the National Archives and Records Administration's *Federal Court Records: A Select Catalog of Microfilm Publications*, James C. and Lila L. Neagles's *Locating Your Immigrant Ancestor: A Guide to Naturalization Records*, and Eakle and Cerny's *The Source: A Guidebook of American Genealogy*.

Locating Naturalization Records

In 1906 Congress passed laws requiring that copies of all naturalization forms be filed with the Bureau of Immigration and Naturalization—which was created by the same act. Naturalization forms were standardized and the information required of an applicant became more detailed (see figures 24 and 25). This law has been a great help to family historians: these forms report where a person was born, where and when the person entered the United States, the court in which the forms were filed, and a personal description of the person. Even without knowledge of where an ancestor filed naturalization papers, you can request a copy of the person's files from the Immigration and Naturalization Service. There, office personnel have access to a nationwide alphabetical index that will make it possible to retrieve your ancestor's file. Check at your local immigration and naturalization office for a copy of the application form. Knowing an ancestor's name, birth date, and place of arrival will expedite the search.

If your immigrant ancestor became naturalized before 1906, you will have to contact the courts for the area in which he or she lived to see which ones have naturalization records. If you are unsure where an immigrant ancestor began the naturalization process, start with the first place you know that person lived. The clerks at the county, city, or federal courts in the area can tell you where naturalization records are kept. Often the federal records are at the nearest regional National Archives. Nonfederal courts generally maintain their records in the court clerk's office, although some of the older records may have been transferred to a state archives or historical society.

Some immigrants filed their declaration of intention to naturalize in the port city of their arrival. They may have completed the naturalization process in the city in which they finally settled. Immigrant ancestors may have completed the requirements for citizenship in several localities. Your search must follow the trail they leave as they move from one community to another. Here, census records may help you. Note the states in

FIGURE 24   *Bureau of Immigration and Naturalization Declaration of Intention*

UNITED STATES OF AMERICA

Department of Commerce and Labor
BUREAU OF IMMIGRATION AND NATURALIZATION
DIVISION OF NATURALIZATION

DECLARATION OF INTENTION

(Invalid for all purposes seven years after the date hereof)

State of Utah.
County of Salt Lake. } ss : In the Third District. Court of Salt Lake County, Utah.

I, *Joso Pejnovic* , aged 37 years, occupation *Liquor Dealer* , do declare on oath (affirm) that my personal description is: Color *White* , complexion *Dark* , height 5 feet 9 inches, weight 200 pounds, color of hair *Black* , color of eyes *Brown* , other visible distinctive marks *None* ; I was born in *Smilan Austria* , on the 20th day of *May* , anno Domini 1871 ; I now reside at *20 N 3rd W St Salt Lake City Utah* I emigrated to the United States of America from *Bremen Germany* on the vessel* *Dresden Hamburg American Line* ; my last foreign residence was *Smilan, Austria* It is my bona fide intention to renounce forever all allegiance and fidelity to any foreign prince, potentate, state, or sovereignty, and particularly to *Francis Joseph Emperor of Austria* , of which I am now a ~~citizen~~ subject ; I arrived at the port of *Baltimore* , in the State Territory District of *Maryland* on or about the 29 day of *April* , anno Domini 1902 ; I am not an anarchist; I am not a polygamist nor a believer in the practice of polygamy; and it is my intention in good faith to become a citizen of the United States of America and to permanently reside therein : SO HELP ME GOD.

Joso Pejnovic
(Original signature of declarant.)

Subscribed and sworn to (affirmed) before me this *Seventeenth* day of *September* , anno Domini 1908

[SEAL.]

J. M. Eldredge Jr ;
Clerk of the Third District Court.

By *H. A. King* , Deputy Clerk.

If the alien arrived otherwise than by vessel, the character of conveyance or name of transportation company should be given.

Source: Utah State Archives and Records Services, Naturalization Records, 1853–1936 (Family History Library Microfilm 1654483)

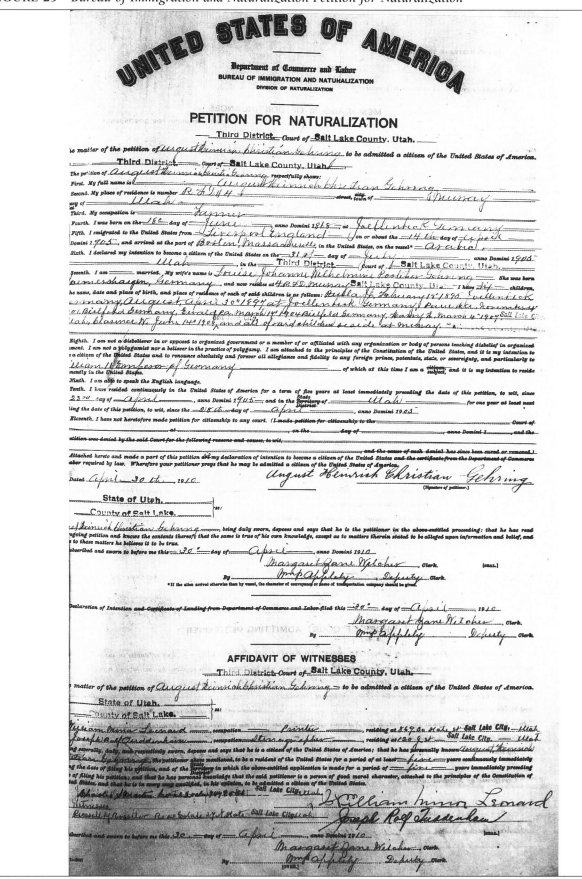

which children were born to these ancestors and use census indexes to identify the communities in which they lived in each state.

For a fee, most courts will provide copies of naturalization papers. Many of these local naturalization records have been microfilmed by the LDS Church and are available at the Family History Library in Salt Lake City or through one of its branch family history centers (see Appendix A). Everton's *Handy Book for Genealogists,* Eichholz's *Ancestry's Red Book,* and Bentley's *County Courthouse Book* all provide addresses of local county clerks and court clerks with information on the availability of local naturalization records. The state historical society or state archives where your ancestors lived may also have information about local naturalization records.

Chapter 3 of the National Archives *Guide to Genealogical Research in the National Archives* provides an excellent discussion of naturalization records. In it you will learn about a photocopy collection and partial index of New York and New England naturalization records. The regional National Archives in New York City has an index to photocopies of naturalization documents filed in New York City courts from 1792 to 1906.

Another area that attracted many nineteenth- and twentieth-century immigrants was northern Illinois. The National Archives–Great Lakes Region in Chicago has a Soundex index to naturalizations in northern Illinois (including Chicago and Cook County after 1871), eastern Wisconsin, eastern Iowa, and northwestern Indiana.

The National Archives and Records Administration continues to microfilm naturalization records from federal courts. For example, in *Prologue,* the journal of the National Archives, you can keep posted on newly available microfilms. In the summer 1992 (volume 4, number 2) issue there were two microfilm publications described that contain naturalization records: *Index to Naturalization Petitions of the United States District Court for the Eastern District of New York, 1865–1957* (M1164, 142 rolls) and *Soundex Index to Naturalization Petitions for the United States District and Circuit Courts, Northern District of Illinois, and Immigration and Naturalization Service District 9* [Chicago], *1840–1950* (M1285, 179 rolls). When you learn about newly microfilmed federal records, contact the nearest regional National Archives to see if it has them. You can also purchase films from the National Archives Publications Services Branch (NEPS) (see Appendix A).

If your immigrant ancestors settled in large urban areas at any time before they became citizens, check with local public and private libraries, historical soci-eties, and regional national archives to learn about their collections involving immigrants in their city. The Newberry Library in Chicago, New York Public Library, Boston Public Library, Historical Society of Pennsylvania, Balch Institute for Ethnic Studies in Philadelphia, and Immigration History Research Center in St. Paul have gone to great efforts to collect records of immigrants who came to their regions. Other libraries and research centers that are in large cities or that specialize in immigrant records are listed in Appendixes A and B. Check both appendixes for research centers near you as well as centers in the regions in which your ancestors lived.

Using Naturalization Records

Although pre-twentieth-century naturalization papers may contain only a few details about your ancestors, they permit you to verify when ancestors arrived and get a look at the spelling of their given names and surnames early in their lives as Americans, since many ancestors changed their names shortly after arriving here. Sometimes their names were changed by clerks who misspelled them, and ancestors may have decided to keep the new spelling as an "Americanized" version of their name. Naturalization documents often help us trace these spelling changes. You may find, for example, that a family spelled its name *Koch* on the passenger list when they arrived but translated it to *Cook* by the time they filed their petition for naturalization. Immigrants commonly used the American translation of their original given names and surnames. It was also popular to choose a phonetic spelling that retained the original sound of a name. *Warnecke,* for example, might become *Varnicky.* You may find the original spelling of a name in the declaration of intention after searching for the changed spelling an ancestor used in the petition for naturalization. This original spelling will be the key to finding the ancestor on passenger lists and in the records of his or her hometown abroad.

Some clerks recorded more details in naturalization records than others. Often an age is mentioned that will be helpful in verifying a birth date. We might learn more than we anticipate—a birthplace, for example—if we will be persistent in seeking out the records that document how our ancestors became citizens.

For most of our history, the wife and minor children of a naturalized citizen enjoyed citizenship also. A woman who married a United States citizen could also claim citizenship by virtue of the marriage. Therefore, you will not find naturalization records for the wives and children of your immigrant ancestors who themselves were also immigrants. Oddly enough, before 1922 a woman marrying a citizen of another nation lost her American citizenship and was treated as a citizen of her husband's country.

Wartime Records

Some ancestors may have obtained their citizenship through military service. As early as 1862, federal legislation permitted aliens who had enlisted in the regular or volunteer army to be admitted as citizens with only one year's residency in the United States. In May 1918, Congress passed an act that allowed any alien with military service during World War I to file a petition for naturalization without proof of five years' residency in the United States. These veterans were not exempt from filing a petition for naturalization, just from residence requirements and the preliminary declaration of intention to naturalize. Look for their naturalization petition in local courts or, after 1906, at the Immigration and Naturalization Service. Today, immigrants can still be excused from some naturalization requirements through military service.

Try to find your immigrant ancestor's military file if you feel that person may have served. As explained in chapter 5, if it was in a local unit, the state archives or historical society can help you find the files. If the ancestor served in the armed forces of the United States, follow the procedures for obtaining military records outlined in chapter 6.

Draft registration records for World War I and World War II contain personal data for many immigrants. This resource was also discussed in chapter 6. Following the instructions there may provide additional data on where and when your immigrant ancestor was born.

Records also have been created to register aliens thought to be a threat to the United States during wartime. German immigrants living in the United States during World War I and Japanese Americans interned in camps during World War II are examples. The National Archives–Central Plains Region has records from the U.S. attorneys and marshals of the Kansas District as part of Record Group 118 (1873–1918), which include "World War I alien registrations and permit applications, 1917–18." The documents were filed by German immigrants residing within the district and include each person's residence, date and place of birth, years of residence in the United States, recent employment history, physical description and photograph, names and personal information about their spouses and children, date and port of arrival, and draft and

naturalization status. This is an example of the type of record you may find in other regional National Archives offices. You must search the catalog for the regional National Archives responsible for federal records in the area where your immigrant ancestors lived if you suspect that they may have been recorded in this type of record. Refer to chapter 6 for help in finding the published catalogs of regional National Archives offices.

Approximately 110,000 persons of Japanese ancestry were affected by federal evacuation and internment orders during World War II. The two agencies set up to direct these activities were the Wartime Civil Control Administration and the War Relocation Authority. These agencies created several types of records that contain a great deal of information about individuals under their authority. Through finding family members in the files of these agencies, you will discover spouses and children, birth dates and places, previous residences, education, employment history, medical history, and citizenship status along with other items of information.

Records of the Wartime Civil Control Administration and the War Relocation Authority are part of Record Group 210, Records of the War Relocation Authority, and are available at the National Archives in Washington, D.C. Records less than fifty years old are restricted to use by evacuees themselves or their legal representatives. Others must obtain written permission from the person whose records are requested or the person's legal representative.

Similar records exist for civilians and military personnel of other national origins excluded from sensitive military areas from 1941 to 1948. The documents are part of Record Group 153, Records of the Office of the Judge Advocate General of the Army. These files record proceedings involving German and Italian immigrants and U.S. citizens of German or Italian ancestry as well as others. Files are arranged alphabetically and detail each person's date and place of birth, marital status, employment, military service, and any legal proceedings involving the individual.

If you have evidence that these files may contain information about one or more ancestors, you can visit or write the nearest regional National Archives or the National Archives in Washington, D.C., depending on which repository has the records you need. Start by contacting the regional National Archives office nearest the place where your relative lived during World War II. You can also write for copies of needed records if they are indexed or arranged alphabetically. To be certain that your request can be filled, telephone first to find out the current procedure for this type of request (see Appendix A).

Native American Records

Native Americans can use tribal records, the records of the Bureau of Indian Affairs, census records, and even congressional records to find forebears. Their unique position as citizens of nations (tribes) within a nation (the United States) benefits the researcher because tribal record keepers chronicled many personal activities. Today records by and about Native American tribes may be found at state historical societies and archives in states in which your ancestor's tribe lived. The records of tribal councils, kept at local tribal offices, also provide personal information about Native American ancestors. The Bureau of Indian Affairs records at agency offices in states in which ancestors lived or at the nearest regional National Archives will also provide information about relations between the federal government and individual members of Native American tribes. Refer to chapter 6 for information about Native Americans in the United States decennial censuses. Because of the role of Congress in approving treaties with Native American tribes, names and other identifying information may appear for individual members of tribes in congressional documents. You will need to be familiar with the history of your tribe and its dealings with the federal government if you wish to find these records. Reference librarians at local college or university libraries or at the state historical society can help you find histories of your tribe. University documents librarians at state universities in states in which your Native American ancestors lived will also be key resources. These librarians will be able to help you determine where the acts of Congress are filed that involve your tribe. Two National Archives publications that will help you find federal records describing your Native American ancestors are Edward Hill's *Guide to Records in the National Archives of the United States Relating to American Indians* and *American Indians: A Select Catalog of National Archives Microfilm Publications.*

Additional valuable resources for researchers include the journals, histories, reports, and diaries of missionaries, pioneers, and others who lived among Native Americans. These records are often found at state and local historical societies (see Appendix A). Other resources include university libraries that collect Native American resources relating to tribes that lived in the area served by the university. In addition, Jimmy B. Parker's "American Indian Records and Research" in *Ethnic Genealogy: A Research Guide*, edited by Jessie Carney Smith, is one of the best guides for persons tracing Native American ancestors.

African American Records

African Americans who were not free did not appear in a United States census under their own names until 1870. Prior to that they were only statistics in the census. (See the discussion of censuses in chapter 6 for more information.) If you are tracing an African American slave heritage prior to 1870 you must use well-known records such as censuses and land records but subject them to methods that are not so common. Trace the names of your ancestors' slave holders in censuses, and then try to find the records of slave sales among local land records.

Often your only source for the names of slave ancestors will be the stories and traditions you have gathered through interviews and searching in family papers. When you have connected each generation back to slave ancestors, look for their names, places of residence, ages, birthplaces, and names of family members in the records of the Freedman's Bureau and Freedman's Savings and Trust Company—both created by Congress in 1865. (These records are available on National Archives microfilms at regional archives and some of the research centers in Appendix A.) The purpose of both government agencies was to provide funds and opportunities for African Americans to own land and provide their own livelihood. Read more about these records in the National Archives and Records Administration's *Guide to Genealogical Research in the National Archives* and Debra L. Newman's *Black History: A Guide to Civilian Records in the National Archives.* Check the indexes of both books under "Freedman's Bureau." For an example of how state, local, and family records can be used to uncover African American family history, check David Thackery and Dee Woodtor's *Case Studies in Afro-American Genealogy* and Thackery's *Afro-American Family History at the Newberry Library: A Research Guide and Bibliography.*

If you know the names of the slave holders of ancestors, check with libraries and historical societies in the counties and states in which they lived for biographies and family histories of the slave holder families. For more help tracing African American families, refer to Charles L. Blockson's "Black American Records and Research" in *Ethnic Genealogy: A Research Guide*, edited by Jessie Carney Smith.

If your ancestors were free African Americans, you will find them in the records described in chapters 5 and 6. Use Denise M. Glover's *Voices of the Spirit: Sources for Interpreting the African-American Experience* to identify the many materials available on African American history. *Black Studies: A Select Catalog of National*

Archives Microfilm Publications by the National Archives will help you identify federal African American records on microfilm.

Among the nearly 24 million African Americans tabulated in the 1990 U.S. census are a number whose families immigrated to the United States from Africa since the middle of the nineteenth century. Discovering information about them will require the use of many of the resources discussed elsewhere in this chapter: passenger lists, naturalization records, religious records, etc.

Religious Records

Almost from the date of the first settlement in North America, religious officials recorded the christenings, marriages, and burials in their congregations. Sometimes the place of origin of immigrant parishioners was listed in these records. This was particularly true in Christian congregations where the language of the church service was not English. Local clerics generally spoke your ancestor's native language and may have been trained or ordained in the mother country. Non-Christian religions also kept records. The key to finding records of this type is an examination of the community's history in which your immigrant ancestors settled. If your ancestors did not have a shrine, synagogue, or church where they lived, they may have traveled to a neighboring town to worship. Community or county histories should tell you where people living in the area attended religious services. Another way to find out about local churches or congregations is to use local directories and telephone books, as discussed in chapter 5.

Were your ancestors Quakers, Huguenots, Shakers, Mennonites, Moravians, Mormons, Muslims, Buddhists, Shintoists, or Hindus? Many of our ancestors came here as part of a religious group that immigrated to America in the hope of a better life. Those who followed often sought out communities where earlier fellow believers had settled. If you are unable to find your immigrant ancestor's place of origin, perhaps learning the origin of your ancestor's local religious leaders will show that your ancestor came from the same locality. You learned in chapter 5 about local histories that describe the communities in which your ancestors lived. Histories of local congregations name members and describe their role in the life of the congregation. Numerous books and periodicals by and about the members of specific religious groups and the societies they formed to preserve their heritage will prove to be valuable resources. In the histories and other publications about religions brought to America by immigrants you may discover

the foreign homeland of an immigrant forebear. Again, you can find out about societies and associations devoted to the history of these groups and the genealogies of their members by consulting the directories of associations listed earlier in this chapter and in the index.

Employment Records

If you know where your immigrant ancestors settled, you can also try to find records about them from their employers. Employee files generally indicate when and where employees were born and provide other details of interest, including names of parents, spouses, and children; evidence of the naturalization process; and medical records. These employee files will also help you understand your ancestor better because they may contain information about job performance and the various assignments they filled on their jobs. Personnel files can give you a view of your ancestor that will be found in no other source. Refer to chapters 5 and 6 for more information about local and national employment records.

Many immigrants who wanted to earn a living from farming, ranching, or other occupations requiring land applied to purchase federal land or participate in the homestead land program. In the files detailing their acquisition of this land will be records of their naturalization process. They could obtain land if they had not been naturalized only upon proof that they had filed a declaration of intention to naturalize. Refer to chapter 6 for help in locating federal land records.

IMMIGRANTS IN FOREIGN RECORDS

Governments in your immigrant ancestors' homelands created records registering people who emigrated to the United States and elsewhere. Some of these records have been copied and brought to the United States where you can use them to learn about your ancestors' origins. Emigration records that remain in archives and libraries abroad can be found and used with a little patient research. Sometimes your immigrant ancestor stopped off in another country before continuing on to the United States. These transit countries also registered transients as they entered and then left.

America via Canada

One of the most important transit countries for immigration to the United States is Canada. Almost since the beginning of immigration to North America, settlers used Canadian ports even though their final destination was somewhere in the present-day United States. Immigration from different parts of the world to the United States was restricted at times by law or maritime regulations enforced to protect the safety of ship passengers. During these times Canadian ports were quite popular. Immigrants felt they could settle temporarily in Canada and move to the United States later. At other times it was cheaper to travel through a Canadian port. Whatever the reason, some of the ancestors that you cannot find in United States immigration or passenger records may have come through Canada. On other occasions, United States citizens—among them naturalized citizens—returning to North America from abroad crossed the Pacific or Atlantic on ships bound for Canadian ports and returned home via a United States/Canadian border crossing station.

Dr. Blair Poelman, a reference consultant at the Family History Library and the library's resident expert on Canadian records, has introduced many researchers to a unique set of records that reflect Canada's important role in United States immigration history: *Soundex Index to Canadian Border Entries through the St. Albans, Vt. District, 1895–1924* (National Archives Microfilm Publication M1461, 400 rolls, 16 mm); *Alphabetical Index to Canadian Border Entries through Small Ports in Vermont, 1895–1924* (M1462, 6 rolls, 16 mm); and *Soundex Index to Entries into the St. Albans, Vt. District through Canadian Pacific and Atlantic Ports, 1924–1952* (M1463, 98 rolls, 16 mm). The *Alphabetical Index* contains some entries not found in the Soundexes. These are not original records but are a collection of cards arranged alphabetically or as a Soundex—by the sound of the immigrant's name. They contain information about immigrants extracted from original passenger ship manifests and registration documents created by the United States Immigration and Naturalization Service and are available on microfilm from the National Archives and Records Service and at some of the centers listed in Appendix A. The original ships' manifests have also been microfilmed: *Manifests of Passengers Arriving in the St. Albans, Vt. District through Canadian Pacific and Atlantic Ports, 1895–1954* (M1464, 640 rolls) and *Manifests of Passengers Arriving in the St. Albans, Vt. District through Canadian Pacific Ports, 1929–1949* (M1465, 25 rolls).

Some scattered passenger lists exist for Canadian ports prior to 1865; an index has been prepared for the lists from 1817 to 1831 and is on National Archives of Canada microfilm reel C-4252. Microfilms also exist for passenger manifests of ships arriving at Québec City, Québec, from 1865 to 1919; Halifax, Nova Scotia, from 1880 to 1919; North Sydney, Nova Scotia, from 1906 to 1919; Saint John, New Brunswick, from 1900 to 1918; Vancouver, British Columbia, from 1905 to 1919; Victoria, British Columbia, and some small Pacific ports from 1905 to 1919. Because these records are not indexed, you must have an idea of when and where an ancestor entered Canada.

The Canadian Employment and Immigration Commission has records on all immigrants arriving at Canadian ports after 1918. Access is subject to Canadian privacy laws. Direct your inquiries to the Query Response Center, Employment and Immigration Canada (see Appendix B).

Americans of Chinese origin who cannot find ancestors' arrival records at United States ports between 1885 and 1949 may want to check the eighteen volumes of registers of Chinese immigrants covering those years that are on microfilm at the National Archives of Canada. They are arranged numerically by serial number and declaration number in rough chronological order. These records may contain the immigrant's village of origin in China as well as date and place of arrival. The National Archives of Canada also has the records of the Chinese Immigration Service, including registration forms, personal files, and name indexes. These latter records have not yet been microfilmed.

Microfilmed records at the National Archives of Canada may be obtained through interlibrary loan at your local public library. Contact the National Archives of Canada for instructions at the address shown in Appendix A. You may also want to request a copy of Janine Roy's *Tracing Your Ancestors in Canada*.

European Emigration Records

Officials for the European ports at which your ancestors boarded ships for America also kept records of departing passengers and ships. These records often contain more information than the lists created on this side of the Atlantic. They may identify the hometown or last residence of an emigrant as well as the person's occupation, age, and marital status.

Some records have been damaged by wars; others perished through neglect. The port of Bremen, Germany, for example, was one of Europe's busiest emigrant embarkation points from the middle of the nineteenth century. Unfortunately, only fragments of its records have survived to turn up at various places. The bulk of the originals held at the Bremen City Archives were destroyed by archivists pressured to find space for incoming documents, and the remaining lists—

post-1907—were destroyed during the Allied bomb-ings of World War II.[2]

If you have been able to find ancestors in passenger lists from the entry port to the United States, note the port their ship sailed from, which is generally given at the beginning of the passenger list. Unfortunately, many European port records are not available in the United States. The government archives for the districts, depart-ments, or regions of the ports may have original passen-ger lists or lists of emigrants. To find the address of the archives nearest the port from which your ancestors embarked for America, visit your local public or college library to use Europa Publications' *The World of Learning 1993.* In it are lists of archives, libraries, learned socie-ties, colleges, universities, and museums in each country of the world. Each entry provides the address, tele-phone number, telefax number, and director's name (or the names of department heads in the case of schools).

Write the archives nearest the port of embarkation to learn about the existence of emigrant or passenger rec-ords and whether or not the archive provides a research service. Although most archives do not maintain a re-search staff, they may have suggestions about how to hire a local researcher to investigate the records for you. If not, consult the *World of Learning* again. A letter to a local college or university asking for the names of stu-dents who would be willing to work as your on-site re-searcher may provide you with the support you need. Write first to language departments or departments of history, which are most likely to have students studying English or studying an aspect of history that may relate to your project. You may also find help by writing to local public and college librarians overseas who may know of local researchers who could help you. Be cer-tain to ask about the fee before you hire someone. If the fee is more than you wish to pay, explain your position in a letter and let the person respond. Perhaps the re-searcher can think of a way to do the work and still stay within your budget.

A number of European emigration research centers have resources of great value to Americans seeking in-formation about European ancestors; several are listed in Appendix B. Before hiring a researcher to dig in the records of European archives, write to the appropriate emigration research center to determine its ability to assist with your research.

European Emigration Records Available in the United States

Among the Family History Library's 1.5 million rolls of microfilmed records are many from other countries.

Before traveling to your ancestor's home country or employing a researcher there, visit a local LDS Family History Center where you can check the Family History Library catalog and determine if records from your family's community are available on loan from Salt Lake City. Using the Family History Library catalog locality search, you can determine if the library has records from the town where your forebears lived. For example, if you looked up the city of Braunschweig in the pre-World War I Duchy of Braunschweig in Germany, you would find microfilms of church registers showing chris-tenings, marriages, and burials from the early nineteenth century; wills, tax lists, and court records from the Middle Ages; and among other records, civil registration of births, marriages, and deaths from about 1805. If your ancestors came from Oberhausbergen in the French department of Haut Rhin, you could look up this town and find that there are microfilmed civil registration records from 1793 and church records from the sixteenth century.

The Family History Library's microfilming program is active in many countries around the world. Space does not permit a complete list of every country from which the Library is acquiring records. Perhaps an excerpt from a now-outdated report of Library microfilming will help you visualize the magnitude of this program. The list of the countries from which records had been received dur-ing 1992 included Austria, Belgium, Greece, Nether-lands, Norway, Poland, Sweden, Yugoslavia (Croatia), England, and Scotland.[3] Unmentioned were continuing projects in other European countries and in South Africa, Australia, Japan, Korea, the Philippines, China, India, and several countries in Latin America. The Fam-ily History Library microfilming program includes only records that identify individuals and families by name. Generally, these records are produced by governments and religious and family organizations in each country.

Copies of emigration records from Denmark, Fin-land, France, Germany, Norway, and Sweden are avail-able in the United States. Records from these countries are available at the LDS Family History Library in Salt Lake City and through its many local LDS Family His-tory Centers. Other libraries also have copies of these microfilms—check with the libraries and research cen-ters listed in Appendixes A and B.

By 1845 Bremen and Hamburg, Germany, were the busiest embarkation points for emigrants from central and eastern Europe. The reason Hamburg and Bremen drew people from many parts of Europe is simple. Hamburg- and Bremen-based travel agents advertised relatively cheap fares on ships bound for America and elsewhere. Many emigrants also traveled to Hamburg and Bremen in hopes of finding work in these bustling trade centers that would provide the money for their ticket to America.

You may examine records created by Hamburg authorities to identify people passing through the city on their way to new homes outside Europe. The passenger lists cover the years 1850 to 1934. The lists for the years 1850 through 1854 are arranged in gross alphabetical order by surnames. That is, if your ancestor's name began with an *A,* you may be required to search the entire *A* section of the passenger list to find him or her. Annual indexes to these records begin with 1855, providing the name of the emigrant, the name of the ship, the date the ship left port, and the page number of the passenger manifest upon which the name appears. Each index is again arranged only by the first letter of the emigrant's surname. The LDS Family History Library has an additional index to records of most of the emigrants leaving through Hamburg from 1856 to 1871 that is arranged as a single alphabetical index. Due to transcription error, some passengers were omitted from this index. If an ancestor does not appear in it, consult the regular index for the year of his or her emigration to America.

When using these lists, keep in mind that from 1854 to 1910 there are two sets of passenger lists and indexes, the "direct" lists and the "indirect" lists. The direct lists and indexes identify passengers who boarded a ship in Hamburg that would take them to their ultimate destination. The indirect lists and indexes recorded those persons who sailed aboard a ship from Hamburg for an intermediate port at which they would board another ship that would carry them to their destination. Refer to the LDS Family History Library's *Resource Guide: The Hamburg Passenger Lists, 1854–1934* by the Church of Jesus Christ of Latter-day Saints for further details. As with today, quick-thinking travel agents were able to put together indirect passage packages that were less expensive than the direct.

The LDS Family History Library also has a collection of passport applications processed by the police officials in Hamburg from 1851 to 1929. Once in Hamburg, law required that migrants, like all inhabitants, register with the police. When emigrants were ready to depart they would de-register with the police and apply for travel papers. Emigrants knew that upon departure from Hamburg and arrival in the United States they would need identity papers showing their last place of residence as well as a birthplace. Those who either had no papers from their hometown or had lived in Hamburg prior to departure sought the needed passport from Hamburg police officials. Among these applicants were many who were on their way to the United States from Scandinavia—

especially Denmark—and central and eastern Europe. This collection of records is indexed by surname, making it easy to determine if a hard-to-find ancestor lived in Hamburg before coming to America. Index entries show the name, birth date, and birthplace of the applicant.

Strasbourg, France, is an example of another type of city that served as a transit point for emigrants bound for America. This city was an important link between central and eastern European emigrants and the ports of France—especially Le Havre. It was at Strasbourg that many people crossed the border from Germany into France. French officials at Strasbourg kept records of persons permitted to enter France. Many German, Polish, Czech, Austrian, and Hungarian ancestors passed through Strasbourg. Some of these records are available at the LDS Family History Library and on loan at local LDS Family History Centers. One set of lists covers 1817 to 1866 and is indexed. Another list on twenty rolls of microfilm at the Family History Library identifies Polish emigrants passing through the Strasbourg area from 1831 to 1870. A third collection of records on thirteen rolls of film identifies about a half-million people living in the Alsatian region from 1871 to 1872—as it was becoming part of Germany after the Franco-Prussian War. These lists are not indexed, but they contain the names of many persons who later emigrated to the United States from that region. Some of those recorded were emigrants from other parts of the German or Austrian Empires who were staying in the area prior to leaving for destinations outside Europe.

The LDS Family History Library has the largest collection of immigration records in the United States. Learn about these collections by checking the latest issue of its catalog at your nearest LDS Family History Center. The Family History Library continues to publish valuable brochures about how to trace immigrant ancestors from different ethnic groups. Write to the address for this library in Appendix A for an up-to-date list of publications.

GeneSys, a division of Dynix, Inc., of Provo, Utah, is now marketing the LDS Church's *FamilySearch* to public and private libraries and other research centers. The Family History Library catalog—a part of FamilySearch—may be available in a library in your community. FamilySearch is discussed in greater detail in chapter 3.

Archives and Libraries in Other Countries

If there are no records for your ancestral hometown in the collections of the Family History Library, research abroad will be needed. In most countries records are kept first by the office or agency that created them. When they become old enough that they are less used or when the office space is insufficient for their storage, they are moved to a records management center or archives. Sometimes local libraries, research centers, or historical societies become the repository for older records. To find where records are in other countries, follow the steps outlined in chapters 5 and 6. First, determine where your ancestor lived, then find the addresses of government offices or private agencies such as religious organizations and employers that are responsible for records in a particular area today. Write and ask them for information about records that will document the life events of your forebears: birth, marriage, death, census, burial or cemetery records, military, tax, school, court, probate, land, and other records for that culture that name individuals and describe their activities.

Just as local libraries, historical or genealogical societies, and archives become your base of operations in the United States, parallel agencies become the focal points of your activities in other countries. In all of your dealings with government officials, librarians, and archivists, remember that it is not their *primary* task to serve family researchers. Be patient. In initial inquiries, ask questions that require yes or no answers or short responses. Be specific in your questions. Instead of asking for a list of all of the records they have, request information about two or three specific types of documents: "Do you have records of birth, marriage, and death?" "Does your office maintain records of land transactions or of court proceedings relating to the estates of deceased persons?" Determine if they can search records for you or if you must do it in person or through an agent.

Most countries have a national archives system; for some, it is in the nation's capital. In some nations the national archives system has branch archives throughout the country that preserve not only the records of the central government but the records of local provinces, states, or regions. Other nations delegate records preservation to provincial, departmental, or state archivists and their staffs. You will also find city archives in many countries of western Europe and in their former colonies.

Employees in the office of the national archivist can generally tell you about how records are cared for in a country. These people may even be able to supply the addresses of local archives for the area in which your ancestor lived. The country's embassy or one of its consulates can give you the address of the national archives. You could also check *The World of Learning,*

cited earlier, or the *International Directory of Archives* compiled by the International Council on Archives and published as volume 33 of its journal *Archivum*. An example will help you understand this approach to finding records in other countries.

Suppose your ancestor came to the United States aboard a ship from Naples. On page 814 of Europa Publications' *The World of Learning,* 44th edition, you find the address of the Archivo di Stato di Napoli, founded in 1808. Among the many libraries listed on the same page is the Biblioteca della Società Napoletana di Storia Patria founded in 1876. You decide to write to both the archives and the library, which appears to collect materials relating to the history of this region. You question them about passenger lists, passport records, and other records of emigrants and request information about indexes or special records created to identify emigrants.

What if your ancestor came from England or France? In *The World of Learning* entry for the United Kingdom you will find a large number of libraries listed but only the address of the Public Record Office in London—equivalent to the National Archives of the United States. A note at the beginning of the entry points out that each county has its own record office (archives) and that they are listed in two publications: *Record Repositories in Great Britain: A Geographical Directory* from the Royal Commission on Historical Manuscripts and *British Archives: A Guide to Archival Sources in the United Kingdom* by Janet Foster. In these publications you will find the addresses and holdings descriptions for each county record office. In *The World of Learning* entry for France many libraries are listed but none of the state-governed departmental archives. There is, however, an address for the national archive administration (Direction des Archives de France). A letter to this address requesting information about archives near the embarkation port of your ancestors should produce the needed address.

One book for quick information as well as brief, up-to-date bibliographies about countries of the world is Brian Hunter's *The Statesman's Year-Book 1993–94.* It will help you understand many things about the countries in which your predecessors lived as well as provide addresses of foreign embassies in the United States and United States embassies in foreign countries. The embassies of the United States in other countries can often help you get in touch with local record keepers abroad. If your attempts to get help from foreign embassies in this country fail, write to the United States Embassy in the country of interest.

If your ancestors came from Germany, Ernest Thode's *Address Book for Germanic Genealogy* will save time. In it are many of the addresses you need, both in the United States and abroad. Although the book's focus is German-speaking Europe, Thode has included addresses of archives and libraries for several other countries as well as many of their embassies and consulates in the United States.

By contacting the nearest embassy or consulate for your ancestors' homeland, you can find the addresses of the archives, libraries, and registrars of vital statistics. *The World of Learning* will also give you addresses of archives, libraries, museums, and universities in the area in which your ancestors lived.

Locating Birth, Marriage, and Death Records Abroad

Birth, marriage, and death records are a key source to use when attempting to place your ancestors in the context of a place, a time, and a family. Today we take it for granted that everyone is registered at birth, usually by state or local officers of the bureau of vital statistics. When someone wants to marry, we assume they apply for a marriage license at the local county or city clerk's office. However, in many parts of the world, these are twentieth-century practices.

The first question you must answer about your family's homeland is how did government or other officials in that country keep track of births, marriages, and deaths. In Europe the church was the first to make an effort to record births in the form of christening records, some of which date from the fourteenth century. After the middle of the sixteenth century, death records and marriage records were kept by most Christian denominations. Where religious custom requires the keeping of sacramental registers (christenings, marriages, burials, circumcisions, bar mitzvahs), shrine registers (of pilgrims), or other documents related to personal participation in religious observances, archives may be maintained by churches or religious bodies in the country. The older local religious records may have been gathered into central religious archives. In other instances, records are kept by local priests and ministers at the church, synagogue, or shrine.

With the French Revolution came that government's desire to lessen the church's influence in citizens' lives. Under the French civil code enacted in 1792, births, marriages, and deaths were to be recorded by civil officers at a local seat of government, usually the mayor's office. Many countries that fell under French influence or direct domination adopted this practice. Thus, you will find civil registration of vital events beginning in many countries between 1790 and 1810. Present-day Netherlands, Belgium, Luxembourg, western Germany, Italy, Spain, Portugal, Switzerland, and Poland are examples.

In the area that became the German Empire in 1871, civil registration of births, marriages, and deaths began in 1876. However, local officials in many of the states that made up the Empire had begun this practice as early as 1848. Civil registration in Bavaria and Baden began during the last decade of the eighteenth century.

In Austria and its dominions, Emperor Joseph II made local Catholic priests responsible for registering births, marriages, and deaths. This edict was dated February 20, 1784.

In England, laws passed in 1836 made government registrars responsible for recording all births, marriages, and deaths. These were filed with a central registrar in London beginning in 1837. The same law became effective in Ireland in 1844 and in Scotland in 1854. Each has its own central registrar's office.

How would you find out about government registration of births, marriages, and deaths in the country from which your ancestors originated? The embassy of that country in Washington, D.C., can help you find the answer. Your local reference librarian may be able to help you find the embassy's telephone number. Several regions of the United States are served by Federal Information Centers that can also provide the address and telephone number of the embassy. If your community is served by a Federal Information Center it should be listed in the federal government pages of your local telephone book.

Notes

1. Suzanne McVetty and Sharon D. Carmack, "Ellis Island: A Research Facility for Genealogists," *NGS Newsletter* 18 (May–June 1992): 68.

2. Angus Baxter, *In Search of Your German Roots*, 3d ed., United Germany Edition (Baltimore: Genealogical Publishing, 1994), 39.

3. RoseMarie Fintner, ed., "European Microfilming Acquisitions," *UGA Newsletter* 21, no. 3 (3d quarter, 1992): 8–9.

CHAPTER 8

⟪⟨ ⟩⟫

Writing Family History

Now that you know how to find your ancestors in original and published sources, you are ready to learn how to reconstruct their lives and share your findings with others through writing a family history. The family history you write should focus on how people interacted with each other and their surroundings. You will want to explain how ancestors thought, reached decisions, and responded to success or disaster. Your descriptions of their houses, clothing, customs, recreation, religion, education, employment, and means of transportation will provide color, context, and reality to ancestors' lives. This chapter is designed to spark your imagination by providing general guidelines for writing your family's history.

The sections that follow explain how to organize your writing project and use information and methods from several disciplines to write your family's history—or at least a part of it. The goal will be an accurate, illuminating family history. You will be reminded again of principles, methods, and resources explained in earlier chapters. Here you will see how they all work together to produce a family's history.

There are several phases in writing a family history: studying other histories, planning your family history, gathering evidence, evaluating evidence, writing, and publishing.

STUDYING THE WORKS WRITTEN BY OTHERS

The first step in your project requires a bit of reading. Reading family histories and biographies others have written will help you visualize how you will accomplish your own writing project. Visit your local library or historical society and ask the librarian to help you find some family histories, genealogies, and biographies. An easy way to do it is by looking up surnames as subjects in the library catalog. Following are a few titles to get you started.

William G. Hartley's *Kindred Saints* is an example of an unusual family history. It does not contain complicated pedigree charts or ancestor lists, and there are no detailed footnotes. Names, dates, and places are used as a frame upon which an interesting story is woven that reads like a novel. The charts and maps that are used are simple and easy to understand. The author has introduced a system of citations or notes that is seldom found in family histories and that some readers feel is easier to deal with than standard citations. The system consists of a paragraph at the end of each chapter that describes the sources and describes how they were used. The citations are brief, including only a title and publication date, and no numbering is used. The people in Hartley's book are not just grandparents, uncles, and cousins; they are people with feelings like you and me. Births, marriages, and deaths are not simply dates and places on a page in the family Bible; they are events that changed the way people lived and the way they felt about themselves and others.

In George Durrant and Noel Barton's *The Case of the Missing Ancestors: The Fun of Sleuthing Out Your Family History,* you learn how to uncover your family's history by following along as the authors trace the history of the Durrant family. Durrant's journey into his family's past begins with memories triggered by the discovery of an old high school letter sweater. Before long, the authors are interviewing old timers from family and neighborhood and tramping through cemeteries to satisfy Durrant's yearning to know where he came from.

Irma Wiese Whipple presents the history of her ancestors by taking the reader along on several exciting research trips to Germany. *In Search of Familie Wiese* introduces you to modern-day family members on both sides of the Atlantic. In Germany, you explore the streets and lanes that were so familiar to the author's ancestors. Any good family history should acquaint the reader with the physical world of ancestors; this book does it without making us sit through a boring lecture about Germany's geography.

Novels about families may also serve as models for a family history. The issues Willa S. Cather deals with in her novel *O Pioneers!* are the ones you could try to explore with your family history. She wrote about family, work, love, being alone, being a woman in a man's world, family conflict, and conflict with neighbors. You see her characters in good times and bad. All of this takes place in the setting of the sometimes bleak and sometimes beautiful rolling hills of western Nebraska. Weather, drought, crop failure, dirt, animals, kindness, and cruelty are woven into the story so deftly that you hardly notice after turning the last page that you, too, have become a pioneer. You lived in the cramped quarters of a log house and sweated behind horses trying to tear up resisting sod to plant a survival crop against the famine that winter could bring.

Biography as a Model

Reading a couple of good biographies will also help you solidify how you want to write about your ancestors. One of the best is Jill Ker Conway's autobiography, *The Road from Coorain*. It details the life of a girl born on the western plains of New South Wales, Australia. You will learn about her parents' lives before she was born and the life she shared with them and her two brothers until she left Australia as a young woman to study in the United States. You see the history of Australia unfold from World War I to 1959 through her eyes and the eyes of family, neighbors, and schoolmates. Her word paintings of the Australian landscape help you understand both the joy and the agony the land brought to her and her family. As you read each page you see how the land, family, neighbors, friends, and teachers all molded the person that the author became. Conway is especially skillful in identifying the real turning points in her life and in the lives of family members and the long-term effects of these milestones.

In *Writing Lives: Principia Biographica*, Leon Edel addresses how we can write biographies that not only teach us about people but contribute to the literature of our time. In his chapter titled "Narratives," Edel outlines three approaches to writing biography that apply to the family history field as well. In the first, the sources are the medium through which characters in the story speak and its setting is presented. With this method you employ carefully selected and arranged excerpts from original documents to depict your ancestors' lives and surroundings. The scribes of the past become the narrators in your story.[1]

The second approach Edel compares to painting a portrait. The writer is less concerned about the whole context or background of a person's life. He or she wants to catch basic traits that describe personality. This type of author provides a brief sketch of what lies beneath the exterior we all show the world. Its focus is on who our ancestors were inside their own minds and hearts. Snippets of ancestors' lives are presented that we believe characterize them, their beliefs, and their emotions.[2] As we reveal the minds and souls of forebears, we often come face-to-face with ourselves.

The last type of biography described by Edel deals with the middle ground between the expansive family history that presents so much carefully arranged documentation and the short interpretive work that zeros in on personalities. Here the author seems more like a novelist—without fictionalizing. It is an in-depth treatment of minds and hearts, but careful attention is also given to personal motivations, events, and the settings of peoples' lives. Sources, too, play their role but more as the foundation for the interpretations of the writer.[3]

Once you understand how your history will be similar to or different from the ones you have studied, it is time to create a plan for the story you will write.

PLANNING A FAMILY HISTORY

Writing a family history will require a substantial investment of time and other resources. Your plan will help you use these resources more effectively than if you tried to complete the project without one. Be flexible. You may discover evidence during the research phase of your study that dictates revisions in your original plan.

Become a Writer

Most of us are talkers: we prefer to explain our ideas verbally. Family historians need to learn how to share their knowledge and ideas in writing. Your family history must deal with issues of enduring value and tell the family's story in a language and style that edifies and motivates. Those reading the sentences and paragraphs you write must find the same pleasure they do when enjoying any other good book. Your words must appeal to their senses and make them a participant in the story.

Review the basic principles of writing by reading a few books about how to write. William Strunk Jr. and E. B. White's *The Elements of Style* is a well-known primer on the subject. William Zinsser's *On Writing Well: An Informal Guide to Writing Nonfiction* will introduce you to some important concepts about communicating through writing. Zinsser uses his experience as a journalist and university professor to offer innovative suggestions on how writers can share their ideas and yet keep readers awake. Writers of family histories can learn a lot from the businesspeople, sports writers, critics, journalists, and others the author uses as examples. When used in conjunction with the two previously mentioned titles, Lawrence P. Goldrup's *Writing the Family Narrative* becomes an excellent outline for anyone aspiring to write family history. The book deals with family history as a literary genre and demonstrates how the facts you uncover about your family can be turned into a description of their lives and their world. Based on years of gathering information about his own family, it also reflects his experience teaching English and writing courses at a local college.

Define the Purpose, Audience, and Scope

First, write a purpose statement that describes why you are writing the history. Perhaps you feel that family members have something to learn from the successes and failures progenitors have experienced. For example, there may be inherited diseases that descendants should understand in terms of the potential impact in their lives. Forebears may have exhibited principles that you feel should be passed on to each new generation. Select a tentative title for the history that reflects this purpose statement. Include in the purpose statement a description of the audience you hope will read the book.

Next, decide how much history you want to cover—the scope of your project. You can describe it in terms of a span of years or in terms of generations. You may want to limit it to a specific place, such as a hometown or state, or follow forebears as they move from one locality to another. Perhaps your history will portray only your life or the lives of your parents and brothers and sisters. Maybe you want to begin with the first

ancestor who came to America or with someone who served in the Revolutionary or Civil War and show how each generation built upon the foundation left by the preceding one, with the last chapters describing present-day descendants of your early ancestors.

The Characters and Setting for Your Story

The term *character* normally refers to fictional persons in plays, novels, short stories, etc. I use the term here to refer to the family members you will describe in your family history. A novelist develops a character by letting the reader see inside the person's mind and heart. The reader comes to know why characters are the way they are because readers see characters' interactions with people, events, and their environment. You can do the same thing. Help those who read your family history understand your ancestors by seeing them as multidimensional persons—like you and me—whose life activities shape their attitudes and actions.

Once you have decided on your purpose, audience, and the time period you wish to portray, list the cast—the characters—in your story. Essential to your story are the pedigree charts and family-group records that you will provide. Decide how you want to present this information. Some authors have a separate section at the back or at the beginning of the history in which charts and sheets outline the names of all persons in the family who lived during the period covered by the story. Other authors prefer to show charts of family members at the end of the chapter describing those lives. If you can find drawings or photographs of ancestors, include a picture pedigree chart to help readers recognize the characters in your story. (Chapter 2 provides help in designing pedigree charts and family-group records.)

You will want to finish this project in your lifetime, so identify only a few key persons in each generation whose lives and actions will carry the story you want to tell. Perhaps at the present time you do not know the names of some of the persons you want to describe; they are ancestors you have not discovered yet. Research will reveal their names and life activities. Just give them a title or some other description for now— "immigrant ancestor," for example—and fill in the facts as you discover them.

Next, list the items you want to learn about that will describe your ancestors' world. Writers call this describing the setting of a story. You will not always know the setting for the lives of each ancestor or family before you start. Research may be needed to provide facts about the world in which they lived. You probably have an idea of some of the conditions that existed at various times in your family's history. Decide to explore living conditions, how people supported themselves, and their relations with the community, family members, and friends. Look into health conditions, the geography, weather, and the events and ideas that were important to people during the times your forebears lived. Add anything you sense will give the reader a feel for the place and time in which progenitors lived.

Finally, identify the turning points you might expect to find in a person's life. A *turning point* is an action that causes a change in a person's life with long-term consequences. Some of these will appear as you research individual lives; others you can plan for in advance: marriage, career choices, emigration, and choosing a religion are examples. Decide to look for what caused these changes, and try to measure their influence at the time of the decision and later in the lives of descendants.

Create a Chapter Outline

The last step in the planning process is to construct a tentative chapter outline. Decide how you are going to present your family's story. Perhaps you are going to devote a chapter to each family in your direct line beginning with your immigrant or soldier forebear and ending with yourself, or you may decide to begin with the present generation and trace the story backward, one generation at a time. Some writers have constructed their story around the major turning points in their family's history. Each chapter explores why decisions were made and how they affected those who made the decision and those who came afterward. Another approach is to devote a chapter to those ancestors who had the most impact on what the family is today. Plan to have an introduction that explains why you wrote the history and describes how it is organized. Also include a conclusion that explains what you learned from the experience.

EVALUATING THE EVIDENCE YOU GATHERED

Chapter 1 taught you some basic principles about judging the accuracy of records used to learn about ancestors' lives. As you prepare to share your findings in a history, the following are some additional ideas you must consider.

Prove the Facts

You learned in chapter 1 that you must verify the content of sources, perhaps by finding other records relating to the same event or persons so you can cross-check each source against the other. For example, some genealogists who are satisfied to find their family in parish registers or local vital records forget that these records only identify a portion of the family—usually one child and the parents. As these genealogists reconstitute families from this single source, they run the risk of including some of the children as siblings when they are really cousins because their parents have the same names and the births occur within a period of about twenty years from a couple's having a first child. To be more certain of who really belonged to the family, it is always good to use censuses, wills, or other records that name several family members.

Family historians want to know the relationship between sources and the events they describe. An eyewitness account of an event is generally more accurate than a description of the event by someone who heard about it. Sometimes, however, even eyewitnesses can mislead us, as shown in the following example.

A minister living in eighteenth-century Connecticut christened a child at the church with the intent of recording the event as soon as he arrived home, where the church registers were kept. An intervening emergency caused him to forget his resolution. When he remembered several weeks later, he recorded the given name of the child as Sylvia instead of the correct name, Cybil. A marriage record for this person was later made at the local town hall. The clerk recorded the correct name and birth date as part of the marriage report. Thus, a later source provided more-accurate information than a source created at the time of the event.

Recognize Your Biases

In your writing, you must be aware of the role that personal feelings and attitudes play. Assessing your feelings about the people and issues in your family history will help you to identify biases and possibly prevent interpretations based solely on feelings. It helps to write down the facts in your life that will bias your view of events and people. The most difficult things to list are feelings. Why are you writing a family history? Can you isolate why you have focused on certain ancestors and stories? There is nothing wrong with being emotionally involved in your project or wishing to make your readers enthusiastic about ancestors' contributions. Remember, however, that these feelings may cause you to accept evidence that other less-emotionally involved persons would not.

Your ethnic background, education, profession, and religious preference all affect your interpretation of documents. The place you grew up will also color your perceptions of what documents are telling you. If your heritage is Italian and you were raised in a large city where you graduated from high school and then from a community college, your interpretation of records describing ancestors in rural Italian villages will be different from those of a cousin who was raised on a farm in California. Your feelings can both detract from and enrich the story you want to tell. You may let personal feelings and biases keep you from exploring all of the issues relating to people and events in your family history, thus robbing readers of the chance to learn about views other than your own.

On the positive side, your personal feelings may inject an air of enthusiasm into a work that makes the story much more fun to read. Also important is your ability to write in such a way that readers become involved in the lives of the people you describe and in the issues and problems you raise. There is nothing wrong in writing to persuade readers to accept your feelings as legitimate. You must, however, be fair enough to share sources and evidence that permit readers to decide whether they can agree or not.

Avoid the Wrong Conclusions

A family historian or genealogist may draw conclusions or make assumptions that are not supported by the evidence in sources. Some refer to this problem as *historical fallacy*. You may be familiar with some of the more obvious errors: assuming that your attitudes about issues such as religion and politics are the same as a forebear's living in the seventeenth century. You may have found him in local religious records and concluded he was as committed a worshiper as you, when in reality he participated only to enjoy full citizenship rights in a community dominated by members of the local congregation. Consider the following scenarios in which researchers could reach false conclusions.

Pretend you find a progenitor's will in which two children are listed and no wife. Can you assume that there were no other children and that his wife had passed away? Perhaps a little more research in local land records will show that he had given considerable amounts of land to two daughters and their husbands as well as to two sons. None of these may appear in the will because the testator had already given them what he considered their fair share of his estate. He may have made a separate agreement with his children to care for his wife until she died and, thus, was using his will to provide for remaining family members who had not yet received any of his estate.

Perhaps you have been fortunate enough to trace an immigrant forefather to his home in Germany. You are able to obtain photocopies of local parish records showing the christenings of your ancestor and his brothers and sisters. You note in the entry for each child that the father is listed as a farmer (*Bauer*). The ancestor who came to this country was also a farmer who owned a large farm in Iowa. You assume that the immigrant's father was likewise a farm owner. A closer look at other christening entries shows that some men were described as farmers and proprietors/owners (*Eigentümer*). In reality your ancestor's father was a tenant farmer and your ancestor came to America because there was nothing for him to inherit except a profession he would have to practice on rented land.

For more on the fallacies that plague historical researchers, see David H. Fischer's *Historian's Fallacies: Toward a Logic of Historical Thought.*

Your research to this point has allowed you to develop some ideas and opinions about your family. You are aware of some of the obstacles that prevent authors from interpreting sources correctly. Now you are ready to share what you have learned by writing about the people, places, and events in your family's history.

WRITING A FIRST DRAFT

Your outline contains ideas about how your family history will be organized, but you may still wonder how to begin. Here is one suggestion for you to consider. Begin by describing what family life was like. Were parents' roles then similar to what exists in your home? How large were families? Did everyone go to school?

Move your analysis from the home to the neighborhood and try to describe the people that lived near your family. Characterize them in terms of their occupations, wealth, religion, and origin. Where did your family fit in? Was your family similar to most neighbors or were they an exception to the norm in their neighborhood?

Next, tell about local institutions. Describe the kind of government there was and how it affected your family. Were there local churches or social groups? If so, what role did your ancestors play in them? If you can, through using newspapers, personal journals, biographies, and local histories, discuss local controversies and make statements about your family's role in them. We take public education for granted today. Explain the roles of education and schools in your ancestors' lives.

The family history you will write becomes the vehicle that explains to readers what you have learned about your family, how you reached your conclusions, and the sources you used. Following are some additional suggestions to help you in this process.

Cite Your Sources

When you read a history, you may assume that the writer is providing an accurate picture of the past, but, as discussed earlier, this expectation is not realistic. Although historians share their personal views of the past, these views are informed but not unbiased. To overcome this problem they have a responsibility to share their sources with us, so that we can draw our own conclusions about their interpretations. One of the measures of a good family history is whether or not the writer cites his or her sources. Another important indicator is whether or not the content of the sources is presented accurately. When we talk of *accuracy,* we really mean presenting the reader with an honest view of the past as the author feels the sources reveal it. Some family histories have neither footnotes nor bibliographies. For all we know, the material being presented is just a family legend. Give your readers a chance to make up their own minds about your conclusions by citing the sources used as evidence for your interpretations or ideas.

At the end of each chapter, or at the end of the book, provide a bibliography of all the books, periodicals, and original sources used or consulted to write the history.

For example, this book provides notes at the ends of chapters and a list of works cited at the end of the book. Use these as examples to learn how to prepare footnotes or endnotes and bibliographies for the family history you write. Whenever you use information from an original document or the words or ideas of another author from a book or periodical, identify it with a footnote/endnote reference number at the end of the sentence or paragraph where the information appears. Begin the numbering of footnotes or endnotes with *1* for the first note in each chapter, *2* for the second, and so on to the end of the chapter.

Write Accurate, Interesting Family History

Your goal should be to describe ancestors' lives in terms that are interesting but factual. Following are some ideas taken from the broader field of literature that may help.

You seldom find family histories on the list of best-selling nonfiction. Autobiographies, biographies, memoirs, and nonfiction adventure stories have been best sellers but not family histories. Many family histories have no story line, no development of characters, no plot, and seldom any setting provided to draw us into the lives of ancestors. The language used in them is unimaginative, and their authors often ignore rules of grammar and usage. The development of characters, plots, and settings based on real people, places, and events requires that family historians use their creative instincts. If historical novels can attract a large audience of readers, why not family histories? The major difference between the two is the treatment of historical reality. Writers of historical fiction describe characters as they *wish* the characters were. The characters genealogists describe are real people whose lives have been captured in contemporary records.

The literary approach to history can be dangerous. Some historians, well aware of the hazards, avoid it. Do not let creative writing lead to creative family history, which in the final analysis is fiction: a story about ancestors that is not rooted in documented facts.

Sometimes, however, the documents you find do not give adequate information about your ancestors. If all you have, for example, are some church records, a will or two, and a census, how can you describe ancestors in terms of their jobs, local politics, the economy, religion, and education? You must extrapolate what ancestors' lives were like from books and articles that describe other people or groups who lived at the same time and in the same community. There are hundreds of books about communities, families, and society in the past. Your local reference librarian can help you find books that describe people in the region or country in which your forebears lived. This kind of family history is authentic because it is based upon sources contemporary with those that describe your family, but they describe other families and communities in the same town, region, or country. Any family history that ignores modern studies about ancestor's contemporaries shortchanges those who read it. An accurate presentation of a family in the setting of its own time and place demands this approach and produces family histories that are fun to read.

Describe the Characters

When we become engrossed in reading a good novel, it is often because of the author's ability to involve us in the thoughts and feelings of the book's characters. Try to draw conclusions about your ancestors' ideas and beliefs. Perhaps they served in wartime, and you want to find out how this experience influenced their thoughts and actions. Perhaps religion played an important role in their lives. Also look for turning points or major events in their lives. Search for facts about these milestones and what caused them. See if you can uncover how your forebears felt during these times of change.

Although retrospective psychoanalysis is, at best, difficult, you can explore original sources and books written by others to learn if they permit a look inside the minds of the people in your story. There may be third-person accounts of these persons' lives that can help you understand your ancestors' feelings. A family historian who avoids dealing with the psychological aspects of an ancestor's life is telling only part of the story.

One way to explore the lives and feelings of the characters in your history is to pretend that you can talk to these ancestors today. What would you want to learn about their lives? Your questions should touch on subjects or areas of life meaningful to you with the aim of comparing the past with the present. Your readers may be interested in the answers to many of the same questions some young people asked my grandfather.

Before he died, at age 97, my grandfather was invited occasionally to speak to youth groups about his life during the turn of the century. These young people asked about things important in their own lives: "What did you think when you saw the first car?" "How did you learn to drive and what was it like to get a driver's license?" "Did you like school?" "What did you do in school?" "Did you have any girlfriends?" "What did you do on dates?"

If you were asking the questions, you might also be interested in how your ancestor thought children should be reared, what roles friends played in your progenitor's life, how he or she viewed women's roles, or what your ancestor did for relaxation. Your forebears had a life that brought enjoyment and happiness as well as a substantial amount of grief and suffering. Your job is to capture these feelings as you describe your forebears.

Capturing in print the lives and personalities of ancestors is a difficult task. All any reader can expect is that you try to draw conclusions from your sources about the feelings behind the events in progenitors' lives. Sometimes your only recourse will be to ask yourself what you would have thought and felt in the same situation. Many things have changed since the time the first human walked upon this planet. The ways we dress, find our food, seek rest, and transmit ideas have changed dramatically and will continue to change. How people feel about what is happening to them has changed little. You are as much an expert on feelings as anyone else, and your interpretations of ancestors' feelings deserve credence.

Describe the Setting

When portraying the world ancestors lived in, it will help if you can isolate specific parts of their lives to depict. Start by identifying the primary components in your life. Your ancestors' lives were similar to yours. You must eat and have shelter and clothing. This area of life we might call the economic side of life. A second aspect of living involves the people we live with and the social or political institutions that play roles in our lives. Finally, there is the world around us, the physical setting in which we live, with real weather, dirt, rocks, rivers, oceans, and wildlife.

To describe the economic setting of ancestors' lives, you will want to explore how they made a living. Include how they trained for their jobs, how much they made or produced, and how they decided upon the work they chose. You would also like to know how much they paid or traded for food, clothing, and shelter. What kind of clothing did they wear, what did they eat, and what was their daily work-life like? If ancestors were farmers, you would want to know how they obtained seeds to plant or animals to raise. How long did it take to plow and sow fields using a horse, mule, or ox? How much did the land yield at harvest time? Today in America the forty-hour week is common; how many hours each week did your forebears work? When did the workday start and end?

A family history must deal not only with individuals but also with how these individuals fit into the various spheres of society—their social settings. What was the role of society in their lives? It is also important to explore relationships between individuals. Question sources to learn if there is any information about how husbands related to wives, parents related to children, or how family members related to other groups in the community. Ancestors were viewed by associates as fellow workers, churchgoers, customers, friends, and enemies. If your goal is to write history that places people in the context of their world, then you must describe how ancestors fit into the fabric of their contemporary society. This fabric includes governmental, religious, educational, and other institutions that impinged on their lives. Use the information documents, books, and eyewitnesses provide to describe these aspects also.

What should you include about the physical setting in which your ancestors lived? Stop for a moment and think about where you live. When you look out the window, what do you see: mountains, an ocean, the wall of an adjacent building, fields as far as the eye can see? When you walk out the door, what do you feel, and does it change according to the season? Pretend you are your ancestor. Walk through his day and project what his life would be like. What would he see and sense? Use these impressions to paint a word picture of the physical setting of your forebear's life. This effort will be easier after gathering and evaluating evidence about the geography, climate, and local history for the area in which your family lived.

EDITING AND PUBLISHING YOUR FAMILY HISTORY

Once you have finished the first draft of your family history, read it carefully from beginning to end. Correct any errors you detect in the way you have expressed yourself or interpreted your sources. Ensure that you have cited the sources you used for the ideas and facts in the history. Read the manuscript a second time to make a content outline of what you have written. Under each chapter list the main topics in the chapter and the subtopics covered under each topic. Perhaps

the history would be easier to understand if you inserted topic headings for the major topics you have identified in each chapter. Check to see that all similar topics are covered together and that the order you used to present the topics still seems correct.

Select two or three family members to read the manuscript and share any ideas for improvements. Find one or two other reviewers who are not family members and ask them to do the same thing. At least one of the nonrelatives should have experience in writing—a teacher, for example. Ask your readers to check for grammar and usage as well as the style you used for your footnotes/endnotes and bibliography. Encourage readers to point out ideas and relationships that are confusing to them. Ask for comments about your organization of the book. Request that they give you their overall impression of the work. Read the comments of your reviewers and make any changes to the manuscript you feel are needed. You may want to pay a professional editor to be one of the final reviewers. If so, the English department at your local college or university may have some people it can recommend. If the college or university has its own press, it could be contacted for advice also.

Most family histories are privately published. That means you hire someone to typeset, print, and bind as many copies of the history as you wish. Most local copy centers will also make as many copies as you wish and bind them for you. Writers who use a computer word processing program to prepare their manuscript can arrange to print the final copy on a laser printer, which will provide a good master for copies of the book from a local copy center or a printer. Of course, you normally can tell the difference between a book published using a local copy center and a book produced by a printer or publisher. That is, the family history made from your laser-printed master at a local copy center will look like a thesis or a school report, but for family historians on a budget, it will serve its purpose well. If you would like to make your family history look more attractive, see if your local library has Mark Beach's *Getting It Printed: How to Work with Printers and Graphic Arts Services to Assure Quality, Stay on Schedule, and Control Costs.* This book will help you create a design for your family history that will make it more appealing.

If you would like to have your book published by a professional publisher, check with your local genealogical or historical society for suggestions about local publishers with experience producing family histories. Once you have published the family history, donate copies to the local genealogical or historical society. Some writers also donate copies to large research centers so that copies will be preserved if the original is somehow destroyed. At the very least, donate a copy to the Library of Congress.

A few family historians have produced their history as a video recording. This approach requires just as much planning, analysis, and writing as a book about your family. The approach presented in this chapter will permit you to prepare a typescript history that can be adapted to become the script for the video presentation. Refer to Duane and Pat Sturm's *Video Family History* for details on producing a family history on video tape.

When you decide to write your family history, be creative. Write history the way you feel it should be written. That does not mean that you make up events. It means that you ask questions of your sources that bring out the truth, are interesting to your readers, and are important to an understanding of ancestors' lives. It means that you try to pass on to future generations the ideals and ideas of your ancestors that have enduring meaning and value.

Notes

1. Leon Edel, *Writing Lives: Principia Biographica* (New York: W. W. Norton, 1985), 176–77.

2. Ibid., 176.

3. Ibid., 181–83.

Works Cited

Abate, Frank R., ed. *Omni Gazetteer of the United States of America.* 11 vols. Detroit: Omnigraphics, 1991. (*See* entry under Omnigraphics for CD version.)

Accelerated Indexing Systems. *Accelerated Indexing Systems, Inc. Microfiche Indexes of U.S. Census and Other Records.* Salt Lake City: Accelerated Indexing Systems, 1983.

American Genealogical Lending Library and Historical Resources, Inc. *Heritage Quest.* Bountiful, Utah: American Genealogical Lending Library and Historical Resources, 1985– .

The American Library Directory: A Classified List of Libraries in the United States and Canada with Personnel and Statistical Data 1923– . 46th ed., 2 vols. New York: R. R. Bowker, 1993.

Ancestry Publishing. *Genealogical Computing.* Salt Lake City: Ancestry, 1981– .

Andereck, Paul, and Richard A. Pence, eds. *Computer Genealogy: A Guide to Research through High Technology.* Rev. ed. Salt Lake City: Ancestry, 1991.

Anuta, Michael J. *Ships of Our Ancestors.* Baltimore: Genealogical Publishing, 1993.

Arnold, Jackie Smith. *Kinship: It's All Relative.* 2d ed. Baltimore: Genealogical Publishing, 1994.

Ash, Lee. *Subject Collections.* 7th ed., rev. and enl. New Providence, N.J.: R. R. Bowker, 1993.

Baxter, Angus. *In Search of Your German Roots.* 3d ed. Baltimore: Genealogical Publishing, 1994.

Beach, Mark. *Getting It Printed: How to Work with Printers and Graphic Arts Services to Assure Quality, Stay on Schedule, and Control Costs.* Cincinnati: North Light Books, 1993.

Beattie, Jerome F., ed. *The Hereditary Register of the United States of America.* Phoenix, Ariz.: The Hereditary Register Publications, 1984.

J. H. Beers & Co. *Commemorative Biographical Record of Middlesex County, Connecticut.* Chicago: J. H. Beers, 1903.

Bentley, Elizabeth P. *County Courthouse Book.* Baltimore: Genealogical Publishing, 1990.

———. *The Genealogist's Address Book.* Baltimore: Genealogical Publishing, 1992.

Berrett, William E. *The Restored Church: A Brief History of the Growth and Doctrines of the Church of Jesus Christ of Latter-day Saints.* 16th ed., rev. and enl. Salt Lake City: Deseret Book, 1977.

Blockson, Charles L. "Black American Records and Research." In *Ethnic Genealogy: A Research Guide,* 309–64. Westport, Conn.: Greenwood Pr., 1983.

Boyer, Carl. *Jacobus' Index to Genealogical Periodicals.* 3d ed. Newhall, Calif.: Boyer Publications, 1988.

Boylston, Adrian F., ed. *The American Blue Book of Funeral Directors.* New York: Kates-Boylston Publications, 1992.

Budd, Ann D., Michael B. Clegg, and Curt B. Witcher. *Periodical Source Index: 1847–1985.* 12 vols. Fort Wayne, Ind.: Allen County Public Libr. Foundation, 1988.

Bullinger's Guides, Inc. *Bullinger's Postal and Shippers' Guide for the United States and Canada.* Westwood, N.J.: Bullinger's Guides, 1871– .

Burek, Deborah M., ed. *Cemeteries of the U.S.—A Guide to Contact Information for U.S. Cemeteries and Their Records.* Detroit: Gale Research, 1994.

Burek, Deborah M., Karin E. Koek, and Annette Novallo, eds. *Encyclopedia of Associations.* 28th ed. 2 vols. Detroit: Gale Research, 1993.

Burgert, Annette K. *Eighteenth-Century Emigrants from German-Speaking Lands to North America.* Breinigsville, Pa.: The Pennsylvania German Soc., 1983– .

Cather, Willa S. *O Pioneers!* New York: Dover Publications, 1993.

Chadwyck-Healey. *Index to Personal Names in the National Union Catalog of Manuscript Collections, 1959–1984.* Alexandria, Va.: Chadwyck-Healey, 1988.

————. *National Inventory of Documentary Sources in the United States.* Teaneck, N.J.: Chadwyck-Healey, 1992.

Ching, Frank. *Ancestors: 900 Years in the Life of a Chinese Family.* New York: Morrow, 1988.

Chorzempa, Rosemary A. *Korzenie Polskie: Polish Roots.* Baltimore: Genealogical Publishing, 1993.

Church of Jesus Christ of Latter-day Saints. *Family-Search: Ancestral File* [Computer file]. Salt Lake City: Church of Jesus Christ of Latter-day Saints, 1993.

————. *FamilySearch: Family History Library Catalog* [Computer file]. Salt Lake City: Church of Jesus Christ of Latter-day Saints, 1993.

————. *Family History Library Catalog* [Microfiche version]. Salt Lake City: Church of Jesus Christ of Latter-day Saints, 1993.

————. *FamilySearch: International Genealogical Index* [Computer file]. Salt Lake City: Church of Jesus Christ of Latter-day Saints, 1993.

————. *FamilySearch: International Genealogical Index* [Microfiche version]. Salt Lake City: Church of Jesus Christ of Latter-day Saints, 1993.

————. *FamilySearch: Social Security Death Index* [Computer file]. Salt Lake City: Church of Jesus Christ of Latter-day Saints, 1988.

————. *Personal Ancestral File, Ver. 2.3* [Computer program]. Salt Lake City: Church of Jesus Christ of Latter-day Saints.

————. *Research Outline: U.S. Military Records.* Series U.S.-Mil., no. 1. Salt Lake City: The Church of Jesus Christ of Latter-day Saints. Family History Libr., 1993.

————. *Resource Guide: The Hamburg Passenger Lists, 1850–1934.* Series EUR, no. 1. Salt Lake City: The Church of Jesus Christ of Latter-day Saints. Family History Libr., 1992.

Clavell, James. *Noble House.* New York: Dell Publishing, 1984.

Clegg, Michael B. *Bibliography of Genealogy and Local History Periodicals with Union List of Major U.S. Collections.* Fort Wayne, Ind.: Allen County Public Libr. Foundation, 1990.

Clegg, Michael B., and Curt B. Witcher. *Periodical Source Index: 1986–1992.* Fort Wayne, Ind.: Allen County Public Libr. Foundation, 1986–1993.

Colange, Leo de. *The National Gazetteer: A Geographical Dictionary of the United States.* 1884. Reprint, Ann Arbor, Mich.: Univ. Microfilms International, 1978.

Coldham, Peter W. *The Complete Book of Emigrants 1607–1776.* 4 vols. Baltimore: Genealogical Publishing, 1990–1993.

————. *Emigrants in Chains.* Baltimore: Genealogical Publishing, 1992.

Colletta, John P. *They Came in Ships.* Rev. Salt Lake City: Ancestry, 1993.

Commsoft. *Roots IV* [Computer program]. Windsor, Calif.: Commsoft.

Connecticut Society of Genealogists. *The Connecticut Nutmegger.* Glastonbury, Conn.: The Connecticut Soc. of Genealogists, 1970.

Conway, Jill Ker. *The Road from Coorain.* New York: Alfred A. Knopf, 1989.

Cordasco, Francesco. *The Immigrant Woman in North America: An Annotated Bibliography of Selected References.* Metuchen, N.J.: Scarecrow Pr., 1985.

Cutler, Carl C. *Queens of the Western Ocean: The Story of America's Mail and Passenger Sailing Lines.* Annapolis: U.S. Naval Institute, 1961.

Davis, Cullom, Katherine Back, and Kay MacLean. *Oral History: From Tape to Type.* Chicago: American Libr. Assoc., 1977.

Deputy, Marilyn, and others. *Register of Federal United States Military Records: A Guide to Manuscript Sources Available at the Genealogical Library in Salt Lake City and the National Archives in Washington, D.C.* 3 vols. Bowie, Md.: Heritage Books, 1986.

Dollarhide Systems. *Everyone's Family Tree Version 3.40* [Computer program]. Bellingham, Wash.: Dollarhide Systems.

Dornbusch, Charles E. *Military Bibliography of the Civil War.* 4 vols. Dayton, Ohio: Morningside, 1987.

Durrant, George, and Noel Barton. *The Case of the Missing Ancestors: The Fun of Sleuthing Out Your Family History.* Salt Lake City: Keepsake Publishing, 1991.

Eakle, Arlene, and Johni Cerny, eds. *The Source: A Guidebook of American Genealogy.* Salt Lake City: Ancestry, 1984.

Edel, Leon. *Writing Lives: Principia Biographica.* New York: W. W. Norton, 1985.

Eichholz, Alice, ed. *Ancestry's Red Book: State, County & Town Sources.* Rev. ed. Salt Lake City: Ancestry, 1992.

Eldridge, Grant J., ed. *Encyclopedia of Associations: Regional, State, and Local Organizations.* 4th ed. 5 vols. Detroit: Gale Research, 1994.

Elliott, Wendy L. "Railroad Records for Genealogical Research." *National Genealogical Society Quarterly* 75 (Dec. 1987):271–77.

Europa Publications. *The World of Learning 1994.* 44th ed. London, Eng.: Europa Publications, 1994.

Everton, George B. *The Handy Book for Genealogists: United States of America.* 8th ed. Logan, Utah: Everton Publishers, 1991.

Everton Publishers. *The Genealogical Helper.* Logan, Utah: Everton Publishers, 1947– .

Faulkner, William. *Absalom, Absalom!* New York: Random House, 1993.

Federation of Genealogical Societies. *Forum.* Salt Lake City: Federation of Genealogical Societies, 1989– .

Filby, P. William. *American & British Genealogy and Heraldry: A Selected List of Books.* 3d rev. ed. Boston: New England Historic and Genealogical Soc., 1983; *1982–1985 Supplement,* 1987.

———. *A Bibliography of American County Histories.* Baltimore: Genealogical Publishing, 1985.

———. *Directory of American Libraries with Genealogy or Local History Collections.* Wilmington, Del.: Scholarly Resources, 1988.

———. *Passenger and Immigration Lists Bibliography: 1538–1900.* 2d ed. Detroit: Gale Research, 1988.

Filby, P. William, Mary K. Meyer, and Dorothy M. Lower. *Passenger and Immigration Lists Index.* Detroit: Gale Research, 1981– ; *1983 Supplement,* 1984; *1984 Supplement,* 1985.

Fintner, RoseMari. "European Microfilming Acquisitions." *Utah Genealogical Society Newsletter* 21, no. 3. (3d quarter 1992): 8–9.

Fischer, David H. *Historian's Fallacies: Toward a Logic of Historical Thought.* New York: Harper, 1970.

Fletcher, William. *Recording Your Family History.* Berkeley, Calif.: Ten Speed Pr., 1989.

Forbes, Harriette M. *New England Diaries, 1602–1800: A Descriptive Catalog of Diaries, Orderly Books, and Sea Journals.* New York: Russell and Russell, 1967.

Foster, Janet. *British Archives: A Guide to Archive Resources in the United Kingdom.* 2d ed. New York: Stockton Pr., 1989.

Gannett, Henry. *The Origin of Certain Place Names in the United States.* 2d ed. 1905. Reprint, Baltimore: Genealogical Publishing, 1977.

Geary, James W. *We Need Men: The Union Draft in the Civil War.* DeKalb, Ill.: Northern Illinois Univ. Pr., 1991.

Gill, Harold B. *Apprentices of Virginia 1623–1800.* Salt Lake City: Ancestry, 1989.

Glazier, Ira, and P. William Filby. *Germans to America.* Wilmington, Del.: Scholarly Resources, 1988– .

———. *Italians to America 1880–1899.* Wilmington, Del.: Scholarly Resources, 1992– .

Glazier, Ira, and Michael Tepper, eds. *The Famine Immigrants.* Baltimore: Genealogical Publishing, 1983– .

Glover, Denise M. *Voices of the Spirit: Guide to Resources in African-American History.* Chicago: American Libr. Assoc., 1994.

Godfrey Memorial Library. *American Genealogical-Biographical Index.* New Series. 171 vols. Middletown, Conn.: Godfrey Memorial Library, 1952– .

Goldrup, Lawrence P. *Writing the Family Narrative.* Salt Lake City: Ancestry, 1987.

Greene, David L. *The American Genealogist.* Demorest, Ga.: David L. Greene, 1937– .

Greenwood, Val D. *The Researcher's Guide to American Genealogy.* 2d ed. Baltimore: Genealogical Publishing, 1992.

Grotefend, H. *Taschenbuch der Zeitrechnung des Deutschen Mittelalters und der Neuzeit.* 11th ed. Hannover: Verlag Hahnsche Buchhandlung, 1971.

Haley, Alex. *Roots.* New York: Doubleday, 1976.

Hansen, Marcus L. *The Atlantic Migration, 1607–1860.* New York: Harper, 1961.

Hareven, Tamara, and Andrejs Plakans, eds. *Family History at the Crossroads: A Journal of Family History Reader.* Princeton, N.J.: Princeton Univ. Pr., 1987.

Harris, Ruth-Ann, Donald M. Jacobs, and B. Emer O'Keeffe, eds. *The Search for Missing Friends: Irish Immigrant Advertisements in the Boston* Pilot. 2 vols. Boston: New England Historic Genealogical Soc., 1991.

Hartley, William G. *Kindred Saints: The Mormon Immigrant Heritage of Alvin and Kathryne Christenson.* Salt Lake City: Eden Hill, 1982.

Havlice, Patricia P. *And So to Bed: A Bibliography of Diaries Published in English.* Metuchen, N.J.: Scarecrow Pr., 1987.

Hayes, Steven. "Hooked on Bulletin Boards." *Genealogical Computing* 12, no. 1 (July/Aug./Sept. 1992): 21–27.

Hays, Samuel P. "History and Genealogy: Patterns for Change and Prospects for Cooperation." *Prologue* 7 (spring, summer, fall 1975): 39–43; 81–84; 187–91.

Hill, Edward E. *Guide to Records in the National Archives of the United States Relating to American Indians.* Washington, D.C.: National Archives Trust Fund Board, 1981.

Hinshaw, William W., and Thomas W. Marshall. *Encyclopedia of American Quaker Genealogy.* Vol. 2. 1936. Reprint, Baltimore: Genealogical Publishing, 1991.

Horowitz, Lois. *A Bibliography of Military Name Lists from Pre-1675 to 1900: A Guide to Genealogical Research*. Metuchen, N.J.: Scarecrow Pr., 1990.

Howe, Hartley E. *North America's Maritime Museums: An Annotated Guide*. New York: Facts On File, 1987.

Hunter, Brian, ed. *The Statesman's Year-Book 1993–94*. 129th rev. ed. New York: St. Martin's Pr., 1992.

Immigration Information Bureau. *Morton Allan Directory of European Passenger Steamship Arrivals*. 1931. Reprint, Baltimore: Genealogical Publishing, 1993.

International Council on Archives. *Archivum*. Munchen: Verlag Dokumentation, 1951– .

———. *International Directory of Archives*. New York: K. G. Saur, 1988.

Jackson, Ronald V. *Utah 1870*. North Salt Lake, Utah: Accelerated Indexing Systems International, 1987.

Jackson, Ronald V., and G. Ronald Teeples. *Connecticut 1850 Census Index*. Salt Lake City: Accelerated Indexing Systems, 1981.

Jackson, Ronald V., and others, eds. *Utah 1880 Federal Census Index*. Salt Lake City: Accelerated Indexing Systems, 1989.

Jacobus, Donald L. *Genealogy as Pastime and Profession*. 1932. Reprint, Baltimore: Genealogical Publishing, 1981.

Jakes, James. *The North and the South*. Boston: G. K. Hall, 1985.

Jones, Henry Z. *More Palatine Families*. Universal City, Calif.: H. Jones, 1991.

———. *The Palatine Families of New York, 1710*. 2 vols. Universal City, Calif.: H. Jones, 1985.

Kaminkow, Marion J., ed. *A Complement to Genealogies in the Library of Congress: A Bibliography*. Baltimore: Genealogical Publishing, 1981.

———. *Genealogies in the Library of Congress: A Bibliography*. Baltimore: Magna Carta, 1987; *Supplement, 1972–1976*, 1977; *Second Supplement, 1976–1986*, 1987.

———. *United States Local Histories in the Library of Congress: A Bibliography*. 5 vols. Baltimore: Magna Carta, 1975.

Kaplan, Louis, comp. *A Bibliography of American Autobiographies*. Madison, Wisc.: Univ. of Wisconsin, 1962.

Kemp, Thomas Jay. *International Vital Records Handbook*. 3d ed. Baltimore: Genealogical Publishing, 1994.

P. J. Kennedy and Sons. *The Official Catholic Directory*. New York: P. J. Kennedy and Sons, 1886– .

Kirkham, E. Kay. *A Survey of American Church Records*. 4th ed. Logan, Utah: Everton Publishing, 1978.

Kludas, Arnold. *Great Passenger Ships of the World*. Trans. Charles Hodges. 6 vols. Cambridge, Eng.: Patrick Stephens, Ltd., 1975–1986.

Lainhart, Ann S. *State Census Records*. Baltimore: Genealogical Publishing, 1992.

Lee, Harper. *To Kill a Mockingbird*. Pleasantville, N.Y.: Reader's Digest Assoc., 1993.

Lemmon, Anne. *Ancestry*. Salt Lake City: Ancestry, 1984– .

Library of Congress. *Genealogies Cataloged by the Library of Congress Since 1986*. Washington, D.C.: Libr. of Congress, 1991.

———. *Library of Congress Subject Headings*. 16th ed. 4 vols. Washington, D.C.: Libr. of Congress, Cataloging Distribution Service, 1993.

———. *National Union Catalog, A Cumulative Author List Representing Library of Congress Cards and Titles Reported by Other American Libraries*. New York: Rowman and Littlefield, 1956–1983.

———. *National Union Catalog of Manuscript Collections*. Washington, D.C.: Libr. of Congress, 1959– .

———. *National Union Catalog of Manuscript Collections: Index 1980–83*. Washington, D.C.: Libr. of Congress, 1984.

Library of Congress, Geography and Map Division. *Fire Insurance Maps of North American Cities and Towns Produced by the Sanborn Map Company*. Washington, D.C.: Libr. of Congress, 1981.

McBride, David N., and Jan N. McBride. *Cemetery Inscriptions of Highland County, Ohio*. 2d ed. Hillsboro, Ohio: Southern Ohio Genealogical Soc., 1990.

McMullin, Phillip W. *Grassroots of America: A Computerized Index to the American State Papers: Land Grants and Claims with Other Aids to Research*. Conway, Ark.: Arkansas Research, 1990.

McVetty, Suzanne, and Sharon D. Carmack. "Ellis Island: A Research Facility for Genealogists." *National Genealogical Society Newsletter* 18 (May–June 1992): 68.

Makower, Joel, ed. *The American History Sourcebook*. New York: Prentice-Hall, 1988.

Makower, Joel, and Alan Green, eds. *Instant Information*. New York: Prentice-Hall, 1987.

Matthews, William. *American Diaries: An Annotated Bibliography of American Diaries Written Prior to the Year 1861*. Boston: J. S. Canner, 1959.

———. *American Diaries in Manuscript, 1580–1954: A Descriptive Bibliography*. Athens, Ga.: Univ. of Georgia, 1974.

Meyer, Mary K. *Directory of Genealogical Societies in the United States and Canada.* 9th ed. Mt. Airy, Md.: Mary K. Meyer, 1992.

Meyerink, Kory L. "Genealogical Periodicals." In *Printed Sources,* edited by Kory L. Meyerink, Anne Lemmon, Matt Grove, and Dennis Sampson. Salt Lake City: Ancestry, 1994.

Miller, Joseph, ed. *Sears List of Subject Headings.* 15th ed. New York: H. W. Wilson, 1994.

Miller, Sally M. *Ethnic Press in the United States: A Historical Analysis and Handbook.* New York: Greenwood Pr., 1987.

Mitchell, Susan L. *The Hewitts of Athens County, Ohio.* Westland, Mich.: S. L. Mitchell, 1989.

Morrison, Joan, and Charlotte Fox Zabusky. *American Mosaic: The Immigrant Experience in the Words of Those Who Lived It.* 2d ed. Pittsburgh: Univ. of Pittsburgh Pr., 1993.

Joel Munsell's Sons. *The American Genealogist, Being a Catalogue of Family Histories: A Bibliography of American Genealogy or a List of the Title Pages of Books and Pamphlets on Family History, Published in America, from 1771 to Date.* (1900) Reprint, Baltimore: Clearfield, 1990.

Joel Munsell's Sons, ed. *Index to American Genealogies and to Genealogical Material Contained in All Works Such as Town Histories, County Histories, Local Histories, Historical Society Publications, Biographies, Historical Periodicals, and Kindred Works, Alphabetically Arranged.* 5th ed. Rev. with *Supplement 1900–1908.* 1900, 1908. Reprint, Oakland, Maine: DanBury Books, 1987.

National Archives and Records Administration. *Abstracts of Oregon Donation Land Claims, 1852–1903.* Microfilm Publication M145. Washington, D.C.: National Archives and Records Administration, n.d.

———. *Abstracts of Washington Donation Land Claims, 1855–1902.* National Archives Microfilm Publication M203. Washington, D.C.: National Archives and Records Administration, n.d.

———. *Alphabetical Index to Canadian Border Entries through Small Ports in Vermont, 1895–1924.* National Archives Microfilm Publication M1462. Washington, D.C.: National Archives and Records Administration, n.d.

———. *American Indians: A Select Catalog of National Archives Microfilm Publications.* Washington, D.C.: National Archives and Records Administration, 1984.

———. *Black Studies: A Select Catalog of National Archives Microfilm Publications.* Washington, D.C.:

National Archives and Records Administration, 1984.

———. *Descriptions of Census Enumeration Districts, 1830–1890 and 1910–1950.* National Archives Microfilm Publication T1224. Washington, D.C.: National Archives and Records Administration, n.d.

———. *Descriptions of Census Enumeration Districts, 1900.* National Archives Microfilm Publication T1210. Washington, D.C.: National Archives and Records Administration, n.d.

———. *Federal Court Records: A Select Catalog of Microfilm Publications.* Washington, D.C.: National Archives and Records Administration, 1991.

———. *Federal Population Censuses, 1790–1890: A Catalog of Microfilm Copies of the Schedules.* Washington, D.C.: National Archives Trust Fund Board, 1993.

———. *Guide to Genealogical Research in the National Archives.* Rev. ed. Washington, D.C.: National Archives and Records Administration, 1985.

———. *Guide to the National Archives of the United States.* Rev. ed. 1974. Reprint, Washington, D.C.: National Archives and Records Administration, 1987.

———. *Guide to Records in the National Archives: Mid-Atlantic Region.* Washington, D.C.: National Archives and Records Administration, 1989.

———. *Guide to Records in the National Archives: Rocky Mountain Region.* Washington, D.C.: National Archives and Records Administration, 1989.

———. *Guide to Records in the National Archives: Southeast Region.* Washington, D.C.: National Archives and Records Administration, 1989.

———. *Immigrant & Passenger Arrivals: A Select Catalog of National Archives Microfilm Publications.* 2d ed. Washington, D.C.: National Archives and Records Administration, 1991.

———. *Index to Naturalization Petitions of the United States District Court for the Eastern District of New York, 1865–1957.* National Archives Microfilm Publication M1164. Washington, D.C.: National Archives and Records Administration, n.d.

———. *Manifests of Passengers Arriving in the St. Albans, Vt. District through Canadian Pacific and Atlantic Ports 1895–1954.* National Archives Microfilm Publication M1464. Washington, D.C.: National Archives and Records Administration, n.d.

———. *Manifests of Passengers Arriving in the St. Albans, Vt. District through Canadian Pacific Ports, 1929–1949.* National Archives Microfilm Publication M1465. Washington, D.C.: National Archives and Records Administration, n.d.

———. *Military Service Records: A Select Catalog of National Archive Microfilm Publications.* Washington,

D.C.: National Archives and Records Administration, 1985.

———. *Military Service Records in the National Archives of the United States.* Rev. Washington, D.C.: National Archives and Records Administration, 1985.

———. *The 1900 Federal Population Census: A Catalog of Microfilm Copies of the Schedules.* Washington, D.C.: National Archives and Records Administration, 1978.

———. *The 1910 Federal Population Census: A Catalog of Microfilm Copies of the Schedules.* Washington, D.C.: National Archives and Records Administration, 1982.

———. *The 1920 Federal Population Census: Catalog of National Archives Microfilm.* 2d ed. Washington, D.C.: National Archives Trust Fund Board, 1992.

———. *Oregon and Washington Donation Land Files, 1851–1903.* National Archives Microfilm Publication M815. Washington, D.C.: National Archives and Records Administration, n.d.

———. *Prologue.* Washington, D.C.: National Archives and Records Administration, 1968– .

———. *Soundex Index to Canadian Border Entries through the St. Albans, Vt. District, 1895–1924.* National Archives Microfilm Publication M1461. Washington, D.C.: National Archives and Records Administration, n.d.

———. *Soundex Index to Entries into the St. Albans, Vt. District through Canadian Pacific and Atlantic Ports, 1924–1952.* National Archives Microfilm Publication M1463. Washington, D.C.: National Archives and Records Administration, n.d.

———. *Soundex Index to Naturalization Petitions for the United States District and Circuit Courts, Northern District of Illinois, and Immigration and Naturalization Service District 9, 1840–1950.* National Archives Microfilm Publication M1285. Washington, D.C.: National Archives and Records Administration, n.d.

———. *Township Plats of Selected States.* National Archives Microfilm Publication T1234, 69 rolls. Washington, D.C.: National Archives and Records Administration, n.d.

———. *Using Records in the National Archives for Genealogical Research.* Rev. ed. General Information Leaflet Number 5. Washington, D.C.: National Archives and Records Administration, 1990.

National Council on Family Relations. *Journal of Family History.* Greenwich, Conn.: JAI Pr., 1976– .

National Genealogical Society. *Index of Revolutionary War Pension Applications in the National Archives.* Bicentennial ed., rev. and enl. Washington, D.C.: National Genealogical Soc., 1976.

———. *National Genealogical Society Newsletter.* Arlington, Va.: National Genealogical Soc., 1975– .

———. *National Genealogical Society Quarterly.* Arlington, Va.: National Genealogical Soc., 1912– .

National Genealogical Society Computer Interest Group. *National Genealogical Society/Computer Interest Group Digest.* Arlington, Va.: National Genealogical Soc., 1982– .

National Historical Publications and Records Commission. *Directory of Archives and Manuscript Repositories in the United States.* 3d ed. Phoenix: Oryx Pr., 1990.

National Society of the Daughters of the American Revolution. *DAR Patriot Index.* 3 vols. Washington, D.C.: National Soc. Daughters of the American Revolution, 1994.

———. *Index of the Rolls of Honor (Ancestor's Index) in the Lineage Books of the National Society of the Daughters of the American Revolution.* 4 vols. Pittsburgh, Pa.: Pr. of Pierpoint, Siviter, 1916, 1940; Washington, D.C.: Pr. of Judd & Detweiler, 1926, 1939; Baltimore: Genealogical Publishing, 1972, 1988.

———. *Lineage Book, National Society of the Daughters of the American Revolution.* Washington, D.C.: Daughters of the American Revolution, 1890– .

National Society of the Daughters of the American Revolution Library. *Continental Columns: Newsletter of the NSDAR Library.* Washington, D.C.: National Soc. Daughters of the American Revolution Libr., 1993– .

Neagles, James C. *The Library of Congress: A Guide to Genealogical and Historical Research.* Salt Lake City: Ancestry, 1990.

———. *U.S. Military Records: A Guide to Federal and State Sources, Colonial America to the Present.* Salt Lake City: Ancestry, 1994.

Neagles, James C., and Lila L. Neagles. *Locating Your Immigrant Ancestor: A Guide to Naturalization Records.* Logan, Utah: Everton Publishers, 1975.

———. *Locating Your Revolutionary War Ancestor: A Guide to the Military Records.* Logan, Utah: Everton Publishers, 1983.

Nelson, Kenneth C. "Civil War Sources for Genealogical Research." *Genealogical Journal* 15, no. 4 (winter, 1986): 187–99; 17, nos. 1, 2 (1988/1989): 89–93.

Newman, Debra L. *Black History: A Guide to Civilian Records in the National Archives.* Washington D.C.: National Archives Trust Fund Board, 1984.

Newman, John J. *Naturalization Processes and Procedures, 1790–1985.* Indianapolis: Indiana Historical Soc., 1985.

New England Historic Genealogical Society. *New England Historical and Genealogical Register.* Boston: New England Historic Genealogical Soc., 1847– .

———. *NEXUS.* Boston, Mass.: New England Historic Genealogical Soc., 1957– .

New York Genealogical and Biographical Society. *New York Genealogical and Biographical Record.* New York: New York Genealogical and Biographical Soc., 1870– .

Oberly, James W. *Sixty Million Acres: American Veterans and Public Lands before the Civil War.* Kent, Ohio: Kent State Univ. Pr., 1990.

Office of the Federal Register. *The United States Government Manual 1993/94.* Washington, D.C.: National Archives and Records Administration, 1974– .

The Ogden Standard-Examiner. Ogden, Utah: Standard-Examiner Publishing, 1920– .

Omnigraphics. *Omni Gazetteer of the United States of America.* (CD Version). Norwood, Mass.: Silver Platter Information, 1992.

Online Computer Library Center, OCLC [Computer network]. Dublin, Ohio: Online Computer Libr. Ctr., 1994.

Parker, J. Carlyle. *Going to Salt Lake City to Do Family History Research.* Turlock, Calif.: Marietta Publishing, 1993.

Parker, Jimmy B. "American Indian Records and Research." In *Ethnic Genealogy: A Research Guide,* 209–38. Westport, Conn.: Greenwood Pr., 1983.

Parsons Technology. Family Origins Version 2.5 [Computer program]. Hiawatha, Iowa: Parsons Technology.

Pennsylvania German Folklore Society. *Pennsylvania German Folklore Society Yearbook.* Allentown, Pa.: Pennsylvania German Folklore Soc., 1936– .

Plunges, Gregory J., Lynn M. Siller, and John J. Grabowski. "Register: Kniola Travel Bureau." MSS. No. 3678. Cleveland, Ohio: Western Reserve Historical Soc., 1977.

Przecha, Donna, and Joan Lowrey. *Guide to Genealogy Software.* Baltimore: Genealogical Publishing, 1993.

Quimby, Peter S., ed. *America: History and Life.* Santa Barbara, Calif.: ABC-CLIO, 1994.

Quinsept. Family Roots Version 3.7 [Computer program]. Lexington, Mass.: Quinsept.

Rand McNally Commercial Atlas & Marketing Guide. 125th ed. Chicago: Rand McNally, 1994.

Redford, Dorothy S. *Somerset Homecoming: Recovering a Lost Heritage.* New York: Anchor Books, 1989.

Reformed Church in America Commission on History. *Historical Directory of the Reformed Church in America, 1628–1992.* Grand Rapids, Mich.: Eerdmans, 1992.

Research Libraries Group. Research Libraries Information Network (RLIN) [Computer network]. Mountain View, Calif.: Research Libraries Group, 1994.

Research Publications. *City Directories of the United States, 1860–1901: A Guide to the Microfilm Collection.* Woodbridge, Conn.: Research Publications, 1993.

Rider, Fremont, ed. *American Genealogical Index.* 48 vols. Middletown, Conn.: Advisory Committee Representing the Cooperating Subscribing Libraries [at] Wesleyan Univ. Station, 1942–1951.

Roberts, Gary B. *English Origins of New England Families: From the New England Historical and Genealogical Register.* 3 vols. Baltimore: Genealogical Publishing, 1984.

Roberts, Jayare. "Beyond the Begat Books." *Genealogical Journal.* 16 (Spring/Summer 1987): 1–112.

Rogers, Colin D., and John H. Smith. *Local Family History in England, 1538–1914.* Manchester, Eng.: St. Martin's Pr., 1991.

Ross, Carl, and K. Marianne Wargelin Brown, eds. *Women Who Dared: The History of Finnish American Women.* St. Paul, Minn.: Immigration History Research Center, Univ. of Minnesota, 1986.

Roy, Janine. *Tracing Your Ancestors in Canada.* 11th rev. ed. Ottawa: National Archives of Canada, 1993.

Royal Commission on Historical Manuscripts. *Record Repositories in Great Britain: A Geographical Directory.* 9th rev. ed. London: Her Majesty's Stationery Office, 1992.

Rupp, I. Daniel. *A Collection of Upwards of 30,000 Names of German, Swiss, Dutch, French, and Other Immigrants in Pennsylvania from 1726 to 1776,* 2d ed. rev. and enl. Philadelphia: Leary, Stewart, 1927.

Schenk, Trudy, Ruth Froelke, and Inge Bork. *The Württemberg Emigration Index.* Salt Lake City: Ancestry, 1986.

Schmidt, Alvin J. *The Greenwood Encyclopedia of American Institutions: Fraternal Organizations.* Westport, Conn.: Greenwood Pr., 1980.

Schmidt, Jack R. *The Redbook National Directory of Morticians.* Youngstown, Ohio: Jack R. Schmidt, 1993.

Schreiner-Yantis, Netti. *Genealogical and Local History Books in Print.* 4th ed. 5 vols. Springfield, Va.: Genealogical Books in Print, 1985–1992.

Schuyler, Michael. *Dial In: An Annual Guide to Online Public Access Catalogs.* Westport, Conn.: Meckler, 1992.

Scott, Donald M., and Bernard Wishy, eds. *America's Families: A Documentary History.* New York: Harper & Row, 1982.

Scott, Sir Walter. *Ivanhoe.* New York: Hewet, Tillotson, 1984.

Smith, Clifford N. *Federal Land Series: A Calendar of Archival Materials on the Land Patents Issued by the United States Government, with Subject, Tract, and Name Indexes.* 4 vols. Chicago: American Libr. Assoc., 1972.

Smith, Eugene W. *Passenger Ships of the World Past and Present.* Boston: George H. Dean, 1978.

Smith, Jessie C. *Ethnic Genealogy: A Research Guide.* Westport, Conn.: Greenwood Pr., 1983.

Steed, John. Brother's Keeper Version 5.2 [Computer program]. Rockford, Mich.: John Steed.

Steiner, Bernard Christian. *History of Guilford and Madison, Connecticut.* 1897. Reprint, Guilford, Conn.: The Guilford Free Public Library, 1975.

Stephens, W. B. *Sources for U.S. History: Nineteenth Century Communities.* Cambridge, Eng.: Cambridge Univ. Pr., 1991.

Stephenson, Charles. "The Methodology of Historical Census Record Linkage: A User's Guide to the Soundex." *Prologue* 12, no.3 (Fall 1980): 151–3.

Stephenson, Richard W., comp. *Land Ownership Maps: A Checklist of Nineteenth Century United States County Maps in the Library of Congress.* Washington, D.C.: Libr. of Congress, 1967.

Steuart, Bradley. *The Soundex Reference Guide.* Bountiful, Utah: Precision Indexing, 1990.

Strassburger, Ralph B., and William John Hinke. *Pennsylvania German Pioneers: A Publication of Original Lists of Arrivals in the Port of Philadelphia from 1727 to 1808.* Norristown, Pa.: Pennsylvania German Soc., 1934.

Strunk, William, Jr., and E. B. White. *Elements of Style.* 3d ed. New York: Macmillan, 1979.

Sturm, Duane, and Pat Sturm. *Video Family History.* Salt Lake City: Ancestry, 1989.

Suelflow, August R. *A Preliminary Guide to Church Records Repositories.* St. Louis: Soc. of American Archivists, 1969.

Swierenga, Robert P. *Dutch Emigrants to the United States, South Africa, South America, and South East Asia, 1835–1880.* Wilmington, Del.: Scholarly Resources, 1983.

———. *Dutch Immigrants in U.S. Ship Passenger Manifests, 1820–1880.* 2 vols. Wilmington, Del.: Scholarly Resources, 1983.

Szucs, Loretto D., and Sandra H. Luebking. *The Archives: A Guide to the National Archives Field Branches.* Salt Lake City: Ancestry, 1988.

Taylor, Robert M., and Ralph J. Crandall, eds. *Generations and Change: Genealogical Perspectives in Social History.* Macon, Ga.: Mercer Univ. Pr., 1985.

Tepper, Michael. *American Passenger Arrival Records: A Guide to the Records of Immigrants Arriving at American Ports by Sail and Steam.* 2d ed. Baltimore: Genealogical Publishing, 1993.

———. *New World Immigrants.* 2 vols. Baltimore: Genealogical Publishing, 1988.

Tepper, Michael, ed. *Immigrants to the Middle Colonies.* Baltimore: Genealogical Publishing, 1992.

Thackery, David T. *Afro-American Family History at the Newberry Library: A Research Guide and Bibliography.* Chicago: Newberry Libr., 1988.

Thackery, David T., and Dee Woodtor. *Case Studies in Afro-American Genealogy.* Chicago: Newberry Libr., 1989.

Thernstrom, Stephan, and others, eds. *Harvard Encyclopedia of American Ethnic Groups.* Cambridge, Mass.: Belknap Pr., 1980.

Thode, Ernest. *Address Book for Germanic Genealogy.* 5th ed. Baltimore: Genealogical Publishing, 1994.

Towle, Laird C., and others, eds. *Genealogical Periodical Annual Index (GPAI).* Bowie, Md.: Heritage Books, 1962– .

U.S. Bureau of Land Management. *Tract Books.* 1265 microfilm reels. Washington, D.C: Bureau of Land Management, 1957.

———. *Land Records: Where They Came from, How We Got Them.* Washington, D.C.: U.S. Bureau of Land Management, n.d.

U.S. Bureau of the Census. *Census Enumeration District Descriptions.* Washington, D.C.: Bureau of the Census, 1977.

———. *Statistical Abstract of the United States—1993: The National Data Book.* 113th ed. Washington, D.C.: Government Printing Office, 1993.

———. *200 Years of U.S. Census Taking Population Housing Questions, 1790–1990.* Washington, D.C.: Bureau of the Census, 1989. Reprint, Orting, Wash.: Heritage Quest, 1992.

U.S. Civil Service Commission. *Official Register of the United States.* Washington, D.C.: U.S. Government Printing Office, 1933–1959. (Supersedes *Register of Officials and Agents,* and *Register of Officers and Agents.*)

U.S. Congress. *American State Papers: Public Lands.* 8 vols. Washington, D.C.: Gales and Seaton, 1832–1861.

U.S. Department of Education. *Directory of Public Elementary and Secondary Education Agencies.* Washington, D.C.: U.S. Department of Education, 1987– .

U.S. House of Representatives. *Congressional Directory for the Second Session of the Thirty-Eighth Congress of the United States of America.* Washington, D.C.: Postmaster of the House of Representatives, 1865.

———. *Congressional Serial Set.* Washington, D.C.: U.S. Government Printing Office, 1817– .

Utah Genealogical Association. *Genealogical Journal.* Salt Lake City: Utah Genealogical Association, 1972– .

Vecoli, Rudolph J., and Suzanne M. Sinke, eds. *A Century of European Migrations, 1830–1930.* Chicago: Univ. of Illinois Pr., 1991.

Walch, Timothy, comp. *Our Family, Our Town: Essays on Family and Local History Sources in National Archives.* Washington, D.C.: National Archives and Records Administration, 1987.

Waldenmaier, Inez P. *Annual Index to Genealogical Periodicals and Family Histories.* Washington, D.C.: Inez P. Waldenmaier, 1956–1963.

Walls, Dwayne E. *The Kidwells: A Family Odyssey.* Durham, N.C.: Carolina Academic Pr., 1983.

Wheeler, Mary B., ed. *Directory of Historical Organizations in the United States and Canada.* 14th ed. Nashville: American Assoc. for State and Local History, 1990.

Whipple, Irma W. *In Search of Familie Wiese.* Rohnert Park, Calif.: Paper Mill Pr., 1983.

James T. White Company. *The National Cyclopedia of American Biography.* 63 vols. New York: James T. White, 1898.

Wigglesworth, Michael. *The Day of Doom.* Tucson, Ariz.: American Eagle Publications, 1992.

———. *The Diary of Michael Wigglesworth, 1653–1657.* Edmund S. Morgan, ed. Gloucester, Mass.: Peter Smith, 1970.

Wolfert, Marion, comp. *German Immigrants: Lists of Passengers Bound from Bremen to New York, 1868–1871, with Places of Origin.* Vol. 4. Baltimore: Genealogical Publishing, 1993.

Wynar, Lubomyr R. *Encyclopedic Directory of Ethnic Organizations in the United States.* Littleton, Colo.: Libraries Unlimited, 1975.

Wynar, Lubomyr R., and Anna T. Wynar. *Encyclopedic Directory of Ethnic Newspapers and Periodicals in the United States.* Littleton, Colo.: Libraries Unlimited, 1976.

Yoder, Don, ed. *Pennsylvania German Immigrants, 1709–1786.* Baltimore: Genealogical Publishing, 1989.

Zimmermann, Gary J., and Marion Wolfert, comp. *German Immigrants: Lists of Passengers Bound from Bremen to New York, 1847–1867, with Places of Origin.* 3 vols. Baltimore: Genealogical Publishing, 1985–1988.

Zinsser, William. *On Writing Well: An Informal Guide to Writing Nonfiction.* 4th ed. rev. and enl. New York: Harper & Row, 1990.

Appendixes

Appendixes A and B provide addresses of selected research centers; most entries also include a telephone number. Because the entries without a telephone number generally describe organizations in which officers and telephone numbers change periodically, the addresses provide a more-reliable contact point.

These lists are not exhaustive. If you wish a more-complete listing of historical and genealogical societies, archives, libraries, and other research centers in a specific state or county, refer to the section in chapter 5 that demonstrates how to use reference books to find addresses of libraries, archives, and other agencies.

Appendix B lists research centers whose collections and services focus on ethnic groups and immigrants to the United States. However, many of the centers listed in Appendix A have collections of United States passenger list microfilms.

APPENDIX A

(((© ©)))

Genealogical Research Centers

Note that the entries for National Archives regional offices include the names of states that fall under the jurisdiction of that office.

Note also that most LDS Family History Centers are listed without zip codes because they have insufficient staff to respond to correspondence. The addresses given are the locations of the Family History Centers. Please contact them by telephone for the hours of operation.

There are more than 1,000 LDS Family History Centers in the United States and Canada. Appendix A identifies at least one Family History Center in each state of the United States and each province of Canada. Write to the LDS Family History Library in Salt Lake City for a complete list of Family History Centers in your state or province.

U.S. NATIONAL ARCHIVES

National Archives Fulfillment Ctr. (NEDC)
8700 Edgeworth Dr.
Capitol Heights, MD 20743-3701
301-763-1872

National Archives General Reference Branch (NNRG)
7th and Pennsylvania Ave. NW
Washington, DC 20408
202-501-5035

National Archives Microfilm Rental Program
P.O. Box 30
Annapolis Junction, MD 20701-0030
800-788-6282

National Archives National Personnel Records Ctr.
  (NCPC)
9700 Page Blvd.
St. Louis, MO 63132
314-538-4201

National Archives Publications Services Branch (NEPS)
7th and Pennsylvania Ave. NW
Washington, DC 20408
800-788-6282

National Archives Reference Services
Washington, DC 20408
202-501-5400

National Archives Trust Fund Board
8601 Adelphi Rd., Rm. 4100
College Park, MD 20740
301-713-6405

National Archives Trust Fund Board
Publication Order Dept.
P.O. Box 100793
Atlanta, GA 30384

U.S. NATIONAL ARCHIVES REGIONAL OFFICES

Alaska

National Archives
Alaska Region
654 W. Third Ave., Rm. 12
Anchorage, AK 99501
907-271-2441

Iowa, Kansas, Missouri, Nebraska

National Archives
Central Plains Region
2306 E. Bannister Rd.
Kansas City, MO 64131
816-926-7271

Illinois, Indiana, Michigan, Minnesota, Ohio, Wisconsin

National Archives
Great Lakes Region
7358 S. Pulaski Rd.
Chicago, IL 60629
312-353-0161

Delaware, Pennsylvania, Maryland, Virginia, West Virginia

National Archives
Mid-Atlantic Region
5000 Wissahickon Ave.
Philadelphia, PA 19144
215-951-5588

Connecticut, Maine, Massachusetts, New Hampshire, Rhode Island, Vermont

National Archives
New England Region
380 Trapelo Rd.
Waltham, MA 02154
617-647-8100

New Jersey, New York, Puerto Rico, Virgin Islands

National Archives
Northeast Region
201 Varick St.
New York, NY 10014
212-337-1300

Idaho, Oregon, Washington

National Archives
Pacific Northwest Region
6125 Sand Point Way NE
Seattle, WA 98115
206-442-4502

California, except southern California; Hawaii; Nevada, except Clark County; Pacific Ocean Area

National Archives
Pacific Sierra Region
1000 Commodore Dr.
San Bruno, CA 94066
415-876-9009

South Dakota, Utah, Colorado, Montana, North Dakota, Wyoming

National Archives
Rocky Mountain Region
Denver Federal Ctr., Bldg. 48
Denver, CO 80225
303-234-5271

Alabama, Georgia, Florida, Kentucky, Mississippi, North Carolina, South Carolina, Tennessee

National Archives
Southeast Region
1557 St. Joseph Ave.
East Point, GA 30344
404-763-7477

Arkansas, Louisiana, New Mexico, Oklahoma, Texas

National Archives
Southwest Region
501 W. Felix St.
P.O. Box 6216
Fort Worth, TX 76115
817-334-5525

NATIONAL DEPARTMENTS AND AGENCIES

Bureau of Land Management
Dept. of the Interior
C and 19th Sts. NW
Washington, DC 20240
202-343-9435

Bureau of Land Management
Eastern States Office
7450 Boston Blvd.
Springfield, VA 22153
703-440-1713

Department of Veterans Affairs
810 Vermont Ave. NW
Washington, DC 20420
202-273-5400

Federation of Genealogical Societies
P.O. Box 3385
Salt Lake City, UT 84110-3385

Railroad Retirement Board
844 Rush St.
Chicago, IL 60611
312-751-4548

Selective Service System
Records Div.
1515 Wilson Blvd.
Arlington, VA 22209-2425
703-235-2274

Social Security Administration
4-H-8 Annex Bldg.
6401 Security Blvd.
Baltimore, MD 21235
Attn: Freedom of Information Officer
401-965-7700

U.S. Department of Commerce
Bureau of the Census
P.O. Box 1545
Jeffersonville, IN 47131
812-288-3300

STATE RESOURCES

Alabama

Alabama Dept. of Archives and History
624 Washington Ave.
Montgomery, AL 36130-3601
205-832-6510

Alabama Genealogical Soc., Inc.
Samford Univ. Library
Special Collection Dept.
800 Lakeshore Dr.
Birmingham, AL 35229
205-870-2749

Alabama Historical Assn.
P.O. Box 870380
Tuscaloosa, AL 35487-0380

Birmingham LDS Family History Ctr.
2768 Altadena
Birmingham, AL
205-967-7279

Birmingham Public Library
Linn-Henley Library for Southern Research
2100 Park Pl.
Birmingham, AL 35203
205-226-3665

Chattahoochee Valley Historical Soc.
H. Grady Bradshaw—Chambers County Library and
    Cobb Memorial Archives
3419 20th Ave.
Valley, AL 36854
205-768-2161

Gadsden-Etowah County Public Library
254 College St.
Gadsden, AL 35999-3101
205-549-4699 x66

Alaska

Alaska Archives
165 E. 56th Ave., #1
Anchorage, AK 99518
907-561-8000

Alaska Genealogical Soc.
8030 Dickerson Dr.
Anchorage, AK 99504

Alaska Historical Library and Museum
P.O. Box G
State Office Bldg., 8th Fl.
Juneau, AK 99811
907-465-2925

Alaska State Library
9706 Trapper Ln., Pouch G
Juneau, AK 99811
907-465-2942

Anchorage LDS Family History Ctr.
2501 Maplewood St.
Anchorage, AK
907-277-8433

Archives and Records Management
Div. of Library and Archives, Dept. of Educ.
141 Willoughby
Juneau, AK 99801-1720
907-465-2275

Arizona

Arizona Dept. of Library, Archives/Public Records
 Research Div.
State Capitol
1700 W. Washington
Phoenix, AZ 85007
602-542-3942

Arizona Historical Soc.
949 E. Second St.
Tucson, AZ 85719
602-628-5774

Arizona State Genealogical Soc.
P.O. Box 5566
Glendale, AZ 85312

Mesa LDS Family History Ctr.
41 S. Hobson
Mesa, AZ 85204
602-964-1200

Arkansas

Arkansas Genealogical Soc.
P.O. Box 908
Hot Springs, AR 71902-0908
501-262-4513

Arkansas Historical Assn.
History Dept.
Old Main, #416
Univ. of Arkansas
Fayetteville, AR 72701
501-575-5884

Arkansas Historical Soc.
422 S. Sixth St.
Van Buren, AR 72956

Arkansas History Commission
1 Capitol Mall
Little Rock, AR 72201
501-682-6900

Little Rock LDS Family History Ctr.
13901 Quail Run Dr.
Little Rock, AR
501-455-0335

California

California Genealogical Soc.
P.O. Box 77105
San Francisco, CA 94107-0105
415-777-9936

California Historical Soc.
2099 Pacific Ave.
San Francisco, CA 94109-2235

California State Archives
Office of the Secr. of State
1020 O St., Rm. 130
Sacramento, CA 95814
916-653-0066

California State Library
914 Capitol Mall
P.O. Box 942837
Sacramento, CA 94237-0001
916-654-0176

California State Library
Sutro Branch
480 Winston Dr.
San Francisco, CA 94132
415-557-0421

Los Alamitos LDS Family History Ctr.
4142 Cerritos Ave.
Los Alamitos, CA
714-821-6914

Los Angeles Public Library
History and Genealogy Dept.
630 W. Fifth St.
Los Angeles, CA 90071-2097
213-612-3317

Oakland LDS Family History Ctr.
4780 Lincoln Ave.
Oakland, CA
510-531-3905

Sons of the Revolution in the State of California Library
600 S. Central Ave.
Glendale, CA 91204-2009
818-240-1775

Colorado

Colorado Genealogical Soc.
P.O. Box 9218
Denver, CO 80209

Colorado Historical Soc.
Stephen H. Hart Library
1300 Broadway
Denver, CO 80203-2137
303-866-2305

Colorado State Library
201 E. Colfax Ave.
Denver, CO 80203
303-866-6728

Denver LDS Family History Ctr.
2710 S. Monaco Pkwy.
Denver, CO
303-758-6460

Denver Public Library
1357 Broadway
Denver, CO 80203-2165
303-571-2190

Div. of Archives and Public Records
Dept. of Administration
1313 Sherman St.
Denver, CO 80203
303-866-2358

Connecticut

Bloomfield LDS Family History Ctr.
1000 Mountain Rd.
Bloomfield, CT
203-242-1607

Connecticut Historical Commission
59 S. Prospect St.
Hartford, CT 06106

Connecticut Historical Soc.
One Elizabeth St.
Hartford, CT 06105
203-236-5621

Connecticut Soc. of Genealogists, Inc.
P.O. Box 435
Glastonbury, CT 06433-1435
203-569-0002

Connecticut State Library
History and Genealogy Unit
231 Capitol Ave.
Hartford, CT 06106
302-566-3690

Connecticut State Library
State Archives
231 Capitol Ave.
Hartford, CT 06106
302-566-5650

New Haven Colony Historical Soc.
Whitney Library
114 Whitney Ave.
New Haven, CT 06510-1025
203-562-4183

Pequot Library
720 Pequot Ave.
Southport, CT 06490-1496
203-259-0346

Delaware

Delaware Div. of Libraries
Dept. of Community Affairs
43 S. Dupont Hwy.
Dover, DE 19901
302-736-4748

Delaware Genealogical Soc.
505 Market St. Mall
Wilmington, DE 19801

Delaware State Archives
Hall of Records
Dover, DE 19901
302-736-5318

Historical Soc. of Delaware
505 Market St.
Wilmington, DE 19801
302-655-7161

Wilmington LDS Family History Ctr.
143 Dickinson Lane
Wilmington, DE
302-654-2145

District of Columbia

Afro-American Historical and Genealogical Society
P.O. Box 73086
Washington, DC 20056-3086

Columbia Historical Soc.
1307 New Hampshire Ave. NW
Washington, DC 20036
202-785-2068

District of Columbia Office of Public Records
1300 Naylor Ct. NW
Washington, DC 20001-4225
202-727-2054

Howard University
Moorland-Spingarn Research Ctr.
500 Howard Pl. NW
Washington, DC 20059
202-636-7239

Library of Congress
Local History and Genealogy Reading Room
10 First St. SE
Washington, DC 20540
202-287-5537

National Soc. of the Daughters of the American
  Revolution
NSDAR Library
Memorial Continental Hall
1776 D St. NW
Washington, DC 20006-5392
202-879-3229

Florida

Florida Genealogical Soc.
P.O. Box 18624
Tampa, FL 33679-8624

Florida Historical Soc.
Univ. of S. Florida Library
P.O. Box 3645, Univ. Sta.
Gainesville, FL 32601
813-974-3815

Jacksonville LDS Family History Ctr.
7665 Fort Carolina Rd.
Jacksonville, FL
904-743-0527

Miami-Dade Public Library
101 W. Flagler St.
Miami, FL 33130-1523
305-375-2665 x5580

Orange County Library Sys.
Genealogy Dept.
101 E. Central Ave.
Orlando, FL 32801
407-425-4694 x380

State Archives of Florida
R. A. Gray Bldg.
500 S. Bronough St.
Tallahassee, FL 32399-0250
904-487-2073

State Library of Florida
Florida Collection
Div. of Library and Infor. Serv.
R. A. Gray Bldg.
500 S. Bronough St.
Tallahassee, FL 32399-0250
904-487-2651

Georgia

Atlanta Public Library
One Margaret Mitchell Sq.
Carnegie Way and Forsythe St.
Atlanta, GA 30303-1089
404-730-1700

Columbus LDS Family History Ctr.
4400 Reese Rd.
Columbus, GA
706-563-7216

Georgia Dept. of Archives and History
Search Room
330 Capitol Ave. SE
Atlanta, GA 30334
404-656-2350

Georgia Genealogical Soc.
P.O. Box 38066
Atlanta, GA 30334
404-475-4404

Georgia Historical Soc.
501 Whittaker St.
Savannah, GA 31499
912-651-2128

Georgia State Law Library
301 Judicial Bldg.
Capitol Hill Sta.
Atlanta, GA 30334
404-656-3468

Hawaii

Genealogical Resource Ctr.
Alu Like Native Hawaiian Libraries Project
1024 Mapunapuna St.
Honolulu, HI 96819-8940
808-836-8940

Hawaii State Archives
Archives Div.
Dept. of Accounting and General Serv.
Iolani Palace Grounds
478 S. King St.
Honolulu, HI 96813
808-586-0329

Hawaii State Library
478 S. King St.
Honolulu, HI 96813
808-548-4165

Hawaiian Historical Soc.
560 Kawaiahao St.
Honolulu, HI 96813
808-537-6271

Honolulu LDS Family History Ctr.
1723 Beckley St.
Honolulu, HI
808-841-4118

Idaho

Boise LDS Family History Ctr.
McMillian and Shamrock
Boise, ID
208-376-0452

The Idaho Genealogical Soc., Inc.
4620 Overland Rd., #204
Boise, ID 83705-2867
208-384-0542

The Idaho State Historical Soc.
Genealogical Library
450 N. Fourth St.
Boise, ID 83702
208-334-2305

The Idaho State Historical Soc.
Library and Archives
450 N. Fourth St.
Boise, ID 83702
208-334-3356

LDS Regional Family History Ctr.
McKay Library
Ricks College
525 S. Center
Rexburg, ID 83460
208-356-2377

Illinois

Illinois State Archives
Capitol Complex
Archives Bldg.
Springfield, IL 62756
217-782-4682

Illinois State Genealogical Soc.
P.O. Box 10195
Springfield, IL 62791

Illinois State Historical Library
Old State Capitol Bldg.
Springfield, IL 62701
217-782-4836

Illinois State Library
300 S. Second St.
Reference Dept.
Springfield, IL 62701
217-782-5430

Newberry Library
60 W. Walton St.
Chicago, IL 60610-3394
312-943-9090

Wilmette LDS Family History Ctr.
2801 Lake Ave.
Wilmette, IL
708-251-9818

Indiana

Allen County Public Library
Fred J. Reynolds Historical Genealogy Dept.
900 Webster St.
P.O. Box 2270
Fort Wayne, IN 46802
219-424-7241 x2242

Indiana Genealogical Soc., Inc.
P.O. Box 10507
Fort Wayne, IN 46852-0507

Indiana Historical Soc.
Indiana State Library and Historical Bldg.
315 W. Ohio St.
P.O. Box 88255
Indianapolis, IN 46202
317-232-1879

Indiana State Library
140 N. Senate Ave.
Indianapolis, IN 46204-2296
317-232-3675

Indianapolis LDS Family History Ctr.
900 E. Stop 11 Rd.
Indianapolis, IN
317-888-6002

Iowa

Iowa Genealogical Soc.
6000 Douglas Ave.
P.O. Box 7735
Des Moines, IA 50322-7735
515-276-0287

Iowa State Archives
Capitol Complex
East 12th St. and Grand Ave.
Des Moines, IA 50319
515-281-3007

State Historical Soc. of Iowa
Bureau of Library Archives
Centennial Bldg.
402 Iowa Ave.
Iowa City, IA 52240-1806
319-335-3916

State Historical Soc. of Iowa
Library
Capitol Complex
600 E. Locust St.
Des Moines, IA 50319
515-281-3007 (Archives)
515-281-6200 (Library)

West Des Moines LDS Family History Ctr.
3301 Ashworth Rd.
West Des Moines, IA
515-225-0416

Kansas

Kansas Genealogical Soc., Inc.
700 Ave. G at Vine St.
P.O. Box 103
Dodge City, KS 67801

Kansas State Historical Soc.
Memorial Bldg.
120 W. Tenth St.
Topeka, KS 66612-1291
913-296-4776

Kansas State Library
Statehouse, 3d Fl.
Topeka, KS 66612
913-296-3296

Wichita LDS Family History Ctr.
7011 E. 13th St.
Wichita, KS
316-683-2951

Wichita Public Library
223 S. Main St.
Wichita, KS 67202
316-262-0611 x262

Kentucky

Historical Confederation of Kentucky
P.O. Box H
Frankfort, KY 40602
502-564-3016

Kentucky Genealogical Soc.
P.O. Box 613
Columbia, KY 42728

Kentucky Historical Soc.
Old Capitol Annex
300 W. Broadway
P.O. Box H
Frankfort, KY 40602-2108
502-564-3016

Kentucky State Archives
Public Records Div.
300 Coffee Tree Rd.
P.O. Box 537
Frankfort, KY 40602-0537
502-875-7000

Louisville LDS Family History Ctr.
1000 Hurstbourne Lane
Louisville, KY
502-426-8174

Univ. of Kentucky
Margaret I. King Library
Dept. of Special Collections and Archives
Lexington, KY 40506-0039
606-257-8611

Louisiana

Baton Rouge LDS Family History Ctr.
10335 Highland Rd.
Baton Rouge, LA
504-769-8913

Le Comité des Archives de la Louisiane
Capitol Station
116 Main St.
P.O. Box 44370
Baton Rouge, LA 70804
504-355-9906

Louisiana Genealogical and Historical Soc.
P.O. Box 3454
Baton Rouge, LA 70821
504-766-3018

Shreve Memorial Library
424 Texas St.
P.O. Box 21523
Shreveport, LA 71120
318-226-5890

State Archives and Records
Office of the Secr. of State
3851 Essen Lane
P.O. Box 94125
Baton Rouge, LA 70804-9125
504-922-1206

State Library of Louisiana
760 Riverside Mall N
P.O. Box 131
Baton Rouge, LA 70821
504-342-4914

Maine

Cape Elizabeth LDS Family History Ctr.
29 Ocean House Rd.
Cape Elizabeth, ME
207-767-5000

Maine Genealogical Soc.
P.O. Box 221
Farmington, ME 04938-0221

Maine Historical Soc.
485 Congress St.
Portland, ME 04111
207-774-1822

Maine State Archives
State House Station #84
Augusta, ME 04333
207-289-5795

Maine State Library
L.M.A. Bldg.
State House Station #64
Augusta, ME 04333
207-289-5600

Maryland

Annapolis LDS Family History Ctr.
1875 Ritchie Hwy.
Annapolis, MD
301-757-4173

Johns Hopkins Univ.
George Peabody Library
17 E. Mount Vernon Pl.
Baltimore, MD 21202
410-659-8179

Maryland Genealogical Soc.
201 W. Monument St.
Baltimore, MD 21201
410-685-3750 x360

Maryland Historical Soc.
201 W. Monument St.
Baltimore, MD 21201
410-685-3750 x359

Maryland State Archives
Hall of Records Bldg.
350 Rowe Blvd.
Annapolis, MD 21401
410-974-3914

Maryland State Law Library
Courts of Appeals Bldg.
361 Rowe Blvd.
Annapolis, MD 21401-1697
410-974-3395

Massachusetts

American Antiquarian Soc. Library
185 Salisbury St.
Worcester, MA 01609-1634
617-755-5221

Archives of the Commonwealth Reference Desk
220 Morrissey Blvd.
(Columbia Point)
Boston, MA 02125
617-727-2816

Bedford Free Public Library
Genealogy Rm.
7 Mudge Way
Bedford, MA 01730
617-275-9440

Boston Public Library
Social Sciences Dept.
666 Boylston St.
P.O. Box 286
Boston, MA 02117
617-536-5400 x261

The Commonwealth of Massachusetts State Library
George Fingold Library
State House, Rm. 341
Beacon St.
Boston, MA 02133
617-727-2590

Massachusetts Historical Soc.
1154 Boylston St.
Boston, MA 02215
617-536-1608

Massachusetts Soc. of Genealogists, Inc.
P.O. Box 215
Ashland, MA 01721

New England Historic Genealogy Soc.
99-101 Newbury St.
Boston, MA 02116-3087
617-536-5740

Springfield City Library
220 State St.
Springfield, MA 01103
413-739-3871 x230

Weston LDS Family History Ctr.
150 Brown St.
Weston, MA
617-235-2164

Michigan

Detroit Public Library
Burton Historical Collection
5201 Woodward Ave.
Detroit, MI 48202-4093
313-833-1480

Grand Rapids LDS Family History Ctr.
2780 Leonard NE
Grand Rapids, MI
616-949-0070

Historical Soc. of Michigan
2117 Washtenaw Ave.
Ann Arbor, MI 48104
313-769-1828

Library of Michigan
717 W. Allegan Ave.
P.O. Box 30007
Lansing, MI 48909
517-373-1300

Michigan Genealogical Council
P.O. Box 80953
Lansing, MI 48908-0953

State Archives
Bureau of History
Dept. of State
717 W. Allegan Ave.
Lansing, MI 18918
517-373-1408

Minnesota

Div. of Library and Archives
Minnesota Historical Soc.
160 John Ireland Blvd.
St. Paul, MN 55102
612-296-6980

Minneapolis LDS Family History Ctr.
2801 N. Douglas Dr.
Minneapolis, MN
612-544-2479

Minneapolis Public Library
History & Travel Dept.
300 Nicollet Mall
Minneapolis, MN 55401-1992
612-372-6648

Minnesota Genealogical Soc.
P.O. Box 16069
St. Paul, MN 55116-0069
612-222-6929

Minnesota Historical Soc.
690 Cedar St.
St. Paul, MN 55101
612-296-2143

Mississippi

Archives and Library Div.
Mississippi Dept. of Archives and History
P.O. Box 571
Jackson, MS 39205-0571
601-359-6876

Clinton LDS Family History Ctr.
1301 Pinehaven Rd.
Clinton, MS
601-924-2686

Historical and Genealogical Assn. of Mississippi
618 Avalon Rd.
Jackson, MS 39206

Mississippi Genealogical Soc.
P.O. Box 5301
Jackson, MS 39296-5301

Missouri

Kansas City LDS Family History Ctr.
103025 Wornall Ave.
Kansas City, MO
816-941-7389

Mid-Continent Public Library
Genealogy and Local History Dept.
15616 E. Hwy. 24
Independence, MO 64050
816-252-0950

Missouri Historical Soc.
Research Library and Archives
225 S. Skinker
P.O. Box 11940
St. Louis, MO 63112-1099
314-746-4500

Missouri State Archives
600 W. Main St.
P.O. Box 778
Jefferson City, MO 65102
314-751-3280

Missouri State Genealogical Assn.
P.O. Box 833
Columbia, MO 65205-0833
816-747-9330

Missouri State Library
308 E. High St.
Jefferson City, MO 65101
314-751-3615

Saint Louis Public Library
History and Genealogy Dept.
1301 Olive St.
St. Louis, MO 63103-2389
314-241-2288

Montana

Helena LDS Family History Ctr.
1610 E. Sixth Ave.
Helena, MT
406-443-0716

Montana Historical Soc.
Memorial Bldg.
225 N. Roberts St.
Helena, MT 59620-9990
406-444-2681

Montana State Genealogical Soc.
P.O. Box 555
Chester, MT 59522

Nebraska

Nebraska State Genealogical Soc.
P.O. Box 5608
Lincoln, NE 68505
402-266-8881

Nebraska State Law Library
Statehouse, 3d Fl. S.
P.O. Box 94926
Lincoln, NE 68502
402-471-3189

Omaha LDS Family History Ctr.
11027 Martha St.
Omaha, NE
402-393-7641

State Archives Div.
Nebraska State Historical Soc.
Div. of Reference Services
1500 R St.
P.O. Box 82554
Lincoln, NE 68501
402-471-4771

Nevada

Las Vegas LDS Family History Ctr.
509 S. Boulder Hwy.
Las Vegas, NV
702-382-9695

Nevada State Genealogical Soc.
P.O. Box 20666
Reno, NV 89515

Nevada State Historical Soc.
1650 N. Virginia St.
Reno, NV 89503
702-688-1190

Nevada State Library and Archives
Div. of Archives and Records
100 Stewart St.
Carson City, NV 89710
702-687-5210

New Hampshire

Concord LDS Family History Ctr.
90 Clinton St.
Concord, NH
603-225-2848

New Hampshire Div. of Records Mgmt. and Archives
Dept. of State
71 S. Fruit St.
Concord, NH 03301-2410
603-271-2236

New Hampshire Historical Soc.
30 Park St.
Concord, NH 03301
603-225-3381

New Hampshire Soc. of Genealogists
P.O. Box 633
Exeter, NH 03833-0633
603-432-8137

New Hampshire State Library
20 Park St.
Concord, NH 03301
603-271-2144

New Jersey

Cherry Hill LDS Family History Ctr.
260 Evesham Rd.
Cherry Hill, NJ
609-795-8841

Dept. of State
New Jersey State Archives
185 W. State St.
CN 307
Trenton, NJ 08625-0307
609-292-6260

Genealogical Soc. of New Jersey
P.O. Box 1291
New Brunswick, NJ 08903
201-356-6920

New Jersey Historical Soc.
230 Broadway
Newark, NJ 07104
201-483-3939

New Jersey State Library
Genealogy Sect.
CN 520
Trenton, NJ 08625-0520
609-292-6274

New Mexico

Albuquerque LDS Family History Ctr.
1100 Montano Rd. NW
Albuquerque, NM
505-345-0406

Historical Soc. of New Mexico
P.O. Box 4638
Santa Fe, NM 87501

New Mexico Genealogical Soc.
P.O. Box 8283
Albuquerque, NM 87198-8330
505-281-3133

New Mexico Records Ctr. and Archives
404 Montezuma St.
Santa Fe, NM 87501
505-827-7332

New Mexico State Library
Southwest Rm.
325 Don Gaspar Ave.
Santa Fe, NM 87503
505-827-3805

New York

American Irish Historical Soc. Library
991 Fifth Ave.
New York, NY 10028
212-288-2263

New York City LDS Family History Ctr.
2 Lincoln Square
New York, NY
212-873-1690

New York Genealogical and Biographical Soc.
122-126 E. Fifty-Eighth St.
New York, NY 10022-1939
212-755-8532

The New York Historical Soc.
170 Central Park West
New York, NY 10024-5194
212-873-3400

The New York Public Library
Research Libraries
U.S. History, Local History, and Genealogy Div.
Fifth Ave. and Forty-Second St.
New York, NY 10018
212-930-0828

New York State Archives
New York Dept. of Educ.
Cultural Educ. Ctr.
Albany, NY 12230
518-474-1195

New York State Historical Assn.
West Lake Rd.
P.O. Box 800
Cooperstown, NY 13326
607-547-2533

New York State Library
Genealogy Sec., Ref. Serv., Cultural Educ. Ctr., 7th Fl.
Albany, NY 12230
518-474-5161

North Carolina

Charlotte LDS Family History Ctr.
5815 Carmel Rd.
Charlotte, NC
704-541-1451

Forsyth County Library
North Carolina Collection
660 W. Fifth St.
Winston-Salem, NC 27101
919-727-2152

North Carolina Dept. of Cultural Resources
Div. of State Library
Genealogical Services Branch
109 E. Jones St.
Raleigh, NC 27601-2807
919-733-7222

North Carolina Genealogical Soc.
P.O. Box 1492
Raleigh, NC 27602

North Carolina Soc. of Historians
P.O. Box 848
Rockingham, NC 28379

North Carolina State Archives
Dept. of Cultural Resources
Div. of Archives and History
State Library Bldg.
109 E. Jones St.
Raleigh, NC 27601-2807
919-733-3952

Public Library of Charlotte and Mecklenburg County
310 N. Tryon St.
Charlotte, NC 28202-2176
704-336-2780

State Library of North Carolina
Archives and History
State Library Bldg.
109 E. Jones St.
Raleigh, NC 27601-2807
919-733-7222

Wake Forest Univ.
Z. Smith Reynolds Library
North Carolina Baptist Historical Collection
P.O. Box 7777 Reynolds Sta.
Winston-Salem, NC 27109-7777
919-761-5472

North Dakota

Bismarck LDS Family History Ctr.
1500 Country West Rd.
Bismarck, ND
701-222-2794

North Dakota State Library
Liberty Memorial Bldg.
Capital Grounds
Bismarck, ND 58505
701-224-4622

State Archives and Historical Research Library
State Historical Soc. of North Dakota
Heritage Ctr.
612 E. Boulevard Ave.
Bismarck, ND 58505
701-224-2668

Ohio

Bluffton College
Musselman Library
Bluffton, OH 45817-1195
419-358-3271

Bowling Green State Univ.
Ctr. for Archival Collections
Jerome Library, 5th Fl.
Bowling Green, OH 43403-0175
419-372-2411

Dublin LDS Family History Ctr.
7135 Coffman Rd.
Dublin, OH
614-761-1898

The Ohio Genealogical Soc. Library
The First Families of Ohio
34 Sturges Ave.
P.O. Box 2625
Mansfield, OH 44906
419-522-9077

Ohio Historical Soc. Archives
Library Div.
1982 Velma Ave.
Columbus, OH 43211-2497
614-297-2510

Public Library of Cincinnati and Hamilton County
Library Sq.
800 Vine St.
Cincinnati, OH 45202-2071
513-369-6900

Soc. of Ohio Archivists
Western Reserve Historical Soc.
Ohio Network of American History Research Centers
10825 E. Blvd.
Cleveland, OH 44106
216-721-5722

State Library of Ohio
65 S. Front St.
Columbus, OH 43266-0334
614-644-6966

Toledo-Lucas County Public Library
Local History and Genealogy Dept.
325 N. Michigan St.
Toledo, OH 43624-1614
419-259-5233

Oklahoma

Office of Archives and Records
Oklahoma Dept. of Libraries
200 N.E. 18th St.
Oklahoma City, OK 73105
405-521-2502

Oklahoma City LDS Family History Ctr.
5020 NW 63rd St.
Oklahoma City, OK
405-721-8455

Oklahoma Genealogical Soc.
P.O. Box 12986
Oklahoma City, OK 73157-2986

Oklahoma Historical Soc.
Library Resources Div.
Wiley Post Historical Bldg.
2100 N. Lincoln Blvd.
Oklahoma City, OK 73105-4997
405-521-2491

Oregon

Archives Div.
Secr. of State
800 Summer St. NE
Salem, OR 97310
503-373-0701

Oregon Genealogical Soc.
P.O. Box 10306
Eugene, OR 97440-2306
503-746-7924

Oregon Historical Soc.
1230 S.W. Park Ave.
Portland, OR 97205
503-222-1741

Oregon State Library
State Library Bldg.
Winter and Court St. NE
Salem, OR 97310
503-378-4368

Portland LDS Family History Ctr.
2215 N.E. 106th St.
Portland, OR
503-252-1081

Pennsylvania

Bucks County Historical Soc.
Spruance Library
84 S. Pine St.
Doylestown, PA 18901
215-345-0210

Carnegie Library of Pittsburgh
Pennsylvania Dept.
4400 Forbes Ave.
Pittsburgh, PA 15213-4080
412-622-3154

Friends Historical Library of Swarthmore College
500 College Ave.
Swarthmore, PA 19801-1399
215-447-7496

Genealogical Soc. of Pennsylvania
1300 Locust St.
Philadelphia, PA 19107-5699
215-545-0391

Historical Soc. of Pennsylvania
1300 Locust St.
Philadelphia, PA 19107-5699
215-732-6201

Lancaster Mennonite Historical Soc.
2215 Millstream Rd.
Lancaster, PA 17602-1499
717-393-9745

Pennsylvania State Archives
Ref. Sect.
Third and Forster St.
P.O. Box 1026
Harrisburg, PA 17108-1026
717-783-3281

Pittsburgh LDS Family History Ctr.
46 School St.
Pittsburgh, PA
412-921-2115

State Library of Pennsylvania
Forum Bldg.
Walnut St. and Commonwealth Ave.
P.O. Box 1601
Harrisburg, PA 17105
717-787-4440

Rhode Island

Rhode Island Genealogical Soc.
507 Clarks Row
Bristol, RI 02809-1581

Rhode Island State Archives
337 Westminster St.
Providence, RI 02903
401-277-2353

Rhode Island State Historical Soc.
121 Hope St.
Providence, RI 02906
401-331-8575

Warwick LDS Family History Ctr.
1000 Narragansett Pkwy.
Warwick, RI
401-463-8150

South Carolina

Columbia LDS Family History Ctr.
4440 Ft. Jackson Blvd.
Columbia, SC
803-782-7141

South Carolina Dept. of Archives and History
1430 Senate St.
P.O. Box 11669
Columbia, SC 29211-1669
803-734-8577

South Carolina Genealogical Soc.
P.O. Box 16355
Greenville, SC 29606

South Carolina Historical Soc.
100 Meeting St.
Charleston, SC 29401
803-723-3225

South Carolina State Library
1500 Senate St.
P.O. Box 11469
Columbia, SC 29211
803-734-8666

Univ. of South Carolina
Thomas Cooper Library
Carolinian and Southern Mtls.
Columbia, SC 29208-0103
803-777-3131

South Dakota

Sioux Falls LDS Family History Ctr.
3900 S. Fairhall Ave.
Sioux Falls, SD
605-361-1070

South Dakota State Archives
Cultural Heritage Ctr.
900 Governors Dr.
Pierre, SD 57501-2217
605-773-3804

South Dakota Genealogical Soc.
P.O. Box 490
Winner, SD 57580

South Dakota State Historical Soc.
900 Governors Dr.
Pierre, SD 57501-2217
605-773-3458

South Dakota State Library
800 Governors Dr.
Pierre, SD 57501-2294
605-773-3173

Tennessee

Chattanooga-Hamilton County
Bicentennial Library
1001 Broad St.
Chattanooga, TN 37402-2652
615-757-5317

Memphis LDS Family History Ctr.
8140 Walnut Grove Rd.
Memphis, TN
901-754-2545

The Tennessee Genealogical Soc.
3340 Poplar Ave., Ste. 327
Memphis, TN 38111
901-327-3273

Tennessee Historical Soc.
War Memorial Bldg., Ground Fl.
300 Capital Blvd.
Nashville, TN 37243-0084
615-741-8934

Tennessee State Library and Archives
403 N. Seventh Ave.
Nashville, TN 37243-0312
615-741-2764

Texas

Dallas Public Library
Genealogy Sect.
1515 Young St.
Dallas TX 75201-9987
214-670-1433

Ector County Library
321 W. Fifth St.
Odessa, TX 79761-5066
915-332-0634

Fort Worth Public Library
Genealogy and Local History Dept.
300 Taylor St.
Fort Worth, TX 76102-7309
817-870-7740

Houston LDS Family History Ctr.
16331 Hafer Rd.
Houston, TX
713-893-5381

Houston Public Library
Clayton Library
Ctr. for Genealogical Research
5300 Caroline
Houston, TX 77004
713-524-0101

San Antonio Public Library
Historical and General Reference Dept.
203 S. Saint Mary's St.
San Antonio, TX 78205-2786
512-299-7813

Texas State Genealogical Soc.
2507 Tannehill
Houston, TX 77008-3052
713-864-6862

Texas State Historical Assn.
2.306 SRH, Univ. Sta.
Austin, TX 78712
512-471-1525

Texas State Library
Information Services Div.
Genealogy Collection
1201 Brazos
P.O. Box 12927 Capital Sta.
Austin, TX 78711
512-463-5463

Utah

American Genealogical Lending Library
P.O. Box 244
Bountiful, UT 84011-0244
801-298-5358

Brigham Young University
Utah Valley LDS Regional Family History Ctr.
4386 Harold B. Lee Library
Provo, UT 84602
801-378-6200

Family History Library of The Church of Jesus Christ
   of Latter-day Saints
35 N. West Temple
Salt Lake City, UT 84150
801-240-2331

Ogden Utah LDS Family History Ctr.
539 24th St.
Ogden, UT
801-626-1132

State Archives and Record Serv.
Archives Bldg.
State Capitol
Salt Lake City, UT 84114
801-538-3013

Utah Genealogical Assn.
P.O. Box 1144
Salt Lake City, UT 84110
801-262-7263

Utah State Historical Soc.
300 Rio Grande
Salt Lake City, UT 84101
801-533-3500

Utah State Library
2150 S. 300 W.
Salt Lake City, UT 84115
801-466-5888

Vermont

Berlin LDS Family History Ctr.
Hersey Rd.
Berlin, VT
802-229-0898

Genealogical Soc. of Vermont
Main St.
P.O. Box 422
Pittsford, VT 05763
802-483-2900

Vermont Dept. of Libraries
Reference and Law Serv.
Pavilion Office Bldg.
109 State St.
Montpelier, VT 05602
802-828-3268

Vermont Historical Soc.
Pavilion Office Bldg.
109 State St.
Montpelier, VT 05609
802-828-2291

Vermont State Archives
Office of the Secr. of State
Redstone Bldg.
26 Terrace St.
Montpelier, VT 05609-1103
802-828-2308

Virginia

Fairfax County Public Library
Fairfax City Regional Library
Virginia Rm.
3915 Chain Bridge Rd.
Fairfax, VA 22030
703-246-2123

National Genealogical Soc. Library
4527 17th St. North
Arlington, VA 22207-2399
703-525-0050
FAX 703-525-0052

Richmond LDS Family History Ctr.
5600 Monument Ave.
Richmond, VA
804-288-8134

Virginia Genealogical Soc.
P.O. Box 7469
Richmond, VA 23221
804-770-2306

Virginia Historical Soc.
428 N. Blvd.
P.O. Box 7311
Richmond, VA 23211-0311
804-342-9677

Virginia State Library and Archives
11th St. at Capitol Sq.
Richmond, VA 23219-3491
804-786-2306

Washington

Div. of Archives and Records Mgmt.
1120 Washington St. SE
P.O. Box 40238
Olympia, WA 98504-0238
206-586-1492

Seattle LDS Family History Ctr.
5701 Eighth Ave. NE
Seattle, WA
206-522-1233

Washington State Genealogical Soc.
P.O. Box 1422
Olympia, WA 98507
206-352-0595

Washington State Historical Soc.
Hewitt Library
State Historical Bldg.
315 N. Stadium Way
Tacoma, WA 98403
206-593-2830

Washington State Library
P.O. Box 2475
Olympia, WA 98504-2475
206-753-4024

West Virginia

Charleston LDS Family History Ctr.
2007 McClure Pkwy.
Charleston, WV
304-363-0116

Div. of Archives and History
West Virginia Library Commission
Dept. of Culture and History
Science and Cultural Ctr.
Capitol Complex
Charleston, WV 25305
304-348-2277

West Virginia Genealogical Soc.
P.O. Box 249
Elkview, WV 25071

West Virginia Historical Soc.
Archives and History Div.
Cultural Ctr.
Capitol Complex
Charleston, WV 25305
304-348-0230

Wisconsin

Madison LDS Family History Ctr.
1711 University Ave.
Madison, WI
608-238-1071

State Historical Soc. of Wisconsin
816 State St.
Madison, WI 53706
608-264-6535

Wisconsin Dept. of Public Instruction
Div. of Library Serv.
Bureau for Interlibrary Loan and Resource Sharing
2109 S. Stoughton Rd.
Madison, WI 53716
608-221-6160

Wisconsin State Genealogical Soc.
2109 20th Ave.
Monroe, WI 53566
608-325-2609

Wyoming

Cheyenne LDS Family History Ctr.
Wyoming County Library
2800 Central Ave.
Cheyenne, WY
307-634-3561

Wyoming State Archives
Research Div.
Barrett Bldg.
2301 Central Ave.
Cheyenne, WY 82002
307-777-7826

Wyoming State Library
Supreme Court Bldg.
2301 Capitol Ave.
Cheyenne, WY 82002
307-777-7281

CANADIAN RESOURCES

Manitoba

Univ. of Manitoba
Elizabeth Dafoe Library
Icelandic Collection
Winnipeg, MB R3T 2N2 CAN
204-474-6345

New Brunswick

New Brunswick Provincial Archives
Univ. of New Brunswick
Bonar Law Bldg.
P.O. Box 6000
Fredericton, NB E3B 5H1 CAN
506-453-2122

Nova Scotia

Public Archives of Nova Scotia
6016 University Ave.
Halifax, NS B3H 1W4 CAN
902-423-9115

Ontario

Metropolitan Toronto Library
Canadian History Dept.
Baldwin Rm.
789 Yonge St.
Toronto, ON M4W 2G8 CAN
416-393-7161

National Archives of Canada
395 Wellington St.
Ottawa, ON K1A 0N3 CAN
613-995-5138

Quebec

Bibliothèque Municipale de Montréal
Salle Gagnon
1210 E. Sherbrooke St.
Montreal, PQ H2L 1L9 CAN
514-872-1631

APPENDIX B

Ethnic and Immigration Research Centers

UNITED STATES

Alabama

W. S. Hoole Special Collections Library
Archive of American Minority Cultures
Univ. of Alabama
P.O. Box 870266
Tuscaloosa, AL 35487-0266
205-348-0500

Arizona

National Assn. for Ethnic Studies
Arizona State Univ.
Dept. of English
Tempe, AZ 85287
602-965-3168

California

Immigrant Genealogical Soc.
1310B W. Magnolia Blvd.
P.O. Box 7369
Burbank, CA 91510-7369
818-848-3122

Univ. of California, Los Angeles
Asian American Studies Ctr.
3230 Campell Hall
Los Angeles, CA 90024
310-825-2974

District of Columbia

Afro-American Historical and Genealogical Soc.
P.O. Box 73086
Washington, DC 20056-3086

Alliance for Maritime Heritage Conservation
P.O. Box 27272
Central Sta.
Washington, DC 20038

National Archives and Records Admin.
8th & Pennsylvania Ave. NW
Washington, DC 20408
202-501-5402

U.S. Holocaust Memorial Council
2000 L St. NW, Ste. 588
Washington, DC 20036
202-653-9220

Illinois

American Soc. for Ethnohistory
60 W. Walton St.
Chicago, IL 60610
219-875-7237

Balzekas Museum of Lithuanian Culture
6500 S. Pulaski Rd.
Chicago, IL 60629
312-582-6500

Ethnic Materials and Information Exchange Round
  Table
c/o American Library Assn.
Office for Library Outreach Serv.
50 E. Huron St.
Chicago, IL 60611
312-944-6780

Evangelical Lutheran Church in America Archives
8765 W. Higgins Rd.
Chicago, IL 60631-4198
312-380-2818

Polish Genealogical Soc.
984 N. Milwaukee Ave.
Chicago, IL 60622
312-229-1493

Swenson Swedish Immigration Research Ctr.
Denkmann Library
Augustana College
3520 Seventh Ave.
P.O. Box 175
Rock Island, IL 61201-2273
309-794-7204

Maine

Penobscot Marine Museum
Church St.
P.O. Box 498
Searsport, ME 04974
207-548-2529

Maryland

National Slavic Convention
16 S. Patterson Park Ave.
Baltimore, MD 21231
301-276-7676

Univ. of Baltimore
Langdale Library
Steamship Historical Soc. of America Collection
1420 Maryland Ave.
Baltimore, MD 21201-5779
301-625-3134

Massachusetts

Council of American Museum Foundation
c/o *USS Constitution*
P.O. Box 1812
Boston, MA 02129
617-426-1812

Irish Genealogical Soc.
21 Hansen Ave.
Somerville, MA 02143
617-666-0877

Peabody Essex Museum
East India Sq.
Salem, MA 01970
508-745-1876

Michigan

Great Lakes Maritime Institute
c/o Dossin Museum
100 Strand Dr.
Belle Isle, MI 48207
313-267-6440

Minnesota

Immigration History Research Ctr.
Univ. of Minnesota
826 Berry St.
St. Paul, MN 55114
612-373-5581

Nordic Bulletin
Univ. of Minnesota
205 Folwell Hall
9 Pleasant St. SE
Minneapolis, MN 55455
612-625-9887

Scandinavian-American Genealogy Soc.
P.O. Box 16069
St. Paul, MN 55116-0069
612-222-6929

Nebraska

American Historical Soc. of Germans from Russia
631 D St.
Lincoln, NE 68502-1199
402-474-3363

Nevada

University of Nevada
Reno Basque Studies Program
Univ. of Nevada Library/322
Reno, NV 89557-0044
702-784-6538

North Dakota

Germans from Russia Heritage Soc.
1008 E. Central Ave.
Bismarck, ND 58501
701-223-6167

New York

American Friends of the Haifa Maritime Museum
192 Lexington Ave., Ste. 901
New York, NY 10016
212-679-8300

Ctr. for Migration Studies of New York, Inc.
209 Flagg Pl.
Staten Island, NY 10304-1199
212-351-8800

Ellis Island Immigration Museum
Statue of Liberty National Monument, Liberty Island
New York, NY 10004
212-363-5804 (Museum)
212-363-6681 (Library)

Hebrew Immigrant Aid Soc.
200 Park Ave. S
New York, NY 10003
212-674-6800

Jewish Genealogical Soc.
P.O. Box 6398
New York, NY 10128
212-427-5395

Maritime Assn. of the Port of New York
17 Battery Pl., Ste. 1006
New York, NY 10004-1194
212-425-5704

New York Public Library
Fifth Ave. and Forty-Second St.
New York, NY 10018
212-930-0828

Panamerican-Panafrican Assn.
P.O. Box 143
Baldwinsville, NY 13027
315-638-7379

Research Foundation for Jewish Immigration
570 Seventh Ave., 3d Fl.
New York, NY 10018
212-921-3871

Russian Nobility Assn. in America
971 First Ave.
New York, NY 10022
212-755-7528

Schomberg Ctr. for Research in Black Culture
Research Libraries of The New York Public Library
515 Malcolm X Blvd.
New York, NY 10037-1801
212-491-2200

World Jewish Genealogy Org.
P.O. Box 420
Brooklyn, NY 11219-0420
718-435-4400

Ohio

Palatines to America
Capital Univ.
P.O. Box 101
Columbus, OH 43209-2394
614-236-8281

Pennsylvania

The Balch Institute for Ethnic Studies
18 S. Seventh St.
Philadelphia, PA 19106-2314
215-925-8090

Ctr. for Immigration Research
c/o Balch Institute
18 S. Seventh St.
Philadelphia, PA 19106-2314
215-922-3454

Scotch-Irish Foundation
1629 Locust St.
Philadelphia, PA 19103
215-546-8585

Scotch-Irish Soc. of the U.S.A.
P.O. Box 181
Bryn Mawr, PA 19010
215-527-1818

Tennessee

Ctr. for Southern Folklore
1216 Peabody Ave.
P.O. Box 40105
Memphis, TN 38174
901-726-4205

Texas

Texas Seaport Museum
2016 Strand
Galveston, TX 77550
409-763-1877

Univ. of Texas at San Antonio
Institute of Texan Cultures
P.O. Box 1226
San Antonio, TX 78294
512-226-7651

Utah

Eastern European Family History Assn.
P.O. Box 21346
Salt Lake City, UT 84121
801-943-8901

Wisconsin

Vesterheim Genealogical Soc. Ctr.
4909 Sherwood Rd.
Madison, WI 53711-1343
608-262-2504

FOREIGN CENTERS

Canada

Canadian Jewish Congress
1590 Ave. Docteur Penfield
Montreal, PQ H3G 1C5 CAN
514-931-7531

Query Response Center
Employment and Immigration Canada
Place du Portage, 10th Fl.
Phase IV Hull
Québec, PQ K1A 1L1 CAN
819-994-4396

England

Maritime Records Centre
Merseyside Maritime Museum
Pierhead
Liverpool, L3 4AA ENG
051-207-0001 x418

Germany

German Emigration Museum
Inselstrasse 6
27568 Bremerhaven, GER

Historic Emigration Office
c/o Tourist Information Am Hafen
Landungsbrücken between Bridges 4 and 5
P.O. Box 10 22 49
20359 Hamburg, GER
0 11 49 40/300-51250

Norway

The Norwegian Emigration Ctr.
Bergjelandsgate 30
N-4012 Stavanger
Norway
47-4-501-274

Norsemen Worldwide Emigration
P.O. Box 451
4001 Stavanger
Norway

Sweden

The Swedish Emigrant Institute
Strandvägen 4
Box 201
S-351 04 Växjö
Sweden
0470-20124

Index

Raymond S. Wright III is an associate professor at Brigham Young University in Provo, Utah, where he teaches courses in family history, genealogy, and paleography. He received his M.A. and Ph.D. in history from the University of Utah. Wright is an Accredited Genealogist of the LDS Family History Library in Salt Lake City, Utah, where he was also manager of library operations before joining the faculty at Brigham Young in 1990. His employment at the Family History Library spanned 18 years and included research assignments in archives and libraries in the United States and many foreign countries. He has twice served as chair of the American Library Association's Genealogy Committee.